D1369739

Putting Econometrics in its Place

Putting Econometrics in its Place

A New Direction in Applied Economics

G.M. Peter Swann

University of Nottingham Business School, UK

Edward Elgar
Cheltenham, UK • Northampton, MA, USA

Published by
Edward Elgar Publishing Limited
Glensanda House
Montpellier Parade
Cheltenham
Glos GL50 1UA
UK

Edward Elgar Publishing, Inc.
136 West Street
Suite 202
Northampton
Massachusetts 01060
USA

A catalogue record for this book
is available from the British Library

ISBN-13: 978 1 85898 305 9
ISBN-10: 1 85898 305 3

Printed and bound in Great Britain by MPG Books Ltd, Bodmin, Cornwall

Contents

List of figures

List of tables

Preface

The advance of econometrics from the early days of the Econometric Society to the present has been a massive intellectual achievement by some exceptionally clever people. But scientifically speaking, it has been problematic. First, despite the impressive methodological advances, the practical results from the use of econometrics are often disappointing. Second, and much more serious, the mainstream economists' preoccupation with econometrics has displaced other essential techniques of applied economics. Economics has treated econometrics as a *universal solvent*, a technique that can be applied to any economic question, that is sufficient in itself, and therefore makes other applied techniques redundant. I shall argue below that this is a serious error. Econometrics has assumed a dominant position out of all proportion, and that is not helpful to the advance of applied economics. I shall argue in this book that *putting econometrics in its place* is an urgent priority for applied economics – so much so that I have made it the title of this book.

So what is the *new direction in applied economics* referred to in this book's sub-title? The advance of economic understanding demands that economists learn to respect and assimilate what I shall call *vernacular* knowledge of the economy. This vernacular includes the knowledge of the economy gathered by ordinary people from their everyday interactions with markets. Such vernacular knowledge may sit uncomfortably with the formal models of economists, because it seems (and often is) unsystematic, informal and anecdotal. But no wise economist should discard the vernacular, because it offers insights that can never be found in formal analysis alone.

Griffiths (1985, p. 166) describes how the French composer, Paul Dukas, advised his pupil, Olivier Messiaen: 'Listen to the birds; they are great masters.' My message is essentially the same. Professional economists can learn much about economics by listening to those who practice economics in their everyday life, because they have acquired their own sort of mastery in our field.

This book has four main purposes. The first is to persuade fellow economists to take the vernacular seriously. But some might ask, don't most economists do this already? And therefore, does such a book really need to be written? Indeed, some economists do use vernacular knowledge some of the time to underpin what they do.[1] But in general, the vernacular is used incidentally to make a piece of high technique more approachable; the vernacular almost never lies at the heart of our work. Outside this limited context, economists do not tend to take the vernacular seriously.

The second purpose is to explain what can be learnt from paying careful attention to the vernacular. In the discussion, I define vernacular very broadly, to include some formal and some less formal techniques used by non-economist researchers (or non-mainstream economists) to analyse economic questions, as well as the real vernacular of ordinary people. When we use a variety of different research techniques, and especially when we use vernacular evidence, we often encounter contradictions and paradoxes, and these can make us uncomfortable. But applied economic researchers should show a certain frontier spirit. Good researchers should seek out these contradictions and paradoxes, because that is the best way to learn. Indeed, we shall have quite a lot to say about paradox-seeking research strategies in the book.

The third purpose is to argue that taking the vernacular seriously is a natural thing for economists to do. After all, economists believe in *economic man*: people are supposed to be rather good at optimising their economic behaviour. The very term optimisation implies a reasonably reliable model of how some part of the economy operates, of how performance depends on actions, and a wise choice of actions. If people have such vernacular models, and we believe that they work, then let us hear them. Indeed, this picture of decentralised vernacular intelligence is thoroughly in keeping with the philosophy of the free market.[2] By contrast, the notion that professional economists alone have a monopoly of wisdom about economic models and methods seems to imply a faith in central economic control which most economists do not believe.

The fourth purpose of the book is to comment on the increasing division of labour within our discipline, and the tendency to specialise in one technique. Is this good for economics research? I doubt it. True, the division of labour in research increases a narrow definition of productivity – in research as elsewhere. But as recognised by Adam Smith, and many since, excessive specialisation can lead to a sort of intellectual atrophy. Moreover, excess specialisation without a respect for the vernacular exacerbates the sense of disconnection between economics and sister disciplines. In the division of manufacturing labour, the manager takes great care to ensure that these discrete packages of labour are re-combined, so that a final product or service can be assembled and sold. Without that, there can be no profit from the enterprise. This re-combination of the fruits of divided labour may not be very harmonious, but it still happens, because it has to happen. Does this happen with the division of intellectual labour? Rarely! There may be much social and intellectual value in the activity of the integrator or encyclopaedist, but too little academic kudos.

Ultimately, I believe this non-dialogue between adjacent disciplines will be very destructive. Politicians are increasingly aware that in a very complex and highly interconnected economy, their actions can have unexpected side-effects some way away from the area where they have focused their attention. Many of them call for evidence-based policy. But academics can only follow through all the unexpected side-effects of a policy measure if we pull together the knowledge of many adjacent disciplines. At the very time when complexity and inter-connectedness are increasing, interdisciplinary dialogue becomes ever more difficult.

TWO PUZZLES

The great Danish physicist, Niels Bohr, is reputed to have said: 'If you are not confused by quantum physics, then you haven't really understood it'. This observation is immensely reassuring to those who are confused by some phenomenon, because they can at least comfort themselves that puzzlement is a step towards enlightenment.

Emboldened, I admit that the origins of this book lie in two observations that have puzzled me for 25 years, since my doctoral studies. First, why does econometrics assume such a privileged position as the dominant technique of applied economics when the results obtained using the technique are often so disappointing? For sure, the econometric pioneers were exceptionally clever people, econometric techniques are very elegant, and doing econometrics is highly enjoyable. But ultimately the test of the technique is the quality and credibility of the results it delivers, and here many great economists have expressed considerable disappointment at the practical results of econometrics.

Second, and even more serious, why do so many applied economists treat other applied techniques (what I here call the vernacular) with such low regard? This might be understandable if econometric results were always well determined and highly accurate. After all, results obtained from such a rigorous method seem more authoritative than results obtained from more informal, impressionistic methods. But this low regard remains a puzzle, first because these alternative techniques can deliver insights that econometrics cannot ever deliver, and second because some (dare I say, many) econometric results have a good deal less credibility than the crude wisdom of the vernacular.

Some readers may think that what follows is too critical of econometrics. If so, I should stress that my criticism is not directed at econometrics as a tool in itself. I have already said that econometrics represents a huge intellectual achievement. I gratefully acknowledge that some of the economic teachers from whom I have learnt most were, first and foremost, outstanding econometricians. I have used econometrics as a tool for 25 years, and will go on doing so. I have published papers using econometrics, and will go on doing so.

Rather, I am critical of the idea that econometrics is the only 'proper' or rigorous applied research tool, a universal solvent which can be applied to any economic problem. This over-optimistic view of what econometrics can deliver on its own has not served us well. Indeed, I would go as far as to say that it has held back progress in applied economics for 50 years or more, and is still doing so.

Despite the provocative title, this book aims to be very positive. How can we advance the tools of applied economics to fulfil the vision of Jevons and Frisch: to illuminate economic theory with the light of real data? For sure, econometrics will always be an important tool of applied economics. My aim in this book is to show how the productivity of our applied economics can be enhanced by harnessing insights from a wide range of other methodologies, and not relying on one alone. Econometrics will work better if we demand less of it, by asking simpler questions, and by harnessing lessons learnt from other techniques.

In concluding this Preface, I should say three things about what the book is and what it is not. First, while the book may at first sight look like a contribution to methodology, I am certainly no scholar of methodology, and the book is rather different from some of the scholarly contributions in that field.[3] The book is really an alternative manifesto for how we should do applied economics, written by an applied researcher who has found this alternative approach essential to his understanding of applied economics. Dasgupta (2002) observed that he could think of few if any economists he knew whose approach to economic problems was much influenced by reading methodology. While I don't entirely agree, I can certainly see what he means: we learn most about how to do applied economics from those who are grappling with applied economic problems at the sharp end. The book describes what I have learnt by trying to do just that.

The second point is that the book is primarily about 'why' rather than 'how'? The book explains why we need to take a more broad-minded attitude to the vernacular in applied economics research, and therefore a different approach to applied economics, but it does not attempt to offer a detailed user's guide to how this should be done. That would be too ambitious for the present volume.

The final point is to define who the book is for. Most of all, the book is written for the puzzled applied economist. We hear an echo of Bohr: if you are not confused at the present trajectory of applied economics, then you may not understand what this book is driving at. I expect the book will be of most interest to those who are not at ease with current practice in applied economic research. But I also hope some who are perfectly at ease with current practice will still find time to read some of the book and think it over.

ACKNOWLEDGEMENTS

This book has its origins in research carried out in 1980, when I was a doctoral student, so in a sense the book has taken 25 years to write! During that time, I have been guided and influenced by many people, and I shall list some of them below. But let me stress that some of those listed would disagree with much of what follows in this book and, moreover, *none of them has any responsibility for remaining errors or eccentricities*.

As a doctoral student, I benefited from many excellent discussions with Peter Skott. I also benefited from discussion and/or correspondence with Tony Atkinson, Angus Deaton, Freeman Dyson, Walter Elkan, Terence Gorman, David Hendry, Tony Horsley, Rudolf Kalman, Wassily Leontief, Michio Morishima and Alan Peacock. Since that time, the ideas here have surfaced repeatedly as I have grappled with research problems in the economics of innovation. I am grateful to the following for discussions about how we should do applied research: Cristiano Antonelli, Rui Baptista, John Barber, Catherine Beaudry, Daniel Birke, Mario Calderini, Martin Cave, Gary Cook, Robin Cowan, Rod Cross, Paul David, Peter Earl, Dominique Foray, Paul Geroski, Peter Grindley, Graham Hall, Michael Hodson, Ray Lambert, Don Lamberton, Stan Metcalfe, Naresh Pandit, Keith Pavitt, Martha Prevezer, Tudor Rickards, Bob Rothschild, Mark Shurmer, Mick Silver, Thea Sinclair, Ed Steinmueller, Paul Stoneman, David Stout, Majid Taghavi, Manouch Tavakoli, Paul Temple, Bruce Tether, Alan Thomas, Steve Thompson, Nick von Tunzelmann, James Utterback and Richard Whitley.

I am especially grateful to Daniel Birke, Ruth Elkan, Ray Lambert, Frank Neffke and Jenny Swann for reading a penultimate draft of the book and making many detailed suggestions. I would like to express special thanks to Edward Elgar for his interest in the idea of this book, his encouragement, and for his patience in waiting a long time for me to complete it. I am also grateful to all his staff for their help with turning my manuscript into a book, especially Nep Elverd, Dymphna Evans, Emma Gordon-Walker, Julie Leppard, Caroline McLin, Emma Meldrum, Alexandra Minton, Francine O'Sullivan and David Vince.

Finally, the greatest thanks are to Jenny, Carri and Emma Swann for all their support.

NOTES

1.   My favourite example is in Gorman's (1976) pathbreaking paper on the applications of separability, where he recalls the observation of an old schoolmaster: 'when you have a wife and child, a penny bun costs threepence'. Gorman notes that this is a compact motivation for the idea of family equivalence scales.
2.   It is also consistent with von Hippel's (2005) recent writings about democratising innovation. The producer does not have a monopoly in the generation of innovation.
3.   I cannot do justice to all the books of that sort that have shaped my thinking, but the following are ones that I like especially: Blaug (1992), Darnell and Evans (1990), Hutchinson (1977, 2000), Mayer (1993) and Seligman (1962).

PART I

What is applied economics?

1. Introduction

J.S. Mill (1859/1929, p. 24) observed that the only way we can know something 'is by hearing what can be said about it by persons of every variety of opinion, and studying all modes in which it can be looked at by every character of mind'. If economists had followed Mill's wise advice, we would by now be making use of an extraordinary repertoire of research methods in applied economics, including the vernacular methods described in this book.

And yet we don't. For the last 50 years or more, applied economics has been completely dominated by econometrics. Indeed, econometrics has been such a dominant force that many (if not most) other approaches to applied economics have fallen out of use. This thinking has shaped economic teaching for several decades. It has shaped research priorities, promotion, and the allocation of research funds. Not everyone thinks this is a good thing.

Some will dispute my assertion. They would argue that some applied economists are quite catholic in their tastes for applied research and will deploy a wide range of methodologies, probably broader than in many other disciplines. I'm sure that's true of some. And I'm also sure that even more applied economists are not catholic in their tastes, favouring applied econometrics and treating less rigorous techniques with some suspicion. How can it be otherwise when there is a bias in almost all economics teaching and almost all economics journals towards econometrics as a dominant technique?

Some may agree with my assertion, but respond with the counter-argument that econometrics is pervasive in applied economics because it dominates any other technique in terms of applicability, efficiency, rigour and accuracy. We use it to the exclusion of other techniques because it can always and everywhere perform better than any other technique. I do not accept that, and as the book progresses, we shall see that this counter-argument is plainly wrong.

I shall argue throughout the book that we must be prepared to use a wide variety of techniques which force us to look at an economic problem from all angles. In Part IV, we shall encounter some approaches that are unusual and some that may seem quite eccentric. In the Preface, I said that these include the *vernacular* economics of everyday experience. But all of these techniques have an important place, because they can tell us things that more conventional approaches will not.

3

There are four main reasons why the domination of economics by a single technique is a bad thing.

NO MONOPOLY OF WISDOM

The first reason is that many people do not believe that economists have a monopoly of wisdom about economics. In particular, many business people and many in government think they have equivalent, and sometimes superior, understanding of the workings of the economy. Is this view justified? In my opinion, it is part right and part wrong. Business people usually have a very clear understanding of particular facets of the organisations and markets in which they work, and see many nuances that are lost to professional economists. Indeed, there should be few things so interesting to the applied industrial economist as to hear an industrialist talk about the workings of his/her business. But business people often do not see how all these components fit together into a system. They see the issues only from the point of view of their own business.

In this respect, our discipline is unlike many others. We study businesses, governments and consumers, and how their economic activities interact. In all cases, the elementary objects of study are people, or collections of people run by managers. All of these have their own mental models with which they seek to understand and react to the economic world around them. Some of these people can and do articulate their mental models. Sometimes these mental models may have some correlation with formal economic theory, but more often they do not. In my view, the best word to describe these informal models is *vernacular*. Sometimes this vernacular knowledge may contradict formal knowledge, and that can pose a serious challenge to the formal because in some respects the vernacular carries greater authority.

Contrast this with particle physics, say, where scientists seek to understand the behaviour of elementary particles. These elementary objects obviously cannot talk about their own vernacular models. Those who work with these materials in industry may have some vernacular knowledge about the properties of materials, and sometimes this will be an important input to scientific research, but this is unlikely to pose a major challenge to formal scientific knowledge.

Because of this difference, the professional economist can find the interface with business difficult. It does not help one's self-respect to be told by a practitioner that our theories or empirical results can be easily disproved by the common sense of the vernacular. The physicist does not face this problem because most practitioners do not have any vernacular knowledge about physics. And if the practitioner believes that some piece of physics defies common sense, then the physicist can comfortably say, as did Einstein, that common sense is just a 'collection of prejudices'. This comes less well from the economist as a riposte to the industrialist!

Preferring to avoid such uncomfortable interactions, it is not surprising that many economists choose to pursue formal economic models and econometric techniques. This mathematical language is very satisfying in its own right, and goes above the head of the practitioner so the academic can limit interaction without loss of face. Another defence mechanism used by many applied economists is to treat vernacular models and vernacular knowledge as 'informal' or 'anecdotal', and therefore 'inferior'.

But is it really wise to say that these vernacular models and vernacular knowledge are inferior to our formal knowledge? I think not. As I argued in the Preface, economics believes in *economic man*, who has good economic models to guide his decisions. Such models are often based on a large amount of experience, and are judged good enough to support risk-taking. We economists have much to learn from these vernacular models.

Imagine that a physicist had the opportunity to 'talk' to the particles he studies; imagine that an astronomer had the opportunity to 'talk' to a traveller from another galaxy; imagine that an animal psychologist could find a way to help animals 'talk'. Would they really shun such an opportunity? Surely not! Even if they treated this talk with some circumspection, it would be fascinating.

And yet here we are in economics with such opportunities to access vernacular knowledge, and yet for the most part we discard it! Indeed, it is my experience from many seminar presentations I have given that some mainstream economists have become rather intolerant of the informal ways in which non-economists talk about economic phenomena, and they discard this vernacular without further attention. That is a very serious mistake. We would do well to remember the wisdom of J.S. Mill, quoted at the start of this chapter.

This myopic and formalist attitude is bad not just because it closes our minds to valuable insights, but also because the associated spirit of isolation does not improve our understanding. As economists, we find ourselves the butt of gentle jokes (and not so gentle jokes) which suggest that our formal methods do not really help us understand the economic world around us.

A memorable example is found in the BBC programme, *Yes Prime Minister* (Lynn and Jay, 1986). The Prime Minister, in conversation with his Principal Private Secretary, expresses dismay at the poor quality of economic advice from Sir Humphrey (his Cabinet Secretary). The Secretary explains that Sir Humphrey doesn't understand economics because, after all, he studied classics at university. The Prime Minister then asks why his economic advice from the head of Her Majesty's Treasury is no better. The

Secretary replies that the latter finds it even harder to understand economics because he is an economist (Lynn and Jay, 1986, pp. 138–9). To our credit, we economists have the sense of humour to laugh at this, and similar jokes at our expense. But it is worth reflecting that if one were to replace the words 'economics' and 'economist' by 'physics' and 'physicist' in this last quote, then there would be no joke!

NECESSARY BUT NOT SUFFICIENT

The second argument is that econometrics on its own cannot deliver an answer to the questions we ask. Some famous economists have been doubtful about econometrics. Keynes, memorably, likened econometrics to alchemy – see Chapter 3. It was trying to do the impossible, to turn the base materials of raw non-experimental data into the pure gold of a parameter estimate – and in any case, Keynes didn't believe that economic parameters were pure gold. Frisch, the great pioneer of econometrics and the Econometric Society was hugely optimistic about the potential of econometrics in the 1930s, but by 1955 had become quite doubtful that econometrics on its own could ever answer all the applied economic questions of the day. Another Nobel prize-winner, Wassily Leontief (1971, p. 3), remarked that while economics had used very sophisticated 'statistical machinery', the results had been pretty indifferent. And yet another Nobel prize-winner, Milton Friedman (1991, p. 36), expressed similar sentiments, observing that the use of mathematics and econometrics in economics had progressed beyond diminishing returns to 'vanishing returns'.

Some would argue that the bulk of Keynes's objections has been addressed by developments in econometrics since the 1940s. Perhaps if he were alive today, Keynes would not be so critical. Nevertheless, many economists have continued to be critical of what they see as an over-reliance on econometric techniques in applied economics. When the critics include Nobel laureates, presidents of the American Economic Association and of the Royal Economic Society, and other economists and non-economists of distinction, then their remarks cannot be lightly dismissed.   The details of the critique of econometrics need a lot of discussion and deserve a chapter in their own right (Chapter 5).

Even the most trenchant critics, however, should recognise that the development of econometrics since the early days of the Econometric Society represents a major intellectual achievement. And most of them do. In general the critique is not an attack on the calibre of those who have created econometrics or the magnitude of their achievement. Rather, it is seeking to establish a basic economic point. Chapter 10 argues that just as any company which invests only in one factor of production and neglects the others finds that these investments exhibit diminishing returns, so prolonged investment in econometrics, to the neglect of other research priorities, is delivering diminishing returns. Or even, as Friedman (1991, p. 36) put it, 'vanishing returns'.

LOSS OF ESSENTIAL DIALOGUE

The third argument is that our limited repertoire of techniques and our low regard for other techniques reinforce the isolation of our discipline from other disciplines and fields.

Would the place of economics in the world of science and humanities be enhanced if economists were more broadminded in their use of research methodologies? The answer must surely be 'yes' – in the same way that the linguist benefits from a working, if imperfect, knowledge of other languages.

In a complex organisation, the division of labour may be used to enhance productivity. But the strategy only works so long as the fruits of the division of labour are marshalled together to culminate in the finished product or service. If this is not done, then there is no finished product or service to sell, or at the very least it must be flawed. For these reasons, the manager takes great care to ensure that these discrete packages of labour are re-combined, so that the final product or service can be sold for profit. Without that, there can be no profit from the enterprise. In Diderot's Encyclopaedia, it all looks rather harmonious; in reality, it is less harmonious, but still happens, because it has to happen.

In the academic world, we are quick to argue for the benefits of specialisation but remarkably unsuccessful at the re-combination of divided intellectual labour. Why so? Because, as Dasgupta and David (1994) have told us, intellectual labour is rewarded by reputation not financial profit, and the greatest rewards usually accrue to the specialists. Professional pressures require most of us to concentrate on research that is highly regarded within one's own discipline; interdisciplinary research, however worthy, is rarely compensation for a weak disciplinary base.

For this reason, a rigid intellectual division of labour is damaging to the position of economics within the wider world of science and humanities. Any economist who travels in an interdisciplinary world can be left in no doubt of the hostility that many other disciplines feel towards us. Those comfortably segregated in the discipline are either unaware of this, or keep well out of the way in splendid isolation. But this non-dialogue between adjacent disciplines will be a loss to all concerned and may ultimately be our destruction. Interdisciplinary divorce is becoming ever more hazardous to our future well-being, while at the same time, interdisciplinary dialogue becomes ever more uncomfortable, and ever more inconsistent with personal professional survival.   This issue is of huge importance, and we revisit it in Part V (Chapter 22 onwards).

NOT SUITED FOR ALL ACTIVITIES

The fourth broad line of argument is that econometrics is plainly not suited for all the activities that the applied economist should be involved in.

We shall introduce in the next chapter (and discuss further in later chapters) the idea of the *applied economist's desk* – a representation of all the activities an applied economist should be involved in if (s)he is really worthy of the title *applied* economist.   There is much more on this desk than the original Econometric Society's formula of theory, mathematics and statistics applied to data.   The contents of the desk include, for sure, testing theory, finding relevant variables and calibrating parameters.   But there is much more: integrating diverse insights, intellectual innovation, developing and using intuition, the regular dialogue with economic theorists, technicians, econometricians and statisticians, dialogue with other disciplines and fields, dialogue with vernacular economists, as well as keeping a careful eye on developments in the field and policy, availability of secondary data sources, literature, media and the Internet.   And, on top of all this, the conscientious teacher will try to bring some of this into the classroom, and hence try to maintain a virtuous circle between research and teaching.   These are very different activities and call for different tools.

Analogies can be dangerous, but we make extensive (and unashamed) use of them in this book, because they are – whether we care to admit it or not – one of the principal techniques by which we learn.   I find the following analogy is useful for considering the methods of applied economics.

Most golfers require a reasonable collection of clubs to complete a round of golf efficiently.   The rules of the game limit you to 14 clubs per bag.   Some golfers carry fewer than this, for reasons of cost, or weight if they do not have a caddy.   Some of the great players can make do with fewer.   It is possible also for the ordinary player to complete a course with fewer, but one is unlikely to score so well as if one had a large selection of clubs.   It is certainly hard to find a single club which is suitable for all shots, and even less one club that is the optimum club for all shots.

The driver is for hitting long shots from the tee, but may not have the accuracy of the 'long irons'.   For a tight situation, the pitching wedge may be required.   The putter is required for the finishing touches and fine detail. Surely economics is more subtle than golf.   So we need a range of clubs.   In principle, one can design a golf course that can be completed with one club. But research, like golf, does encounter bunkers and rough. How are you going to get out of these with a driver?

Moreover, the analogy goes further than just the clubs in the bag. It also says something about the proficiency required with each of the clubs. There is a saying in golf that 'driving is for show, but putting is for dough'. The player who concentrates simply on driving bravura but neglects his putting will not achieve the best score. There may be a lesson here for the applied econometrician!

In general, eclectic methodologies do not command great respect. Eclectics, as philosophers who select such doctrines as please them in every school, may not appear to have a 'hard core'. Be that as it may, the message of the book has to be that there is no 'universal solvent' for applied economics. The good applied economist should seek to master several applied techniques, and combine them in solving each problem. If that seems eclectic, and hence untidy, so be it; but it is essential.

SPECIALISATION: MERITS AND RISKS

Some readers will still be thinking that the above criticism does not capture the essential merit of specialisation. Yes, indeed, there is a legitimate role for division of labour and specialisation in research as in production.

The founding father of economics, Adam Smith (1776/1904), put the division of labour at the centre of his analysis. So influential was it that Prince Albert said that the division of labour was the 'moving power of civilization'.[1] Equally, the division of intellectual labour is a central organising principle in academic research. Rather as the divisions and sub-divisions of a complex organisation must shut themselves off from the irrelevant activities of other divisions and sub-divisions, so economics must shut itself off from other disciplines. We cannot dispute that much of the advance in our discipline since the early pioneers has come about because of the intellectual division of labour.

Now, since Smith and Rae, we know that the division of labour progresses alongside process innovation. For each tool that is invented, it is efficient that some specialise in the use of that tool. So too with the invention of new research techniques. How can we make progress in the application of econometric methods to economic data without specialisation in econometrics and the sub-divisions of econometrics? From this point of view, it makes no sense for specialists to waste time using a panoply of techniques. Better that they master one, and use it well.

But specialisation is not all good.   While Smith's *Wealth of Nations* started with a eulogy about the division of labour, by the end he had delivered one of the most damming critiques (Smith, 1776/1904, Volume II, p. 267). He argued that persistent repetition of a few standard operations would lead to stupidity, ignorance and a sort of intellectual stagnation.[2]

The reader may think that this remark applies only to the lowly manual labourer performing mind-numbing mechanical tasks, and cannot apply to the specialised intellectual labour of the academic. If so, I suggest that the reader has a long and hard think about Smith's remark, for I believe it applies to any specialism – including our own.[3]   For as Shaw (1903, p. 214) put it, with admirable brevity: 'No man can be a pure specialist without being in the strict sense an idiot'.

These ideas all come to a head again in the concept of creative marginality (Dogan 1994, 1999; Dogan and Pahre, 1990). Dogan argues that much of the invention in each discipline depends on exchanges with other fields. From this point of view, the *marginal scholars* play an especially important role in intellectual invention. Indeed, Dogan goes as far as to suggest that progress in academic disciplines is concentrated at the periphery, where there is cross-fertilisation with other disciplines. By contrast, the core of the discipline becomes stagnant. As a result, Dogan describes a 'paradox of density', which asserts that in densely populated core fields, productivity per head is lower than in marginal fields. In core fields, a large part of the really innovative work is completed before the field becomes densely populated. Overcrowding simply encourages the spread of jargon, intense debates about niceties, and safe but routine work carried out by the large community of intellectual foot soldiers.

AIM AND STRUCTURE OF THE BOOK

This book is about how our thinking as economists can be enhanced by what we can learn from many other disciplines and traditions. We learn both how to do economics better, and also how to talk about economics to others.

The main objective of the book is to chart a new direction in applied economics. While there follows some criticism of econometrics, that is not my principal objective. Indeed, I have used econometric analysis in much of my published work, and will continue to use it with enthusiasm. Like many applied economists, I take many econometric estimates with a pinch of salt, and am aware there are some settings – notably in my own field, the economics of innovation – where econometrics is of limited use. Nevertheless, I am in no doubt that the results of applied econometric studies and indeed econometric theory, taken together, have enhanced our understanding of the way the economy works.

Rather, the aim of the book is to demonstrate that econometrics is not – and never can be – a universal solvent for all economic puzzles and problems. Answering questions in applied economics invariably requires us to use a portfolio of techniques, perhaps indeed some techniques not yet invented, and certainly techniques not yet in general use. Econometrics is undoubtedly a powerful tool, but we cannot expect to see the full power unless we harness it properly to other methods of applied economics. Econometrics will always have a place in applied economics, but it will be a more modest role than it assumes at present, and it needs to be kept in that place.

For the sake of the young researcher, or doctoral student, I feel obliged to attach a health warning. As Machiavelli (1513/1908, p. 121) famously observed, it is risky to pursue an idealistic agenda if that means we neglect what the world expects us to do. Econometrics may not be a universal solvent, but demonstrating expertise in the subject is currently viewed as an essential part of an economist's education. For many schools, a thesis in applied economics without advanced econometrics is not a thesis. This may frustrate the student but it is a fact. Similar constraints apply in all other disciplines, so we have to grin and bear it. But when we emerge from these professional constraints, then it is time to be bold.

The rest of the book is in five parts. The rest of Part I sets the scene by discussing what it is that applied economics is trying to achieve. Why is empirical work essential in economics (Chapter 2)? And what can we learn from Keynes's use of the metaphor, 'statistical alchemy', to describe econometrics (Chapter 3)?

Part II looks at the attraction and the problems of the formal techniques in applied economics. Why was econometrics such an exciting prospect (Chapter 4)? And why have some of the results been so disappointing? What do people think is wrong with econometrics as a tool to develop such empirical analyses (Chapters 5 and 6)?

Part III then describes the character of the vernacular methods of applied economics. Here we interpret vernacular in a very broad sense to include all the techniques unfamiliar in formal economic analysis. Some of these are rigorous and respected techniques used in other fields and disciplines, and it is perhaps less than complimentary to call them vernacular. However, I want here to maintain a simple dichotomy: the formal applied techniques of applied economics and the rest. Chapter 8 argues that vernacular economic knowledge is what one would expect to find in an economic system with decentralised intelligence, and as a result it should not be a big leap for economists who believe in the decentralising power of the market to accept that vernacular economic knowledge can be of great value. Chapter 9 draws a parallel between applied economic research and photographic composition.

Part IV then describes ten approaches to applied economics (Chapters 11 to 20) – from applied econometrics and experimental economics, at the formal end of the spectrum, to common sense, intuition and metaphor at the vernacular end of the spectrum. Chapter 10 introduces this major part of the book by reflecting on what we gain by using this plurality of techniques. Chapter 21 describes why there always will and should be an essential miscellany of other research techniques.

Part V reflects on the dangers inherent in the current econometrics-dominated trajectory (Chapter 22), and sets the priorities for changing attitudes to the use of vernacular in applied economics (Chapter 23). Chapter 24 discusses some of the obstacles in the way of this change in attitude. Chapter 25 concludes.

NOTES

1. See Pevsner (1960, p. 40).
2. In the same way, Ruskin (1904b, p. 196) wrote memorably of how the division of labour damages the labourer.
3. Durkheim (1893/1984, p. 307) argues that damaging effects of division of labour apply equally to the scientist who spends all his time trying to solve a few equations, and to the labourer who spends all his time making pinheads.

2. Economics will only be applied if it is applied

To describe the character of applied economics as a subject of enquiry could deserve a whole book in its own right. We do not attempt to do this here. Our aim in this chapter is simply to justify an assumption that underlies this book. I believe this is a reasonable assumption, though not above question.

This assumption is summarised in the title of this chapter: *Economics will only be applied if it is applied.* In fact, the studied ambiguity of the title confounds two statements, and I believe that both of them are true. First, that economics will only be used ('be applied') by practical people if economists seek to illuminate theoretical models with reference to real data ('it is applied'). Second, that economics will only obtain the necessary data with which to get to grips with the real world ('be applied') if practitioners use it ('it is applied').

The first is a common assertion: that economics is only useful if theory is illuminated with real data. The core of traditional economic theory does perhaps contain some results whose character does not depend on the precise magnitudes of different relationships. For example, under traditional conditions of perfect competition and full information, markets will clear. This proposition holds irrespective of the values of parameters describing demand and supply curves. However, the character of most economic results does depend on the magnitudes of several parameters. So, for example, the effect of a change in marginal direct rate of tax on labour supply will depend on the balance between income effect and substitution effect. If we have no knowledge of these, then it is very difficult to make an authoritative prediction about the net effect.

If economics is to achieve real usefulness as a science,[1] then we have to learn as much as we can about the sizes of economic parameters. Now these parameters may not be like the great constants of the physical sciences – this is discussed below. They may change sharply over time. Nevertheless, far from reducing the need for careful empirical observation, this property increases it. Without that knowledge, our theoretical apparatus is of limited use – though I certainly don't suggest that pure theory is useless.

The second statement is less common, but equally important: that data availability is limited by the extent to which practical people actually use economic principles. Most applied economists do not invest a large amount of time in collecting their own data – though there are some honourable exceptions. As a result, we often give little thought to where our data come from. I find it useful to think of data coming from four generic sources:

(a)   Data collected and documented by companies for their own business purposes
(b)   Data collected and published for profit by companies whose business is to sell data to others
(c)   Data collected by the government and its agencies for the purpose of economic management
(d)   Data collected by researchers for interest but not for profit

Some would argue that data in categories (a) and (b) has been collected for many centuries, without any explicit economic theory to guide it. Nevertheless, there can be no doubt that much of the data collected by companies is guided – whether explicitly or implicitly – by some underlying economic principles. Data collection is expensive, and busy managers will only invest resources in collecting that data if they can see a business case for having it.

When we turn to data of types (c) and (d), it is clear that the collection of these data is more closely related to developments in economic principles. Keynes's macroeconomics, which defined an active role for government in economic management, was the trigger for a major investment in the development and refinement of National Account Statistics (Stone and Stone, 1961).

However, it is fair to say that the greater part of the data we work with as economists is collected by colleagues who are not professional economists. This fact means that we do not have control over our data in the way that an experimental scientist would. Does this matter? Yes it does, if the mental models which data collectors use to collect their data are different from our own. We shall return to this issue later in this chapter.

APPLIED IN WHAT SENSE?

In what sense is economics an *applied* science? Or to put it another way, can it be applied in the same way as the natural sciences? To clarify this, we need to retrace our steps into the history of economic thought.

Pioneering economists such as Smith and Marx were theorists and empirical economists at the same time. There was no division of labour between theory and empiricism in their time, or if there was, they at least straddled both fields. But their empirical analysis could be described as informal. It had more substance than the empirical bases of many modern-day theorists, but did not claim any comparability with empiricism in the natural sciences. The main advances in economics of the nineteenth century were contributions to theory.

Jevons (1871/1970, p. 90) was perhaps one of the first to argue that economic theory on its own would not make economics into a science. It had to be supplemented by systematic collection and analysis of real data. He was realistic about the difficulties involved, but also quite optimistic about the prospects of success (Jevons, 1871/1970, p. 90). Marshall also saw this empirical endeavour as an essential part of the future development of the subject. In a letter to Edgeworth, summarised in Stone (1978, p. 2), Marshall argued that economics proper involved both theoretical reasoning and a thorough study of facts. Only by combining these activities could the economist disentangle all the complex causes found in economic activity.

How is this complex to be disentangled? The vision of the Econometric Society was that the combination of economic theory, mathematics and statistics was the best approach to disentangling. As Frisch (1956, p. 302) described it, this vision involved a combination of mathematical tools, an understanding of theory and the use of statistical data. But in commenting on progress during the first 25 years of the Econometric Society, Frisch (1956, p. 301) observed how difficult it was to turn Jevons's dream into reality.

Keynes's critique of econometrics will be examined further in Chapters 3 and 5, but one aspect deserves mention here. Quite apart from any problems with the methodology, Keynes was doubtful that economics was the sort of empirical science that would be amenable to such analysis. This concern is clearly apparent in his correspondence with Harrod. Keynes argued that economics is a moral science and not a natural science (Moggridge, 1973, pp. 296–7).[2] He argued that in chemistry and physics the objective is to measure parameters and constants, and once that has been done it is done for good. In economics, by contrast, Keynes believed that any parameters that might be measured in a particular study at a particular time would not apply to the economy in future. As a result, the inappropriate pursuit of quantification in economic models would reduce, rather than increase, their value in economic analysis (Moggridge (1973, p. 299).

In effect, Keynes is saying this. Even if econometric techniques can turn non-experimental data into parameter estimates, they would not be *real* parameters. There are no *gold-standard* parameters in economics: they are at best local approximations applying only to a given time and place. In fact, this view is shared by many modern econometricians who would be ready to accept that the parameters of economic model are not great constants, but useful simplifications in trying to make sense of the world. See the discussion between Hendry, Leamer and Poirier summarised in Hendry et al. (1990).

In my view, Keynes establishes a very simple but very important point. If there are no standard parameters in economics – like the great constants of the physical sciences – then this has huge implications for the potential division of labour in economics. What are these implications?

The economics of standards and the economics of transaction costs teach us a very important lesson. Standards facilitate the division of labour by reducing transactions costs. Suppose that one firm A requires a given input X as an input to its production process. It faces a 'make or buy' decision: it can make X in house or buy it in from a specialist supplier of X.   What determines the best strategy? Crudely speaking, the make or buy decision depends on the balance of scale economies and transactions costs.   The specialist supplier can make X at lower cost because it enjoys scale economies which A cannot expect to achieve. On the other hand, A may face transaction costs in buying X from a specialist supplier. If the provision of X is outsourced, it may be costly to monitor and ensure that X is produced to the required specification and required quality. These monitoring costs are lower if X is produced in house.

Now if the specification of X is defined by a commonly accepted and carefully codified standard, then this must reduce transaction costs. A can order X from a specialist supplier, confident that it will meet the standard – or if it does not, that he can demand a replacement or repair. For this reason, A does not incur substantial costs in monitoring the production of X.

In many natural sciences, parameters are real standards, and this fact facilitates the intellectual division of labour.   Theoretical physicists can confidently make use of standard estimates of the great constants of physics without getting involved in the actual estimation of those constants. This estimation of constants can be 'outsourced' to specialists in such measurement, who in turn need not know about all the uses to which theorists may wish to put such parameters.

On the other hand, if Keynes is right, and economic parameters are not standards, then the division of intellectual labour cannot work so well. Those who require an estimate of an empirical price elasticity of demand for a given product, for example, cannot simply look up a standard estimate in a book. We know that measured price elasticities depend on a number of factors: the degree of commodity aggregation, the stage of the product in its life cycle, the availability of alternative products, the properties of the data used, and so on. If we take a particular parameter estimate from the published work of other teams, we cannot know if it is suitable for our purposes unless we know how the measure was produced, and that involves us in monitoring the work of the other team. In the end, it may be best to estimate the parameter we need in house.

To my mind, this non-standardisation of economic parameters has huge implications for the appropriate division of labour in economics. If there are no standards, the division of labour cannot progress so far without running into substantial transaction costs. We must do many more activities in house, and cannot expect to outsource so many activities.

The reader may object to this as follows. Surely the economics profession exhibits a high degree of specialisation. Surely the division of intellectual labour in economics has progressed just as far as in the physical sciences. I would make two points in response.

First, I don't actually think our intellectual division of labour has progressed as far in economics as it has in sciences. One index of this is the average number of authors per published paper. In economics, it is rare to find journal articles written by more than three authors. In the sciences, by contrast, it is quite common. And at the same time, it is more common to find single-authored journal articles in economics than in the physical sciences.

Second, I would assert that the degree of intellectual division of labour in economics has essentially been driven by the demands of professional recognition, and it does not represent an optimum division of labour to maximise the quality of applied economic research. Faced with the continuing pressure to publish, researchers tend to specialise in a narrow field. Forays into different fields or across disciplinary boundaries are a bit risky – even if they would make for better applied economics. Such forays tend to be made by those who are getting on in years!

In short, I think we can conclude from the exploration in the history of economic thought that economics is an applied science in the sense recognised by Jevons. Theory is made useful by empirical research. However, economics is not yet – and may never be – applied in the same way as the physical sciences, because it does not have the same standard parameters. This fact has very important implications for the organisation of applied economics.

VIRTUOUS CIRCLES

The lessons of the last section about the role of standards in the intellectual division of labour seem to me sufficiently important that I shall look at these issues from a rather different perspective – though in the end the two perspectives have a lot in common.

The reader will readily see that the two statements wrapped up in the title of this chapter suggest a *virtuous circle*. Thus, if economic analysis is illuminated by empirical data, that will make it more useful to practical people. And the more it is useful to these practical people, the more data they are likely to collect. Once again, armed with these new data, applied economists can make further advances with our analytical tools, which will further extend their utility to practical people. And so on. Hence the virtuous circle. Without this virtuous circle, professional applied economics is too abstract while vernacular economics is too vernacular.

Let us look a little closer at this virtuous circle. There are in reality two parts to it. The first virtuous circle is between economic theory and applied economics. This posits that theory informs applied research and data collection, and that the fruits of this applied research feed back into the construction of better economic theory.

Now indeed, if all data used in applied economics were collected by the applied economists themselves, this would be the complete virtuous circle. However, in practice, much of the data we use in economics is not data we collect ourselves as economists, but it is collected by companies, government department and agencies, and others, and we use their data.

For this reason, there is a second part of the virtuous circle. This is from applied economics to vernacular economics. If we depend on vernacular economists for our data, then it is helpful for us if their vernacular models are similar to formal models, for then the data they collect will be of greater use to us. With this better data, we can produce better applied economic models, of use to the vernacular economist, who in turn will reward us with more useful data.

However, this sharing of models is not a one-way process. Vernacular economists often have their own models, and these are often rather different from our own. We may think that ours are more rigorous and therefore superior. Vernacular economists, on the other hand, often think that their models are more relevant, if cruder.

Some mainstream economists seem to act as if a bit of imperialism is required: they need to displace these 'primitive' vernacular ideas with our more sophisticated methods. In general, that is not a successful strategy: the vernacular economist tends to react to that with a mixture of resentment and amusement! And above all, such imperialism is unlikely to succeed in getting the vernacular economist to adopt our models. What is actually required is for us to absorb the models of vernacular economists and refine them to an end product that is useful for both of us. Then we can hope to share a common model which is essential for the functioning of this virtuous circle. The issue of *common standards* surfaces once again!

Now, it seems to me that neither part of this virtuous circle is in very good repair. The link from economic theory to applied economics is quite weak, and the reverse link from the results of applied economics back to economic theory is weaker still. Equally, the link from applied economics, as a discipline, to vernacular economics is a bit weak – though efforts at dissemination have improved this to some extent in recent years. And the link from vernacular economics back to applied economics is especially weak. The precise reasons for this poor repair are different in each case, but the general principle is the same. We have developed an intellectual division of labour in our subject which is not supported by a system of common standards. As a result, the division of labour does not work very well.

Let us start with the first part of the virtuous circle from economic theory to applied economics, and back. The original vision of Frisch, and other founding fathers of the Econometric Society, was of econometrics as a union of economic theory, mathematics and statistics, and this econometric technique would be applied to real data to estimate real economic relationships. The pioneering econometricians like Frisch, Leontief, Stone and others were equal to this challenge, but as early as the 1950s, mathematical economic theory was splitting apart from what we now call econometrics. Indeed, the rift between mainstream economic theory and empirical economics has since become quite wide. Theory was only of limited use to the applied econometrician, because theoretical restrictions were not very relevant to the sorts of practical data that were actually available. And equally, because econometric analysis could only rarely provide a convincing test of hypotheses from economic theory, the theorist started to lose interest in applied econometric results. Theory did not meet the standards required by the applied econometricians, and econometric tests did not meet the standards required by theorists. Result: the division of labour into theory and econometrics without common standards led to a breakdown in the virtuous circle. It is interesting to note that experimental economics – rather than econometrics – has emerged as the favoured applied technique for testing economic theory, as we shall see in Chapter 12.

Turning to the second part of the virtuous circle, the pioneering econometricians could keep the circle in good repair because they took such care to understand the data they worked with and where it came from. Leontief in particular wrote at length about the engineering processes and engineering data which he and his associates used in some of their input–output work. Leontief was not just an econometric specialist: his understanding of the necessary adjacent fields meant that there was no communication breakdown from a lack of common standards. Later applied econometricians have tended to be more specialised, and have concentrated their energies on refining their techniques, and spend less of their energy in dialogue with the vernacular economists who provide their data. This specialisation without common standards has damaged the virtuous circle.

The dialogue between the economics discipline and vernacular economics deteriorated further when it was realised that the productivity of econometric analysis was running into diminishing returns and that a well-informed vernacular observer could estimate economic relationships with comparable accuracy (Ward, 1972). Indeed many critics of economics were – by the early 1970s – becoming sceptical about the relevance of much economic analysis, whether theoretical or even applied. As a result, the British Conservative Governments of 1979–97 cut back expenditures on public data collection, and few outside the academic profession expressed much regret.

While it is a big task to repair this circle, some progress has been made, and more can be done. It is an important task because, as I said before, without the virtuous circle professional applied economics is too abstract and vernacular economics is too vernacular. The essential requirement, as I see it, is for applied economists to raise their understanding of, and respect for, the vernacular. Only through this dialogue can we expect to create the common standards required to sustain the virtuous circles described above. This will be discussed at more length in Parts III and IV of the book. For now, we shall introduce our concept of the applied economist's desk, a description of the activities that the applied economist must be involved in if the virtuous circle is to work well.

THE APPLIED ECONOMIST'S DESK

Keynes (1972, pp. 173–4) gave us a memorable description of the qualities of the master economist. He argued that the master economist must combine skills in mathematics, history and philosophy. The master economist must be prepared to examine all aspects of man's nature and all human institutions. He must be able to combine abstract thinking with an understanding of concrete realities. And on top of all this, he must be a statesman. A tall order, indeed! This is, moreover, a much wider range of activities than captured in the Econometric Society's original conception of applied research. It is not enough to combine theory, mathematics and statistics with data. The real applied economist has much more on his/her desk than that. So, what do we find on the applied economist's desk?

Figure 2.1 shows a series of activities on the desk (within the rectangle), and also shows a number of communications with others. This is a busy applied economist, and not a specialist. However, as I shall argue throughout this book, this is what the master applied economist must be able to do.

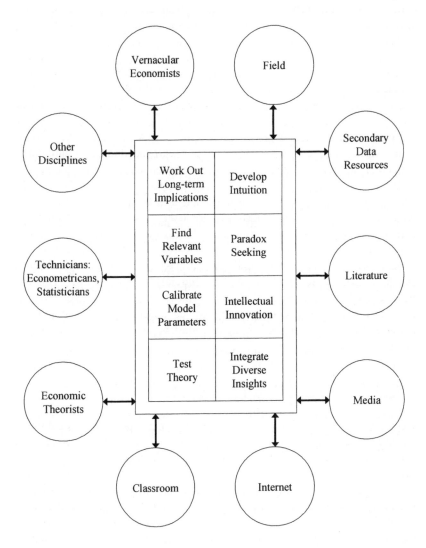

Figure 2.1   The applied economist's desk

Take the desk activities first. One of the first things we are taught as students of applied econometrics is that our job is to 'test theory'. Indeed, a part of our activity in applied econometrics is testing theory – though in my view it is only a fairly small part. (I have commented above on the limited extent to which econometrics is able to provide a test of theory.) To my mind, a greater part of applied econometrics is about calibrating model 'parameters'. But while these two items on our desk are amongst the more enjoyable activities, we cannot do them without data. In some areas of applied economics, data are easily available, but in most this is not so. Accordingly, a large item on our desk is the selection of relevant variables, and through interrogating various sources of data, building up the data sets necessary for our work.

For many applied econometricians, these are their three main desk activities (apart from writing, of course). But there is another in the top left-hand corner of the desk which often receives insufficient attention – in my view. Once we have calibrated an economic model, surely we should use it? What does the model say will be the long-term implications of some change in economic conditions, or some change in policy? Having gone to the trouble of calibrating a model, it is a bit strange if we don't do this. It seems to imply that we have rather little faith in the model! (If that is really true, then we need to reflect long and hard on our whole approach to applied economics.)

In addition to these left-hand column activities, however, the applied economist should have a series of rather different activities on the right-hand side of the desk. One is a constant imperative to integrate diverse insights from different methods. Why is this so important? We shall see in the remainder of the book that it is important for at least three reasons. First, it is one of the most productive routes to intellectual innovation. Second, it is an essential part of what I shall call a *paradox-seeking* strategy in applied economics. Third, integration, innovation and paradox-seeking are essential components of a strategy to develop our economic intuition.

How does integration lead to innovation? How does it support paradox-seeking – and why indeed would we want to seek paradoxes? And how does integration develop intuition? To answer these questions fully is the task of successive chapters in the rest of the book, but let me offer a very brief account here.

First, let us start with the role of integration in innovation. As we shall see in Chapter 9, the literature on creativity sees combination and reorganisation as fundamental to the process of creative thought. People create new knowledge or ideas by combining and reorganising existing concepts or categories. Creativity is therefore a combinatorial activity: it is all about bringing together different perspectives on the same issue. And to the extent that creative thought is a necessary (if not sufficient) condition for innovation, then the role of integration in promoting intellectual innovation is clear.

Second, let us turn to the role of integration in supporting a paradox-seeking strategy. There are two parts to this. To begin with, how does integration help paradox-seeking? This is quite straightforward. Judging from my own experiences, and all those other applied economists I know who work with a variety of different research techniques, it is very common to find that when we use several techniques to analyse a question we tend to find some contradictions or paradoxes. Technique A finds that X is important while technique B finds that X is unimportant. For the single-technique researcher, this problem (if it is a problem) does not arise. With a strict division of labour in different academic fields, this contradiction may never be noticed, because the literature review of each field concentrates only on its own, and edits out contradictions or paradoxes from adjacent fields. The problem (again, if it is a problem) cannot escape the notice of the multi-technique researcher, or the interdisciplinary traveller. But I shall argue that these paradoxes are not so much problems as opportunities.

So why should we want to adopt a paradox-seeking strategy? This is perhaps one rather controversial aspect of this book, and it is developed below (in Part IV, and especially in Chapter 23). But in essence the point is that resolving paradoxes is – in artificial intelligence at least – one of the key ways in which learning takes place. If we can resolve the apparent paradox of why X happens in case A but doesn't happen in case B, then we have learnt some new principle (call it F). If we never encountered the paradox, we would not learn F.

Third, how do integration, innovation and paradox-seeking help to develop our intuition? We shall discuss this below (especially in Chapter 19). One view of intuition is that it is like a neural network model built up from the integration of different empirical results and the resolution of a series of paradoxes.

Finally, the applied economist must communicate with a variety of other communities and resources. These include economic theorists, econometric specialists and statisticians. Most of us do this already. But the enlightened applied economist will reach out wider – and the importance of this will emerge as we progress through the book. The master applied economist will speak to other related disciplines, vernacular economists (described in Part II) and people in the field and policy. All applied economists interrogate secondary data sources, and keep an eye on the conventional literature, but of equal importance – in my view – are the vernacular accounts in the media and internet sources. Finally, the classroom can be an important laboratory for the applied economist – and not just a workhouse!

NOTES

1. In a fascinating book, Szostak (1999) argues that much of modern economics would be better understood as art and not science. This perspective would help to explain some features of our subject.
2. Parsons (1997) has analysed Keynes's views on economics as a moral science.

3. Econometrics as alchemy?

To conclude this part of the book I want briefly to revisit what is, perhaps, the most famous (if less than complimentary) metaphor for what econometrics is trying to achieve. Commenting on Jan Tinbergen's econometric studies of investment for the League of Nations, Keynes (1939) memorably described econometrics as a form of 'statistical alchemy'. What did he mean by this? It is generally assumed that he was referring to an attempt – forlorn, as he saw it – to turn the base metal of imprecise data into the pure gold of a true parameter estimate. Indeed, that was certainly a part of Keynes's message, but I believe there was more to it than that.

Keynes's metaphor of 'statistical alchemy' is in some ways a rather curious one. Statisticians have always been concerned with measurement, and with knowing the accuracy and reliability of measurement. To the alchemist, by contrast, measurement was not of great importance. Holmyard (1956) documents how at the time of peak alchemical activity, remarkably accurate balances were available, but they were little used by alchemists. For all their other failings, the alchemists could not be accused of seeking to produce unrealistically accurate measurements.

Alchemy (at least in the Middle Ages) was considered to have had three essential goals. The first was the transmutation of base metals into gold. The second was the discovery of an elixir of life. The third, less widely discussed, was the search for a universal solvent, to which Paracelsus – perhaps the greatest of the alchemists – gave the name *alkahest*.

Which of these aspects of alchemy did Keynes have in mind when referring to econometrics? As I have said already, it is most commonly assumed that he was referring to the first: the goal of *transmutation*, by which the base metals of imprecise non-experimental economic data are turned into the pure gold of a parameter estimate. Chapter 5 assesses his critique, and whether any parts of it still stand. I shall argue there that two of the problems identified by Keynes, when taken together, pose a very serious problem for applied econometrics in many contexts – even if neither on its own is such a cause for concern.

Of course, as we saw in the last chapter, Keynes clearly had his doubts about whether parameter estimates were made of pure gold. But figuratively speaking, of course, economics as a subject matter is all about how people turn base metals into things of higher value. And in the economic domain this transmutation is feasible. So, while the pursuit of physical transmutation may be a fallacy, the pursuit of economic 'transmutation' is not.

However, it is also worth reflecting on the two other aspects of alchemy. Ben Jonson famously described the huge power of the elixir (*The Alchemist*, 1610; Act II, Scene 1). An elixir would, amongst other things, bring the user honour, respect, safety and a long life. Did Keynes mean that econometrics was a form of elixir!? It is amusing to speculate on this. For certain, a striking characteristic of many econometricians is that they wear their age very well. Some of them have lived to a healthy old age (Frisch and Tinbergen, to give just two examples). Moreover, econometrics has conferred honour, respect and the safety of tenure on many of its followers. But as far as I am aware, not even at their most exuberant did any econometricians claim that they had uncovered the elixir of life!

No, the interpretation that interests me the most is the third one: the idea that econometrics could have the power of universal solvent. Paracelsus used the term *alkahest* to describe the alchemist's universal solvent, which could turn stone into water. Did the early econometricians see econometrics as a universal empirical technique for solving all applied economic problems? I think the answer has to be, 'yes'.

The triad structure of econometrics, described by the founding fathers of the econometric society, in which econometrics consists of the combined application of theory, mathematics and statistics, was seen as a universal tool. Because of that, applied economics discarded earlier applied techniques. By the 1950s, Frisch himself had recognised that this was a mistake, and it would be essential to revive some of these discarded techniques if we were to extract the full potential of econometrics. We discuss this further in Chapter 5. However, most econometricians seem to have ignored this message of Frisch's.

Finally, it is worth reflecting on Keynes's recognition that Newton and other great scientists dabbled with alchemy. While a prevailing view of alchemy during the early stage of real science was that alchemy represented bad science, with undesirable associations, some more recent writers have been a little kinder to it. Some have gone as far as to call alchemy the mother of chemistry, even if on its own it was misguided (Holmyard, 1956; Feyerabend, 1978, p. 305).

It seems to me that this broader interpretation of Keynes's famous metaphor captures exactly what has gone wrong with our over-reliance on econometrics in the second half of the twentieth century. Econometrics was seen as a universal solvent. That optimism was misplaced and unfortunate because it led us to discard older techniques as informal and non-rigorous. In fact, we should have kept them going, not because they would displace econometrics but because they would strengthen it.

If this book is critical about what has happened in applied economics from the 1950s onwards, I must stress again that my aim is not to criticise econometrics itself. What I am criticising is the mistaken idea that econometrics could be a universal solvent, for all problems in applied economics. But econometrics is not this universal solvent, and never can be. Answering questions in applied economics invariably requires us to use a portfolio of techniques, perhaps indeed some techniques not yet invented, and certainly techniques not yet in general use. The mastery of applied economics demands that we recognise this.

I believe that this *idea of econometrics as a universal solvent* has held back progress in applied economics for 50 years, and is still doing so. But let me stress again that I do not mean that econometrics in itself is holding us back: it is not. The errors of applied economists who make exclusive use of econometrics are sins of omission, not commission.

PART II

The formal in applied economics

4. The surveyor's dream

In this chapter, I want to explore one particular reason why econometrics seemed such an exciting prospect as a general tool of applied economics. This is only one such reason, but it is an especially interesting one. As I see it, econometrics appeared to offer applied economics what the technique of *triangulation* (invented in 1533 by Gemma Frisius) offered cartography and surveying. When we think of all that has been achieved using triangulation and some relatively straightforward trigonometry, then it is little wonder that an equivalent technique in applied economics should attract such a surge of interest.

To explain this similarity between triangulation (as originally defined by Frisius) and econometrics, I shall start by describing the background to triangulation and what could be achieved using it. I shall then show how this is similar to what econometrics appeared to offer applied economics.

I need to clear up one possible source of confusion before I start, however. I shall be talking here about triangulation as defined by Frisius and used subsequently for cartography by Mercator and followers. The same word *triangulation* has been borrowed by some social scientists to describe the methodology of using two or more independent research techniques to obtain a more reliable understanding of some phenomenon. Now the reader of this book will quickly see that I make enthusiastic use of metaphor myself, and moreover I do of course approve of such methodological plurality. But Frisius gave us a very precise concept of triangulation – as we see below – and in my view that is not a very good metaphor for methodological plurality. Be that as it may, this later use of the word triangulation is now in standard use in social sciences. I should simply stress that this chapter has nothing to do with triangulation in the modern social scientific sense.

FRISIUS AND TRIANGULATION

In 1533, Gemma Frisius, a professor at the University of Louvain (Belgium), made a major contribution to the development of surveying techniques. He expounded the principle of triangulation. Figure 4.1 offers a simple illustration of his method. (Taylor, 1957, describes this in more detail.)

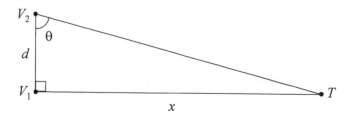

Figure 4.1   Triangulation – as invented by Frisius in 1533

The surveyor takes two bearings of a distant geographical feature (T) from either end of a relatively short baseline (of length d). The first bearing is taken at point V_1 and the second at point V_2. For simplicity, Figure 4.1 is drawn on the assumption that the baseline is perpendicular to a straight line from V_1 to T. (This is not essential but it simplifies the mathematics.) In that case the bearing at V_1 is $\pi/2$, a right angle, while the bearing at V_2 is given by the angle θ. From these three pieces of data (d, θ and $\pi/2$) the surveyor can compute the distance x between the first viewpoint and the distant object (T).

In Frisius's era, x could be calculated graphically. The surveyor would reconstruct Figure 4.1 on paper, but on a much reduced scale. He would start by drawing a horizontal line (as between V_1 and T). He would then draw the vertical baseline (V_1V_2) of length d (in the appropriate scale). He would then draw a downward-sloping ray from point V_2 at an angle of θ to the baseline. Where this ray crosses the horizontal point would locate point T. The distance to the distant object, defined as x, could then be read from the diagram, and converted to a real-life distance using the appropriate scale. Today, using trigonometry, we can compute the distance directly using a trigonometric formula: $x/d = \tan(\theta)$.

Why is this so significant? Because it allows the surveyor or cartographer to measure distances of distant objects and plot maps without travelling large distances.[1] The only distance measurement required is that of the baseline. This was hugely important in an era of high transport costs. It massively expanded the scope of surveying, and meant that far more detailed maps could be attempted with a given amount of labour. To appreciate this fully, imagine the travelling required when a cartographer has to compute 100 distances, each of them several miles, but does not have use of triangulation. That would involve many, many days walking on foot, but could easily be accomplished in a day using triangulation (Skelton, 1958).

The technique sounds too good to be true. And in one sense it is. It is susceptible to error when applied in the field. It depends on very accurate measurements of angles at each end of the baseline, and this only became possible with subsequent advances in measuring techniques. Moreover, errors in drawing would lead to errors in measurement. There is a trade-off between cost and accuracy. If the surveyor uses a longer baseline (d) then the measurement of x is less susceptible to error in measuring the angle θ. But, obviously, it is cheaper to use a short baseline as it involves less walking.

ECONOMETRICS AS TRIANGULATION?

As I see it, econometrics has two striking similarities to triangulation as described by Frisius. First, triangulation is a method of measuring the locations of many distant objects with a minimum of travel. In the same way, econometrics is a method of calibrating economic models which can be done at the desk, and involves little or no travel to visit any factories or markets described by those economic models. Second, triangulation may require considerable accuracy in the measurement of angles, and especially so when the baseline is short relative to the distance to the object (that is, d/x is small). In the same way, econometrics requires considerable accuracy in measuring data, and especially so when the explanatory variables of interest show little variation in our data. This is the theme of Chapter 6.

In view of the first similarity, and in view of all that was achieved with triangulation, we should not be surprised at the huge early enthusiasm for econometrics. It offered the prospect of calibrating models of an entire economy, covering many different relationships, but could apparently do this without any need for the researcher to visit a mass of companies, markets, consumers in different regions and countries. Whereas interview research would require a huge amount of travel, econometrics seemed to offer the prospect that a team of desk-based researchers could model an entire economy. In short, econometrics, like triangulation, appeared to promise a massive increase in productivity. Unfortunately, for reasons we discuss in Chapter 5, 6 and 11, this increase in productivity was to some degree illusory.

One of the reasons for this has been that the application of econometric methods in complex multivariate settings requires more accuracy in our data than we can expect to achieve. This may surprise the reader: does a bit of measurement error really matter? In triangulation, it matters when the rays from either end of the baseline are nearly parallel. This happens when the baseline is relatively short compared to the distance from our object of interest (that is, the ratio d/x in Figure 4.12 is small). In other words, measurement error matters when the triangle formed by triangulation has a very sharp point at the distant object of interest.

Roughly speaking, the same intuition applies to econometrics. Measurement error matters when our observations are not far enough apart. More precisely, measurement error matters when the (partial) variance in our explanatory variables is small. We call this a problem of the signal-to-noise ratio and discuss it further in Chapter 6. This problem is distressingly common in complex multivariate settings where different explanatory variables are closely collinear.

To my knowledge, this similarity between triangulation (as practised by Frisius) and econometrics has not been remarked before. The reader may not find it convincing, but to my mind it is of crucial importance. If you want to map and measure the world quickly, and can't afford to travel to all the points of interest, then triangulation must look attractive. The same logic applied to the econometric experiment. So, in retrospect, it is no surprise at all that econometrics was welcomed with such enthusiasm by applied economists in the 1930s. We shall see in the next chapter what critics think went wrong.

NOTES

1.   This shows why the modern social science use of the term triangulation is unfortunate. Frisius took two fixes on the distant object T to establish how far away it was (x). He did not do this to reassure himself that it was indeed the object T.

5. What do the critics say is wrong?

For a dominant method in one of the main social sciences, econometrics has attracted its fair share of criticisms – or perhaps more than its fair share of criticisms. These have come from other social scientists, from non-econometric economists, and – perhaps most disturbing of all – from some of the early pioneers of econometrics. The aim of this chapter is to summarise some of these critiques, not because the present author agrees with all of them but because it is useful to build up a clear picture of what the critics think is missing from our methodology of applied economics.

We can organise this discussion in two ways: first, according to the source of the critique, or second, according to the substance of the critique. While there would be some attractions in following the first approach, it is more useful for the purposes of this book to organise the discussion in the second way. I have organised these under nine headings:

- Economics is not a natural science
- Econometrics is a flawed tool
- Restricted domain
- A methodological revolution only
- Trained incapacity
- The isolation of economics
- Bricks from straw?
- Diminishing returns
- Generalised unease

To some extent these overlap, but I think there is an important distinct lesson in each critique.

ECONOMICS IS NOT A NATURAL SCIENCE

Of all the critiques of econometrics, perhaps Keynes's (1939) is the most famous, and arguably the most telling. After all, here is arguably the finest social scientist of the 20th century, an accomplished mathematician and logician who could have easily mastered the technical side of econometrics, had he chosen to do so, but who argued from an early stage that he thought it misguided, a sort of 'statistical alchemy'.

Keynes's critique was in two parts. One is his criticisms of the idea that economics can be studied in the same way as the physical sciences. Much of this is captured in his correspondence – notably with Harrod – and we have described the main elements of that already in Chapter 2. The second part is his specific critique of Tinbergen's (1938) method in his econometric study for the League of Nations. We turn to this shortly.

As we saw in Chapter 2, Keynes did not believe that the parameters of economic relationships were like the great constants of physics. Moreover, he was opposed to the idea that economics could be turned into a natural science. More generally, he was sceptical about the use of mathematics in economics. Wiener (1964, p. 91) also argued that the idea of a parameter estimate as a constant to be estimated is a myth. He argued that economics as a game is one where the rules keep changing, and in the circumstances it is unwise to try to assign a precise measurement to the quantities in economic models. He believed that it was 'neither useful nor honest' to assign precise values to vague parameters.[1]

Wiener (1964, pp. 89–90), moreover, had a sceptical interpretation of the economist's use of mathematics. He felt that economists were jealous of the success of mathematical physics, and as a result had sought academic respectability by describing our imprecise ideas in an inappropriate mathematical language.

On the matter of parameters as local (and temporary) approximations, there is less distance between Keynes and Wiener on the one hand and some modern econometricians on the other. Some applied economists make it clear that they do not believe model parameters are real constants. Nevertheless, model parameters are useful – even if they only have the status of a local (and temporary) approximation. But some econometricians would still maintain that models are only useful if their parameters are constant. The exchange between Hendry, Leamer and Poirier on this question (Hendry et al., 1990, pp. 195–7) gives a fascinating insight into the different views held by three leading econometricians on these issues.

ECONOMETRICS IS A FLAWED TOOL

Even if Keynes's objections to the principle of estimating and using parameters are set aside, Keynes (1939) was still concerned that the econometric technique could not hope to estimate parameters with any reliability. In retrospect, we could say that he had recognised some of the econometric problems that needed to be solved before the technique would be truly reliable. Many econometricians would say that all these issues have now been resolved. In my view, that is almost right. I shall argue that when two of these properties are found together then econometrics has not handled – and arguably cannot handle – the ensuing problems. That will be the subject of Chapter 6.

The six main parts of Keynes's (1939) critique of econometric procedure are:

(a) Multiple regression should operate on a complete list of causes

This is the issue of omitted variables bias, which is well understood in modern econometrics. If omitted variables are correlated with included variables, then the estimated parameters will be biased. On the other hand, if omitted variables are orthogonal to all included variables, then parameter estimates will be unbiased, though the sampling error attached to the parameter estimates will be higher than it need be.

(b) The failure to establish a connection need not imply there is none

There are two interpretations of this. First, 'failure to establish a connection' can mean that a parameter estimate has such a high standard error that we cannot reject a null hypothesis of 'no effect'. Keynes was of course right that strong correlation between different factors would cause high parameter standard errors. Second, 'failure to establish a connection' can mean that a true connection between two variables is not observed because – for example – omitted variables bias causes the estimate to be biased towards 0.

(c) If factors are not independent, we can have spurious correlations

'Spurious correlation' means that regression analysis identifies a connection between two variables when in fact they are unrelated. If all relevant factors are included, then the inter-correlation of explanatory variables should not actually be a problem on its own. Modern econometrics established that correlation between different explanatory variables – on its own – does not lead to bias in regression estimates. But the combination of inter-correlated explanatory variables and either (i) omitted variables, or (ii) measurement errors can certainly lead to spurious correlations – see (a) above and (d) below.

(d) Significant factors must be measurable

This can be interpreted at two levels. First, in order to estimate a regression model, it must be possible to produce some measure of each significant factor to be considered in a regression analysis. Second, this measure must be accurate. At one level, these observations are right. In most practical cases, the inability to measure a variable means that it will be omitted from a regression – and that can lead to omitted variables bias, as in (a) above. Equally, if an explanatory variable is measured with error, and one does nothing about it, then traditional Gaussian regression will lead to a biased estimate. This was known to Gini (1921), if not before.

In principle, however, it can be argued that it is not actually essential that factors should be measurable. Econometricians have developed techniques for handling estimation with latent (unobservable) variables (Griliches, 1974, made an early survey of this). Equally, an errors-in-variables estimator can be used to handle cases where variables are measured with error. Or, alternatively, instrumental variable estimators can produce consistent estimators even when data are measured with error – so long as suitable instruments are forthcoming.

The operative words here are, *in principle*. In practice, the errors-in-variables estimator requires precise knowledge about the correlation structure of measurement errors, which we almost never have. In practice, a good instrument is most likely to be a variable that is related to the inaccurate measure, and we cannot be sure that any measurement errors in the instrument are independent of any measurement errors in the original variable.

A prevailing intuition amongst many applied economists has been that *a little measurement error hardly matters*. This may be too optimistic. Surely, in benign circumstances this is a reasonable assumption. In less benign circumstances, the combination of multicollinear regressors and measurement error can be very serious. Chapter 6 explains why.

(e) Is linearity an appropriate assumption?

If we assume that a relationship is linear when it is not, then ordinary regression techniques will produce biased estimates. An error in the functional form, like many other mis-specifications, can be interpreted as a case of an omitted variable, and so the problem of omitted variables bias raises its head again. Alternatively, in the confluence analysis techniques pioneered by Frisch (1934) and revived by Kalman (1982a, 1982b) and Klepper and Leamer (1984), errors in functional form can be interpreted as another manifestation of errors-in-variables.

In principle, again, there is no great difficulty in progressing beyond linearity, and getting functional forms right. For example, many of the limited dependent variables models (summarised by Maddala, 1983) take non-linearity very seriously. Nevertheless, when we come to look at average practice in econometrics – as opposed to best practice – then this may be a more common problem.

(f) Time lags and trends must be adequately dealt with

Again, Keynes was spot on. If we do not get the dynamics of a model correct, then at the very least we can expect autocorrelation of the equation residuals – and that will need to be adjusted for since it violates the assumptions of the basic linear regression model. More serious, we can suffer from biases in parameter estimates: it is not just that we get the time sequences of any effects wrong, but the net long-run effect of x on y may be calculated inaccurately. While we argued before that econometrics has not taken the issue of measurement errors especially seriously, it is fair to say that econometricians have taken the issue of dynamics very seriously. A huge amount of work has been done to handle time lags and trends (see Hendry, 1995, for a most comprehensive summary of the state of the art). Even if average practice does not necessarily deal satisfactorily with all problems, best practice surely does.[2]

The 'Lady Bracknell' principle

One additional flaw in the technique which has been mentioned by other critics is the practice of making a sequence of anonymous data points from different objects. Some have suggested that this is tantamount to throwing away the baby with the bath-water, or at least throwing away lots of rich insights on each individual case.

Boulding (1970, 1971) argued that econometrics has driven out important parts of the economist's education, and indeed has imbued economists with the belief that they do not need to know about institutions, the reality behind data, or the sorts of qualitative information that cannot easily be quantified and used in a regression. We shall take a closer look at his comments below. Hicks (1979) also disliked the practice of creating populations of observations by combining data on very different cases. He noted that different observations often came from different countries or industries, and that although we often have relevant information about these different entities, the econometric procedure ignores any such information. He argued that it was fine to plot such very different observations in a graph, but it made no sense to 'suppress their names'. Phelps Brown (1972, p. 6) made a similar point about the use of time series data. He argued that different years had different 'personalities' and that it was not right to treat each annual observation as if it was just another timeless piece of experimental data.

Of course, sometimes we have no option but to anonymise data observations. In data on individual consumption patterns, for example, we are obliged – ethically and legally – to treat each observation anonymously. But in many cases, we could identify the character of individual observations – if we wished to.

The econometrician is in a difficult spot here. If any anomalous observations or outliers in a presumed relationship can always be explained away by special circumstances pertaining to a particular observation, then it could be argued that our empirical analysis is unscientific because our hypothesis is in essence irrefutable. Many econometricians prefer therefore to keep themselves in a state of blissful ignorance about the identities corresponding to their observations. This attitude reminds us of that bastion of the English upper classes, Lady Bracknell, who observed (Wilde, 1899/1954, p. 266): 'I do not approve of anything that tampers with natural ignorance.'

RESTRICTED DOMAIN

A number of critics argue that econometrics is applicable only to a restricted domain of problems. In that sense, econometrics cannot be a universal solvent which will take any empirical facts and dissolve them into a uniform solution. It only works in a restricted domain of problems.

Some might respond, whoever said that econometrics was a universal solvent? Answer, quite a few undergraduate and graduate schools in economics. After all, most undergraduate courses and graduate courses in economics have for many years taught econometrics as the one serious method of applied economics. Many leading journals have chosen to select only empirical work that is fluently econometric. I don't think we need to labour the point here.

Worswick (1972, p. 79) made some telling points of this sort. He argued that much econometric research was an elaborate exercise in making 'pretend-tools' which would be wonderful 'if ever a set of facts should turn up in the right form'. And he criticised the econometricians' reluctance to accept this point (Worswick, 1972, p. 83). He spoke of a 'doctrine of econometric escalation' according to which any unsatisfactory econometric results call for further research using even more sophisticated econometric methods. In his view, the profession had little respect for simpler methods – what we call 'vernacular' in this book.

Mayer (1980, p. 18) made a similar comment. As the econometric technique had its weaknesses, economists should accept that economic truth is not always written in the form of equations, and we should be open to other, older methods. A very influential applied economist, Summers (1991, pp. 129–30) made some telling points in the same vein. In particular he argued that formal econometric work has had rather little influence on thinking about substantive questions. Instead, the empirical work that had truly been influential was actually based on very different methodological principles – again, the 'vernacular' of this book. And Summers (1991, p. 146) concluded bluntly that it is easier for the researcher to develop technical bravura than it is 'to make a contribution to knowledge'.

A METHODOLOGICAL REVOLUTION ONLY

Karl Popper (1957, p. 60n) made a very optimistic assessment of econometrics, arguing that 'one social science at least has gone through its Newtonian revolution'. A number of critics seized on this, because they felt that Popper was wide of the mark. Hutchinson (1977, p. 40) for example responded that this revolution in economics was one of form and not of substance. And Ward (1972, p. 43) argued that while the change in economics by 1965 might look like a major scientific revolution, 'it was essentially methodological rather than substantive'.

Leontief (1971, p. 3) made some memorable criticisms of the econometric revolution in his speech as President of the American Economic Association. While econometricians had used a lot of highly sophisticated 'statistical machinery' the results were frankly 'indifferent'. Leontief argued that our priorities had become severely distorted. The profession considered it a 'greater scientific achievement' to develop a new econometric procedure than to gather additional data. Leontief (1971, p. 4) was also highly critical of the excessive reliance on 'indirect statistical inference' to estimate economic parameters, rather than the imaginative collection of new data.

Harry Johnson (1972, p. 20) also observed that there was something of an imbalance in the econometric revolution. He noted that the best work on econometrics was mostly theoretical and bore little resemblance to the vision described by Frisch. And Norbert Wiener (1964, pp. 90–91) also felt that econometricians had missed the point of the scientific method. In emphasising mathematics and neglecting data collection, econometrics was trying to imitate the appearance of physics without following its actual procedures.

TRAINED INCAPACITY

This is a theme that has concerned several critics of the econometric revolution. Most prominent amongst these critics, perhaps, was Kenneth Boulding. He felt that econometrics and mathematical economics were doing economics a great disservice because they were driving out traditional skills, and displacing other essential parts of the economist's training (Boulding, 1970, p. 156). As he put it, the 'quick returns in economics in the last thirty years' accrued to those of mathematical ability who analysed existing data rather than spend time collecting new facts. And moreover, this tendency was accentuated by the training methods used in graduate schools, to such an extent that we 'perhaps have actually regressed in the training of people who are skilled at finding out what the real world is like'. He argued that graduate schools were responsible for what Veblen had called, 'trained incapacity'.

Boulding also made a memorable attack on what he calls the 'anti-historical method' in modern applied economics (Boulding, 1971, pp. 232–3). He said that economics is producing clever technicians who have little idea of economic reality. The anti-historical approach leads us to discard information that is not amenable to econometric analysis, and this does nothing to improve our understanding of reality. Elsewhere, Boulding (1970, p.155) takes a more mellow line, but argued that such an approach is running into diminishing returns. He argued that 'no science can rise above its original data collection', and he urged economists to give more attention to the collection of all forms of data and not just those data amenable to econometric analysis.

Peter Wiles (1984, p. 293) offered a very succinct critique in this vein: 'The main thing that is wrong with economics is its disrespect for fact'. Wiles (1984, p. 293) then listed the various manifestations of this disrespect:

- Failure to gather primary data
- Neglect of others' research findings
- Excessive use of axioms
- Excessive honour to theory
- Tendency to disregard contradictory evidence
- Preference for algebra over arithmetic
- Interest in puzzles not problems
- Use of stylised facts (that is, convenient half-truths)

J.K. Galbraith (1971, p. 41) gave one of the bluntest statements about this problem of trained incapacity. He said that paying excessive attention to mathematical exercises would lead to 'atrophy of judgement and intuition' when in fact these were the key intellectual skills required to find real solutions to economic problems. He also felt that the use of mathematics had sometimes led to a 'habit of mind which simply excludes the mathematically inconvenient factors from consideration'. It is interesting to compare these remarks with what Smith said about the hazards of the division of labour – see Chapter 1.

Leontief (1982) argued that our preference for deductive reasoning over fact-finding meant that we had lost the art of using the data around us unless it appeared in the right form. He was dismayed at the huge amount of detailed information that was neglected by economists simply because it did not appear in an econometrically-convenient form.

Morishima (1984, p. 70) argued that economists had a preoccupation with mathematics 'because mathematics is powerful'. However, he was not optimistic that scientific necessity would overcome the deeply ingrained power of vested intellectual interests. Those economists who have been successful in this paradigm would not welcome any change which would devalue their human capital.

THE ISOLATION OF ECONOMICS

A number of critics have argued that our preoccupation with econometrics to the exclusion of other empirical techniques has not helped our communication with other disciplines – which, on the whole, have a rather low regard for econometrics. Leontief (1971, p. 4) argued that our 'sense of self-sufficiency' resulting from a reliance on indirect inference was making it hard to collaborate across disciplinary boundaries. He was also highly critical of the positivist view that truth of assumptions is irrelevant to the usefulness of a theory (ibid., p. 5). He considered that this view was in large measure 'responsible for the state of splendid isolation in which our discipline nowadays finds itself'.

Leontief (1983, p. 904) argued that a rigid division of labour between theory and empirical work was hazardous, even in the 'exact sciences'. But he went on, 'in softer disciplines, it is bound to bring about a total impasse'. It is interesting to compare this observation with our remarks in Chapter 2 about the virtuous circles that must turn if applied economics is to be successful.

BRICKS FROM STRAW?

A recurrent critique of econometrics has been the idea that we are trying to build bricks from straw. The raw data we have are not (and cannot be) accurate enough for use with advanced econometric methods. Perhaps the most famous critique of this sort was the work of Morgenstern (1963). Morgenstern argued that economic data were not and probably could not be as accurate as econometricians seemed to assume (Morgenstern, 1963, p. 116n). He noted a comment made by Weiner after reading the first edition of Morgenstern's book, *On the Accuracy of Economic Observations*: 'Economics is a one or two digit science'. Morgenstern urged his readers to think carefully about this remark, especially when some economic data are reported to six or more significant digits. Moreover, Morgenstern argued that we should not really be ashamed about the fact that our data cannot be more accurate than that. We must just resist using techniques which demand unattainable accuracy. He noted that some physicists would say that a measurement that is accurate to 10 per cent is actually 'a very good measurement' (Morgenstern, 1963, p. 97).

However, Morgenstern and von Neumann (1953) were not just concerned with measurement accuracy as such, but also with the definition of economic categories. They argued that these definitions are poor because we have not done the empirical labour in the field that the physical sciences had done before creating a mathematical science (von Neumann and Morgenstern, 1953, p. 4). Leontief (1971, p. 6) was equally concerned about the lack of standardisation in our categories and our data. This resonates with the arguments in Chapter 2, that without standards of this sort we should not expect to progress to the division of labour found in the physical sciences.

DIMINISHING RETURNS

A number of critics have suggested that increasing investment in econometric technique, unmatched by comparable investments in data collection or other methods, must ultimately run into diminishing returns to econometrics. This is really just the same point as the argument that the company that employs ever more labour, but without investing in capital equipment or plant, must eventually run into diminishing returns to additional labour.

Ward (1972, p. 49) made this point early on. He argued that the availability of additional econometric data was having little effect on the quality of econometric results, and he argued that some sort of 'upper limit' was emerging, and the quality of econometric results 'is not strikingly superior to that achieved by the well-informed intuitive observer'. And as we saw above, Friedman (1991, p. 36) argued that economists had invested in mathematics and econometrics to a point of 'vanishing returns'. If the cost of performing regressions is vanishingly small, while the cost of collecting data is high, then it is not perhaps surprising that we go on performing additional regressions of vanishingly small value, while we are seemingly reluctant to invest in data collection.

GENERALISED UNEASE

Some critics have expressed a general sense of unease with the state of econometrics – without focusing on any one specific defect. Understandably perhaps, such criticisms are often ignored when they come from outside the field, but when they come from two of the great pioneers of econometrics, Frisch and Stone, we should sit up and listen.

Though a most enthusiastic pioneer of econometrics in the 1930s, by the mid-1950s Frisch had become very disappointed at the development of the subject. One of his main concerns was that it was so much easier to 'sit down and develop refined abstract schemes' than to use the econometric vision to produce better applied economics (Frisch, 1956, p. 301). And near the end of his life, Frisch (1970) wrote an essay that expressed even greater alarm about the state of econometrics. He warned the econometricians that econometric practice must help us to understand 'concrete realities' or otherwise it would degenerate 'into something that is not worthy of the name econometrics, but ought rather to be called *playometrics*' (Frisch , 1970, p. 163, his emphasis). In the same way, Stone (1978, p. 1) argued that 'econometrics proper' – meaning the use of econometric methods to improve applied economics – had not been advancing. Indeed, when he compared the econometrics of the late 1970s with that of 30–40 years earlier, he thought that the earlier work was superior.

WHAT OF THESE CRITIQUES?

What are we to make of this stream of complaints? Some econometricians seem weary with these criticisms and tend to ignore them. And perhaps that is justified. Should the econometricians necessarily feel any obligation to respond to this steady stream of complaints?

As I stated at the start of this chapter, I don't necessarily agree with all of the above critical remarks. Some econometricians may argue that most if not all of the above points can be answered, and that none of them needs detain us – though I think that some of them do still have validity. I personally am especially concerned with the issue of the signal-to-noise ratio – and will discuss this in the next chapter. But my purpose in listing them here is different. I wanted to form an overview of what the critics think is wrong.

The most important point for me is not whether econometrics can defend itself against these charges, or whether the future development of economics should adjust to embrace these criticisms. Rather, this list of criticisms gives us an idea of what a distinguished collection of applied economists think is missing – if I may put it like this – from the applied *econometrician's* desk. What should the real applied economist be doing that the econometrician is not?

After all, econometrics may have its shortcomings. But if we use complementary techniques that fill in the gaps left by econometric technique, then the shortcomings of econometrics hardly matter. Econometrics has been on the receiving end of this stream of complaints because econometricians have acted as if their technique is a universal solvent for all economic research problems. If econometrics had not achieved such a dominant position as a universal technique, but had simply been one of the techniques we use amongst others, then the critics would probably have directed their energies to showing how other techniques can fill these gaps rather than criticising econometrics per se.

Accordingly, my aim in the rest of this book is to identify some of the things that the applied economist should do to fill in the gaps listed above. This agenda will include a variety of activities other than applied econometrics. With one exception, in the next chapter, it is not my intention to comment on the future development of econometrics itself.

NOTES

1. In informal discussion, Freeman Dyson made an almost identical point to me that economics is not really like a science because the rules of the game keep changing.
2. A further assumption – that the environment should be homogeneous or uniform over time – is one that we have discussed above, and which Keynes (1939) rejected.

6. The problem of the signal-to-noise ratio

I said at the end of the last chapter that I did not intend to delve deeper into the various critiques of econometrics, except to see what other techniques we need to use to fill the gaps referred to by the critics. There is one exception, however. In the last chapter, we mentioned the view of some critics that economic data often are not and probably cannot be accurate enough for the purposes of econometrics. I call this the problem of the *signal-to-noise ratio*, and I personally believe it is a serious problem for many econometric studies. This chapter explores what this problem is and why it comes about. In keeping with the non-mathematical character of the rest of the book, I have tried to keep most of the mathematical details in an appendix, but a few essential formulae appear in this chapter.

THE SIGNAL-TO-NOISE RATIO: AN INTRODUCTION

The term signal-to-noise ratio originates in electronic engineering – for example, in the study of radio, hi-fi and television. To put it crudely, when we listen to the radio, we want to hear the signal without distortion from the noise. A good radio or hi-fi system is one which has a high signal-to-noise ratio. Indeed, it is this ratio – rather than the *absolute* level of noise – that matters, because we can always increase both signal strength and noise by use of an amplifier. On the other hand if the signal-to-noise ratio is too low, then it is hard or impossible to hear the radio broadcast clearly.

In hi-fi, the signal-to-noise ratio is measured in decibels, and defined on a logarithmic scale as follows:

$$S/N = 10*\log_{10}\left[\frac{\text{signal}}{\text{noise}}\right] \qquad (6.1)$$

So, for example, if the strength of the signal is 10 times greater than the strength of the noise, the signal-to-noise ratio is 10 decibels.[1]

How high does a signal-to-noise ratio have to be for us to listen to the radio in comfort? A good quality signal-to-noise ratio for a hi-fi system is probably in the region of 60 decibels or higher. If the ratio is less than that, then the system is of poor quality. Note what this means. Because the ratio is computed on a log scale, a signal-to-noise ratio of 60 decibels means that the signal is 10^6 (or 1 million) times stronger than the noise! To the economist, at least, this seems like a very high figure. Do we find such high signal-to-noise ratios in econometrics? I think we can safely say, 'never'!

THE SIGNAL-TO-NOISE RATIO IN ECONOMETRICS

This concept of a signal-to-noise ratio carries over more or less exactly into econometrics, and I find it a very clear and intuitive way to understand the problem of data accuracy in complex regression models.

What is the signal-to-noise ratio in econometrics? There are perhaps two possible interpretations:

(i)   Noise is the set of all other influences on our endogenous variable besides the explanatory variable(s) of interest

(ii) Noise is the error of measurement (defined broadly) in the explanatory variable(s) of interest

In what follows, we shall focus on (ii), because arguably there is no problem with (i). Why is there no problem with (i)? Because the whole point of our regression techniques in econometrics is that we can take account of multiple measurable explanatory variables and also, by use of the equation error, of unmeasured factors like (i). There is no problem with noise of type (i), and in fact standard regression methods assume that there is indeed such noise in the system.

However, there can be a problem with noise of type (ii). Let us see why in the context of a simple bivariate regression model. Assume an underlying bivariate regression model with two normalised variables, with zero means:

$$y = bx + u \qquad\qquad (6.2)$$

But x cannot be measured exactly, only with error:

$$\tilde{x} = x + v \qquad\qquad (6.3)$$

We can show that the usual ordinary least squares (OLS) estimator which uses the measured values rather than the true values (of x) is inconsistent (see Appendix, Result 1). The extent of the bias is given in the following formula:

$$\frac{p\lim \hat{b}}{b} = \frac{1}{1 + \dfrac{1}{\sigma_{xx}/\sigma_{vv}}} \tag{6.4}$$

where σ_{xx} is the variance of the true signal and σ_{vv} is the variance of the noise (or measurement error), and hence σ_{xx}/σ_{vv} is the signal-to-noise ratio.

What does the formula tell us? The left-hand side compares the estimated value[2] of b with its true value. The right-hand side shows how this depends on the signal-to-noise ratio. If the signal-to-noise ratio is very large, then the right-hand side of the equation will be close to 1, and that means there is very little difference between the estimated value of b and the true value. In short, if the signal-to-noise ratio is very large, then any bias is very small. That is the good news. But if the signal-to-noise ratio is very small, then the right-hand side of the equation will be substantially less than one, and that means that the estimated value of b is substantially less than the true value. In short, if the signal-to-noise ratio is small, then econometric estimation will be subject to large bias.

Immediately, then, we see that the same sort of intuition applies to the signal-to-noise ratio in econometrics as in hi-fi. A high signal-to-noise ratio means a good clear radio broadcast, and a good clear estimate of the econometric parameter we want to measure. But a low signal-to-noise ratio means a poor radio signal, and an inaccurate measure of the econometric parameter.

THE MULTIVARIATE CONTEXT

Is this really an issue in applied work? Does a bit of measurement error really matter? I would tend to answer that it is probably not a big deal in a bivariate context, but it may well be a serious issue in a multivariate context. To see this, consider the simplest extension of equation (6.2) with two explanatory variables:

$$y = xb + zc + u \tag{6.5}$$

where x is measured with error as in equation (6.3), while the other explanatory variable (z) is measured accurately.

Then, once again, we can show that that the usual multivariate OLS estimator which uses the measured values rather than the true values (of x) is inconsistent (see Appendix, Result 2). Using the Frisch–Waugh theorem (1933), we can show that the extent of the bias is given in the following formula:

$$\frac{\text{plim } \hat{b}}{b} = \frac{1}{1 + \dfrac{1}{\sigma_{xx.z}/\sigma_{vv}}} \tag{6.6}$$

where $\sigma_{xx.z}$ is the *partial* variance of the true signal x and σ_{vv} is the variance of the noise (or measurement error in x), and hence $\sigma_{xx.z}/\sigma_{vv}$ is the *partial* signal-to-noise ratio. But what is this partial variance in x? It is a measure of the signal in x which is unrelated to variations in z. More precisely:

$$\sigma_{xx.z} = \sigma_{xx}\left(1 - R_{x.z}^2\right) \tag{6.7}$$

where $R_{x.z}^2$ is the R-squared from a regression of x on z. Clearly, if x and z are unrelated, then this R-squared is approximately 0, and in that case the partial variance is roughly equal to the full variance. But if x and z are very closely related, so that this R-squared is nearly 1, then the partial variance of x is much less than the full variance.

So what does equation (6.6) tell us? The story is essentially the same as in equation (6.4). If the partial signal-to-noise ratio is very large, then there is little bias. But if the partial signal-to-noise ratio is very small, then econometric estimation will be subject to large bias. There is, however, an important difference between equations (6.6) and (6.4). In equation (6.6) the partial variance may be small for two different reasons: first, because the full variance of x is small; second, because x and z are closely related.

It is for this reason that I believe that a low (partial) signal-to-noise ratio may be a common problem in complex multivariate models. If different explanatory variables are closely related – and this multicollinearity property is commonly found in econometric data – then the partial variance in any one regressor (x) is liable to be quite small, even if the full variance in x is large. This means that the partial signal-to-noise ratio is low even though the full signal-to-noise ratio is large.

The above result (equation (6.6)) generalises to the case of a general multivariate model with many other explanatory variables (see Appendix, Result 3). The basic character of the result is the same, but in a sense things can get even worse because the *R*-squared from a regression of *x* on all other explanatory variables is liable to be higher than that in equation (6.7).

DOES MEASUREMENT ERROR REALLY MATTER?

In summary, we can conclude from the above that measurement error doesn't matter very much if it is small relative to the independent signal (or partial variance) of any regressor. But measurement error may well matter when it is large relative to the partial variance of the regressor. Another way of putting this is to say that measurement error may not matter too much in a simple regression model, but it may well matter in a complex regression model with multicollinear regressors. In short, it is the combination of measurement error and multicollinearity that causes the problems.

As a practical matter, how can we assess in any specific regression model whether measurement errors may be biasing the results? Answer: we need to estimate the signal-to-noise ratio.

There are two problems in obtaining such an estimate. The first problem is that while we can readily estimate the variance of the measured signal, this is not the same as the variance of the true signal. Consider the following result, derived from equation (6.3) – see Appendix, equation (A.5):

$$\sigma_{\tilde{x}\tilde{x}} = \sigma_{xx} + \sigma_{vv} \tag{6.8}$$

This says that the measured variance of *x* is equal to the true variance of *x* plus the variance of noise (or measurement error). In other words, the measured variance is systematically greater than the true variance. The second problem, of course, is that almost by definition we do not know the variance of measurement error.

However, we easily derive the following formula for the true signal-to-noise ratio from equation (6.8):

$$\frac{\sigma_{xx}}{\sigma_{vv}} = \frac{\sigma_{\tilde{x}\tilde{x}} - \sigma_{vv}}{\sigma_{vv}} \tag{6.9}$$

So if we can estimate the approximate size of the measurement error variance, then we can readily estimate the signal-to-noise ratio.

How do we assess the likely size of measurement errors for any variable? It is common to say that a figure is accurate to plus or minus some fixed percentage. For example, we might say that the retail price index is accurate to ±*p* per cent. If we interpret this interval as a (say) 95 per cent confidence interval for the real value of the index, then we can compute the variance of measurement errors from that. The derivation is not difficult, but it is messy, so the reader is referred to the Appendix (Result 4).

Another way of looking at this, which I have found very helpful, is to ask what level of measurement error would drive the true signal-to-noise ratio towards zero. If the true signal is zero, then from equation (6.8), all the measured signal must be noise! This would correspond to a decibel level of minus infinity! We can call this the 'critical level of measurement error' (CLME). Additionally, we can ask what level of measurement error would drive the signal-to-noise ratio towards one. In this case, the measured signal is half true and half noise. This would be a decibel level of zero! We can call this the 'half-critical level of measurement error' (HCLME). See the Appendix (Result 4) for the definition of these.

This CLME can sometimes be computed from published regression summaries, if sufficient information is published, but usually it cannot. But it can be calculated as an adjunct to any regression calculations. I have applied it in a number of contexts – for example, a study of complete systems of demand equations (Swann, 1985a) estimated the Deaton and Muellbauer (1980) 'Almost Ideal Demand System'. This study used nine commodity groups, with price indices in logs. In this case I computed CLME at about ±2 per cent and HCLME at about ±1 per cent. These are very low numbers! This means that if the price indices are accurate to ±2 per cent, then all the measured signal is noise, and the signal-to-noise ratio is zero. In this case, regression is pointless. We cannot estimate any true parameters; all we get is noise. If the price indices are accurate to ±1 per cent, then the picture is a little better in that half the measured signal is true and half is noise, but regression estimates will still be subject to very serious bias. In fairness, this may be a rather atypical example, for it is well known that the multiple price indices used in complete systems of demand equations tend to exhibit a high degree of collinearity.

How accurate are economic data? In the last chapter, we noted Wiener's famous statement that, 'Economics is a one or two digit science'. I take this to mean:[3]

'one digit': accurate to about ±10 per cent
'two digit': accurate to about ±1 per cent

In the last chapter, we also noted Morgenstern's (1963, p. 97) view that a measurement in physics that is accurate to within 10 per cent should be considered 'a very good measurement'. So we should probably be content with economic measurements that are accurate to ±10 per cent. Maurice

(1968) was a bit more optimistic, and reckoned that components of consumer expenditure are accurate to between ±3 per cent and ±10 per cent.

What do we conclude from this? We should not place much trust in regression estimates where the critical level of measurement error (as defined above) is as little as plus or minus a few per cent. It seems very unlikely that much of the economic data we have is good enough to calibrate such a demanding econometric model.

UNCERTAINTY IN REGRESSION ESTIMATES

An alternative way to assess whether measurement error really matters is provided by the work of Gini (1921) and Frisch (1934). Gini's paper was a famous early attempt to allow for measurement errors in regression analysis.

When we estimate a conventional bivariate regression of y on x (as in equation (6.1)), we are in effect assuming that measurement errors in x are very small. Or, to put it another way, we are assuming that equation errors completely dominate errors in x. But if this is quite wrong, and if instead measurement errors in x dominate equation errors, then Gini demonstrated that we should really run the regression in reverse: a regression of x on y. He also showed that if we didn't really know what was the truth, and which type of error dominated, then we could put a bound on our uncertainty as follows. Frisch (1934) extended this argument to the multivariate case, and also deepened our understanding of Gini's procedure.

First, run a regression of y on x:

$$y = x b + u \qquad (6.10)$$

Then run a regression of x on y:

$$x = y c + w \qquad (6.11)$$

Then construct the interval $[\hat{b}, 1/\hat{c}]$ from the two parameter estimates. Gini shows that the true value for b lies somewhere in this range. If equation error dominates, it will lie towards the lower end of the range; if measurement error in x dominates, it will lie towards the upper end of the range.

This interval is a measure of our uncertainty about the value of b due to our uncertainty about the character of errors in our equation. It is conceptually quite distinct from the standard confidence interval due to sampling uncertainty. However, Swann (1985b) showed that the width of this Gini range (GR) could be compared to the standard 95 per cent confidence interval (CI) using the following very simple result (see Appendix, Result 5):

$$\frac{GR}{CI} = \frac{T-k}{4t} \tag{6.12}$$

where t is the standard t-statistic for the null hypothesis that $b = 0$, T is the number of observations in the regression and k is the number of explanatory variables.

To illustrate the significance of this result, suppose we run a regression with 100 degrees of freedom ($T - k = 100$). Then:

$$\begin{aligned} &\text{If } t < 25,\ GR > CI \\ &\text{If } t = 25,\ GR = CI \\ &\text{If } t > 25,\ GR < CI \end{aligned} \tag{6.13}$$

In my experience, t-statistics of 25 are fairly rare in econometric results, especially so when we have as few as 100 data observations. For example, a t-statistic of about 2.5 is a more common occurrence. In that case, with $T - k = 100$, equation (6.12) yields $GR/CI = 10$. In this case, the width of the Gini range is 10 times that of the 95 per cent confidence interval.

In short, I suspect that in the vast majority of cases the Gini range must be wider than the 95 per cent confidence interval. What does that mean? It means that uncertainty in regression estimates due to measurement errors is very probably more important than the uncertainty in regression estimates due to small samples of data. Measurement errors (in their various manifestations) do matter a lot – a good deal more so than sampling uncertainties!

Frisch (1934) extended Gini's work to the multivariate case – what he called 'Confluence Analysis'. Arguably, the multivariate picture is even more problematic. Kalman (1982a, 1982b), Klepper and Leamer (1984) – amongst others – have provided a modern interpretation of Confluence Analysis.

HOW DO WE INCREASE THE SIGNAL-TO-NOISE RATIO?

What can we do to make things better? Is there any way we can increase the signal-to-noise ratio? The answer is, 'yes'. What we must do is seek to impose *valid* restrictions on our regression models, so as to reduce their dimensionality. That is, we reduce the number of parameters that need to be estimated.

By this, I *do not* mean that we should omit important variables from our regressions. We know well enough from basic econometrics that 'omitted variables bias' is an ugly problem. What I *do* mean is that we should seek restrictions on our model that we know to be valid from research we have done using another research method. These valid restrictions reduce the dimensionality of our regression models. And we can show, using a most elegant theorem due to Goldberger (1964), that imposing valid restrictions will increase the partial variance in our regressors, and therefore increase the signal-to-noise ratio – see the Appendix (Result 6).

When applying his confluence analysis, Frisch frequently found that his multi-dimensional equivalents to Gini ranges were very wide indeed. He concluded (Frisch, 1948, p. 370) that it is very rare to find cases where statistical data alone can determine parameters with accuracy, and he argued that economists need to look for other approaches to estimating parameters. It is interesting to note that he picked the interview method as a possible way to gain further information about parameters. This information could be used to impose valid restrictions on our models, reduce the dimensionality of our regression problems and increase the signal-to-noise ratio. Actually, as we shall see in Part IV, there are a variety of other approaches in addition to the interview method from which we can obtain this additional information.

In the rest of this book, I shall argue that the other techniques described in Part IV have many other uses besides this. We should not see them simply as a way to solve the problem of a low signal-to-noise ratio in our econometric work. But the committed econometrician, who has little regard for the other techniques described in Part IV, may still find it worthwhile to use them as a way to improve his regression work.

CONCLUSION

In view of the above, I think it fair to conclude that without doubt econometrics has a problem with the signal-to-noise ratio. I believe it ranks as one of the biggest practical problems in econometrics. In view of that, it has always mystified me why econometricians pay so little attention to the issue of measurement error. Maddala (1998) gave a fascinating insight here. He observed that when he was preparing a new edition of his econometrics textbook, the reviewers all suggested that he should remove the chapter on errors in variables because it is 'never used' (Maddala, 1998, p. 414). But as Maddala (1998, p. 414) noted, applied economists 'have to face the problems of errors in variables all the time'.

NOTES

1. $S/N = 10*\log_{10}(10/1) = 10$ decibels.

2.   Strictly speaking, the numerator of the left-hand side is the probability limit. Roughly speaking, this is the value that this estimator will converge to when we use a very large sample for estimation.

3.   The logic of these calculations is as follows. If we say that a measurement of 5 is accurate to one digit, we mean that the true value is between 4.5 and 5.5. This is a proportionate margin of error of $\pm 1/10$ or ± 10 per cent. If we say that a measurement of 50 is accurate to two digits, we mean that the true value is between 49.5 and 50.5. This is a proportionate margin of error of $\pm 1/100$ or ± 1 per cent.

PART III

The vernacular in applied economics

7. Vernacular economics

By *vernacular* economics, I mean the understanding of economics developed by non-professional economists. This is a very broad definition. I include the understanding of economics developed in other academic disciplines. I include the understanding of senior business people, government officials and politicians who need to develop their own mental models of how their part of the economy works in order to keep their businesses solvent. I include rank and file members of the workforce who, while they may not be charged with any great strategic decision-making, still need to understand how the economy affects their business, and therefore their employment prospects and the condition of the labour market. And I include the understanding of ordinary consumers, who find that they get a better deal from their limited resources if they have some understanding of the working of markets. Probably everybody of teenage years and above has some vernacular understanding of economics.[1]

Is this vernacular economics really different from formal economics? Keynes (1936, Chapter 24) famously argued that practical people who think they are unaffected by any theory 'are usually the slaves of some defunct economist'. In that case, we might ask if there is anything to be learnt from vernacular economics but a half-digested account of the economic theory of a century beforehand? I am in no doubt that Keynes was right, and that business people are guided by the ideas of academics far more than they would ever concede. However, this observation, in itself, does not imply that vernacular economics is just the same as formal economics. The two forms of economics may have some common intellectual heritage, but they have developed in different ways, just as the great-grandchildren of a great late-Victorian entrepreneur may be found in many different walks of life and with many different degrees of intellectual, economic and social achievement.

In my experience, vernacular economics has something in common with our formal economics, but some very important differences. That is what makes it so interesting. One of the best examples I can give relates to a study of the market for *Virtual Reality* (VR) software which I carried out between 1996 and 2000. I was privileged to have good access (through the British Government's Department of Trade and Industry) to many of the VR pioneers in the UK and some from other countries, and spent a lot of time talking to them about their understanding of the market for their VR systems. I suppose at the start I had a mild missionary objective (not an imperialist one) that I might persuade them that their understanding of their markets (and hence the success of their businesses) could be modestly improved if I taught them some economic tools. In practice, most of the learning was in the reverse direction. I found that these pioneers often had rather sophisticated mental models of how their markets work, and to be honest, I learnt more from recording and assimilating their models than they learnt from the economists' models.

Were these models just the same as our own, however? Emphatically not! The style was completely different. They were usually rather informal, back of the envelope models, explained using diagrams and flow-charts, and rarely using any maths. Use of metaphor was widespread. Many of these pioneers had a background in science or mathematics, so I don't think that lack of mathematical ability was a constraint on their use of sophisticated models. Rather, my sense after talking to them was that to apply the economists' models to their world would be a matter of bending their world to their models, and that didn't seem a very good idea to me – or indeed to them! Much better to try to modify the economists' tools to their world.

What did my fellow economists make of this endeavour? My business school colleagues were typically quite supportive. But I also gave a couple of presentations of this work to mainstream economics audiences. I presented some of the mental models of these VR pioneers, complete with diagrams, flow-chart, metaphors and anecdotes, and without any axioms, formal models, mathematics or econometrics. Some members of the audience sat quietly, courteous enough to let me have my say even if it all seemed a bit peculiar. But others responded with a mixture of exasperation and hostility. To them, this was just not proper economics.

I conclude from this foray that vernacular economics is interesting, even if it is very different in style, and we have much to learn from it, even if some mainstream economists do not feel comfortable with it. However, I do not mean to imply that the interest of vernacular economics makes our own formal economics redundant. Each vernacular understanding of economics is local and incomplete. It refers to a particular part of the economy, and generally speaking does not contain a good systemic overview of the economy as a whole. Senior business people with an extraordinarily good understanding of their own business usually do not have such a clear perception of the whole economy as a complex system. And, indeed, even those social scientists who have been very critical of economics as a discipline have had to concede that economics provides a powerful systemic model of the whole economy.

THE MEANING OF 'VERNACULAR'

I have chosen the word *vernacular* to describe this informal economics, because it is such a rich term, and captures exactly the sort of economic understanding that interests me. Ilich (1982) wrote a memorable essay about vernacular values in which he gives many examples of the vernacular. So, for example, vernacular weaving is home spun, and destined for home use rather than the market. Vernacular food production is food gathered from our own garden or common land, and destined for home consumption. It is not sold or bought in a market. As such, it is in a sense the opposite of a commodity. And vernacular architecture is the building whose design follows local norms and conventions in house design, which in turn have evolved carefully over many years to reflect local conditions, materials and requirements. Vernacular architecture is, in a sense, the opposite of the architect-designed building.

Another familiar use of vernacular is in the context of vernacular language, and it is useful to dwell on this at length. This again is an evolving local language or dialect as opposed to a formal, standardised or professionally defined language. The vernacular may vary from region to region, or even from district to district, from industry to industry, or even from one job to another. Is this diverse collection of vernacular languages a good thing? Should we ever try to turn such a collection of vernacular dialects into a standardised language?

Ilich (1982) gives a fascinating account of the pioneering attempt of Don Elio de Nebrija to do just this in the fifteenth century. Nebrija was concerned that the Castilian language had degenerated into a 'loose and unruly' collection of vernacular dialects, and it was his objective to turn this into a 'standard coinage'. In 1492, Nebrija produced the first grammar of the Castilian language – and indeed the first grammar of a modern European language. He dedicated this great undertaking to Queen Isabella.

However, Queen Isabella was not entirely enthusiastic about this venture, which she felt was misguided (Ilich, 1982, p. 74). She argued that the ordinary man should be allowed to have 'perfect dominion over his tongue' and it was not the monarch's job to interfere. Ilich (1982) considered this an exceptional piece of royal wisdom, for he argued that the vernacular language is what ordinary people use to ensure their survival in a difficult world. Deny them this, force them to communicate in a standard language, and some will not be able to survive. Many totalitarian regimes in more recent times have sought to abolish particular dialects, and this is generally an instrument of repression. Queen Isabella's remark also anticipates Hayek's ideas on the role of local knowledge in a decentralised economic system – we shall return to this in Chapter 8.

WHY DOES A NEW VERNACULAR EMERGE?

Dalby (1998) has argued that there are two opposing forces at work in the evolution of languages. There are a variety of forces that lead languages to converge. These include the economic forces of globalisation and international trade, and also those technological developments (radio, television, film and Internet) that increase communication over long distances. There are also a variety of forces at work that lead languages to diverge. These include the economic forces of specialisation, division of labour and innovation. A group of specialists concentrating their professional attention on a narrow area of new technology little understood by ordinary people will soon evolve their own vernacular.

Just as vernacular languages emerge, so we must expect vernacular economics to emerge. These latter are the local languages and 'models' used by economic actors to make sense of their part of the economy. They may be highly informal, non-standardised, and will probably not conform to the language of economic professionals (that is academic economists) – even if they have some intellectual heritage in common (following Keynes). And to the extent that innovation and the division of labour proliferate different linguistic vernaculars, then so also would we expect them to proliferate different economic vernaculars.

Let me be very clear about one point however. In saying that innovation and the division of labour tend to lead to a new economic vernacular, I do not mean that the economics of the 'new economy' is quite different from the economics of the old economy. Though some prophets argued that the advent of the Internet and the dot.com would create a new economics, we have seen that post-Internet economics actually has a lot in common with old economics. What I do mean is that new industries built on new technologies with highly specialised labour will tend to develop their own distinctive language in which to describe the workings of their industry. This language grows out of deep experience, and can provide a remarkably accurate summary of local conditions and peculiarities.

A work of literature written in an obscure language can be translated from its original language into English, but something is lost in translation. In the same way, the vernacular economics of a particular industry can be translated into the standard language of the professional economist, but again something is lost in translation. In my view, the economics of the virtual reality market is best understood in the vernacular of that industry, even if mainstream economists prefer to hear it in our standard economic language.

Having said that, there can be no doubt that some of the vernacular methods that I will describe in Part IV of the book tend to be viewed with suspicion by professional economists. Common criticisms are that these methods are 'informal', 'vague', 'woolly', or 'unscientific'. To some degree these are fair criticisms, and we can perhaps understand why those with a high regard for econometrics and other formal techniques of applied economics would tend to disregard the vernacular. But for those who hold a less rosy (and in my opinion, more realistic) view of what can be achieved with econometrics (and what cannot), these vernacular methods start to look rather attractive.

Above all, the attraction of the various forms of vernacular economics is that each one has its own distinct vantage point. We shall see in the next chapter why this must be important to those who follow Hayek's ideas on the role of local knowledge in a decentralised economic system. We shall also see in Chapter 9 why it makes sense to treat applied economic methodology akin to photographic composition, where we look at the world from a number of distinct vantage points, and then select the one that gives the best and clearest picture.

NOTES

1. Indeed, quite young children now have experience as consumers, and many people consider there is something wrong in this. The Archbishop of Canterbury has written of his regret at this loss of innocence (Williams, 2000, Chapter 1).

8. The vernacular as local knowledge

In a most influential article, Hayek (1945) noted that it is almost considered a heresy to suggest that there is any important knowledge apart from scientific knowledge. But he argued that without doubt there was a large body of 'very important but unorganized knowledge' which should not be called 'scientific'. This is the specific, local knowledge 'of time and place'. This knowledge was economically important because almost everyone 'possesses unique information of which beneficial use might be made' (Hayek, 1945, p. 521).

Most mainstream economists accept Hayek's (1945) arguments about the superiority of decentralisation over central planning. An essential part of his argument was that local economic efficiency requires the use of specific local knowledge which cannot be used (and perhaps cannot be known) by a central planning authority. I shall argue that this local economic knowledge is exactly the vernacular knowledge that I described in the last chapter. It is really rather strange therefore that the same mainstream tradition that accepts Hayek's arguments seems to have such a low regard for vernacular economic knowledge.

In the last chapter, I described vernacular economic knowledge as 'interesting'. Here I shall go further. If Hayek is right, and such vernacular knowledge ensures the superiority of decentralisation over central planning, then vernacular knowledge must be an essential object of study for the applied economist.

HAYEK ON 'THE USE OF KNOWLEDGE IN SOCIETY'

The aim of Hayek's (1945) famous article was to explain the superiority of decentralised economic systems over centrally planned economic systems. But at various points, Hayek also describes the similarity between these issues of efficient economic organisation, and some similar methodological questions.

Throughout the article, Hayek notes the essential role of local knowledge – the specific knowledge of time and place. He argues that economic knowledge never really exists in a concentrated form, but instead is found as a dispersed collection of incomplete and often contradictory items. For that reason, the problem of economic organisation is how we can and should use knowledge which is not available in its totality to any one individual or agency.

Hayek puzzles why this dispersed and incomplete knowledge is generally regarded with a kind of contempt. But he is clear that modern economics has little use for knowledge of the particular circumstances of time and place. He suggests that this tendency has been reinforced by the predilection for use of mathematics and statistics within economics. This sort of local knowledge cannot be completely captured in a statistical form.

Hayek concludes that economic efficiency requires that decisions needing specific knowledge about the circumstances of time and place must be left to the 'man on the spot', because only such a person can have such specific knowledge. Central planning can never achieve that sort of efficiency because it cannot use (and probably cannot obtain) the local knowledge of the 'man on the spot'.

When I talk of vernacular knowledge in this book, I mean the sorts of knowledge referred to by Hayek. This is loose, informal, dispersed, and does not necessarily lend to statistical aggregation. As Hayek suggests, professional economists tend not to take it very seriously. But a deep understanding of the economic system depends on our being receptive to such vernacular knowledge, and requires that we respect the vernacular methods used to acquire it – even if these are very different from the research methods which we use as professional economists.

If the vernacular economics described in this book is the economics of decentralised decision-makers, then formal economics is the economics of the central planner. Formal applied economics, as described by the current mainstream, is preoccupied with statistical and quantifiable knowledge, and uses this very well. But it only rarely uses vernacular knowledge and it would be better if it did this more often.

TAKING INFORMAL METHODS SERIOUSLY

Part IV describes some of these vernacular methods. They include case studies, common sense, intuition, introspection and metaphor. These seem highly informal techniques compared to the rigour of econometrics and experimental economics. Why should we take these informal methods seriously? There are two reasons.

First, it is customary in modern economics to assume that *economic man* is a good economist. If that is true, then there is no reason why economic man should not use that capability to choose an appropriate method to develop his understanding of the economic world around him. For this reason, we must respect the methods he uses to obtain the knowledge essential to his decisions. These techniques of assembling vernacular knowledge may seem rather crude, just as some vernacular tools of production seem crude. But they serve the required purpose in the specific context.

Second, we shall see in Part IV that these vernacular methods are in fact not as crude as they appear at first sight. For example, intuition may be a much deeper source of reliable knowledge than we tend to assume. In Chapter 19, where we review some of Herbert Simon's research on intuition in decision-making, we shall see that intuition is perhaps best understood as a form of subconscious pattern recognition built up from extensive local experience. Simon saw a direct parallel between some human thinking and some of the methods of artificial intelligence. We shall explore a simple model of machine learning through which the computer can build a mental model of some complexity, through repeated and diverse experience. This has something in common with the development of human intuition.

Ultimately, the most important thing about vernacular knowledge is that it is built up from the specific circumstances of time and place. The vernacular economic knowledge of one location does not deny the different vernacular economic knowledge of another location. The vernacular economic knowledge of one age does not deny the vernacular economic knowledge of an earlier age. Each economic agent builds up a mental model from his experience, and if we contrast these different mental models, that gives us a powerful insight into how changes in economic circumstances influence economic behaviour. A collection of vernacular knowledge is attractive because it comes from so many vantage points. In the same way, we argue in Chapter 16 that one of the reasons why the history of economic thought is so interesting is because it offers us so many different vantage points. In that chapter, we argue that old economic theories still tell us something about how an economy works – or perhaps I should say, how it *used* to work – even if these old theories are not really applicable to the economy of today.

9. Economic research as composition

I believe that the applied economist can learn how to do better applied economics by understanding how the professional photographer approaches the problem of composition in photography. In his classic, *Principles of Composition in Photography*, Feininger (1973) considered the reasons why professional photographers take better photographs than amateurs. He argued that this was not because professionals have better equipment or better technology. No, the reason why professionals take better photographs is because of a difference in attitude. Before the professional takes a photograph, 'they study their subject from all sides and angles, and in every respect' (Feininger, 1973, pp. 130–31).

This is remarkably similar to the philosophy of J.S. Mill quoted at the start of Chapter 1. If J.S. Mill had been a photographer, one suspects he would have approached the challenge of taking a photograph in just the same way as Feininger's professional.

In this chapter, I shall argue that good applied economic research is very similar to good composition. We need to look at the subject, 'from all sides and angles, and in every respect'. I shall also argue that the view of econometrics as a universal research technique has tended to encourage an approach to applied research which is similar to Feininger's amateur.

EXPLORATION AND COMPOSITION

Economists rarely talk about exploration or composition. But any study in applied economics involves some exploration and then requires careful composition.

Exploration requires a certain frontier spirit. The explorer travels into the unknown, enduring danger, showing endurance, expecting the unfamiliar, and in many ways, delighting in discovery of the unfamiliar. Exploration entails reconnaissance, orienteering, voyage, investigation, rummaging, excavation, experiment, serendipity, discovery, surprise and the likelihood of encountering some eye-opening objects or occurrences. The objects found on an exploration may not conform to our norms, and indeed may challenge our norms, sometimes very vigorously. Those without the explorer's enthusiasm may be uncomfortable with that. The explorer must try to be broad-minded, to set aside preconceptions, prejudices and rigidities of mind. If (s)he can do this, then (s)he can come closer to understanding.

Indeed, we could go as far as to say that the intellectual explorer seeks out paradoxes and contradictions, because if we can respond to these in the right way, we can learn much from them. In drawing together some of the themes in the book, Chapter 23 will describe a *paradox-seeking* approach to research in applied economics.

If exploration is an unfamiliar way to describe economic research, then composition is perhaps even more so. Nevertheless, there is much in common between the approach to applied research described in this book and the approach to composition described in Feininger (1973).

As summarised at the start of this chapter, Feininger (1973, pp. 130–31) argues that the reason why a good professional photographer produces better photographs than an amateur is not that the professional has superior equipment, nor superior developing and printing facilities, nor that professionals are better informed about the 'technical' side of photography, nor that they have access to better subjects. The difference stems from a difference in attitude or approach.

There are three components to this difference (Feininger, 1973, p. 131). First, Feininger says that the amateur tends to 'stumble on' a subject and take a photograph. The professional, on the other hand, develops an interest in specific subjects. Before (s)he takes a photograph, (s)he thinks about the subject from all points of view. Second, the amateur photographer tends to have a favourite camera which (s)he thinks can do everything. The professional, by contrast, realises that different subjects call for different types of camera, and chooses his/her equipment accordingly. Third, while the amateur may be satisfied with a single shot, the professional never settles for just one photograph. Professionals know that it is best to take a sequence of shots, because the quality of these will often improve as more are taken and the photographer develops a better understanding of the subject.

These three principles – studying the subject from all sides and all angles, selection of appropriate equipment for the particular subject and repeated exploration while taking photographs – are all essential parts of the approach to research described in this book. I shall talk about these principles in the remainder of this chapter.

BISOCIATION

In my view, the creativity literature provides additional support for the research approach described in this book: studying the subject from all sides and all angles. The creativity literature sees combination and reorganisation as fundamental to the process of creative thought. People create new knowledge or ideas by combining and reorganising existing concepts or categories (Mumford and Porter, 1999). This has been recognised for some time (if in an informal way) in the aphorisms of the great minds. The 19th century painter, Henry Fuseli (1831, p. 137), wrote of artistic invention that it: 'discovers, selects, combines the possible, the probable, the known, in a mode that strikes with an air of truth and novelty'.

Koestler coined the term *bisociation* to describe what happens in creative thinking. Koestler's (1964, p. 35) aim was to distinguish between routine thinking which operates on a 'single plane' and creative thinking which 'operates on more than one plane'. And to Koestler (1964, p. 35), bisociation is about perceiving and understanding 'in two self consistent but habitually incompatible frames of reference'.

If this is right, and I believe it is, creative research requires us to look at phenomena in just such a way. This is the clear attraction of research using the different vernacular economics of very different groups. As we have argued above, vernacular understanding is the understanding built up from the particular circumstances of time and place. Any individual vernacular is 'self-consistent', but the vernaculars of different times and places may be very different. Moreover, to the extent that the vernacular outlook is only local, the different vernaculars will be 'habitually incompatible frames of reference', as Koestler put it. If the researcher can try to understand the world from these different vantage points and – most important of all – understand why these different perspectives appear to contradict each other, then he can make a creative contribution to research.

Bisociation is therefore a combinatorial activity. It need not necessarily be a social activity, though some have argued that the scope for bisociation is greatest when there can be creative interaction in heterogeneous groups. At any rate, the creative researcher needs to explore. In writing this book, I have learnt just how much my thinking as an economist has been enhanced by what I have learnt from many other disciplines and traditions. One learns how to do economics better, and how to talk about economics to others. By following Feininger's principle for the professional photographer, we look at economic questions 'from all sides and angles', and we learn things that more conventional approaches will not tell us.

THE *ALKAHEST* AND THE AMATEUR

The second difference between amateur and professional photographer, in Feininger's view (1973, p. 131), was that the amateur tends to have a favourite camera which (s)he thinks can do everything, while the professional realises that different subjects call for different types of camera. The third difference between professional and amateur was that the professional never settles for just one photograph.

Amongst some of those who consider that applied econometrics is the alchemical *alkahest*, a universal solvent for economic research questions, we find an attitude to research which is similar to Feininger's amateur. Econometrics is thought of as a favourite tool that can do everything, and there is little recognition that different questions require different tools. And if an econometric study fails to provide convincing or useful results, a typical response from such a researcher is to conclude that we need more of exactly the same. Repeat the econometric study with more data! There is no need to change the tool, nor to take a different perspective.

The approach to research recommended throughout this book is closer to that of Feininger's professional. If a particular tool doesn't work, try another. Be ready to concede that a favoured tool is not suitable for all purposes, and be prepared to use another. If a particular perspective doesn't work, then try another. If necessary, be prepared to construct a special tool – or even a special vantage point – for your particular purpose. This last possibility is what we shall call innovative economics – and is discussed in Chapter 21.

PART IV

Ten approaches to applied economics

10. Plurality: why and what?

This part of the book summarises ten approaches to applied economics. Some chapters deal with several research techniques together, but even so the topics covered in these chapters are by no means an exhaustive list. At the end of this part of the book, we include a brief chapter on what I shall call *innovative economics*. The good applied economist should also make occasional use of an essential miscellany of techniques to provide insights that don't seem to be available from any other technique. Moreover, the innovative applied economist will always be looking to create new research tools.

Before we start on this overview of different approaches to research, it is useful to have a brief recap of why we want to use a plurality of techniques, and to describe what we are looking for in that plurality.

Let us start with 'why'? In the previous chapters we have seen a variety of reasons why plurality is attractive. The most compact way to summarise these is to observe that there are many items on the good applied economist's desk, and different activities require different tools.

We argued above that econometrics is not a universal technique. In fact, we should go further and make it clear that neither is there any other universal technique. Excessive use of one technique, to the neglect of any others, will run into diminishing returns – just as the manager who employs more and more labour without investing in plant and equipment will usually run into diminishing returns to labour.

This is a basic point from first year economics. Figure 10.1 shows the familiar isoquant diagram summarising the relationship between inputs of two factors of production (econometrics and other techniques) and output (in the form of economic knowledge). If we continually expand our use of the first (so moving to the right along ray A) while doing very little of the second, then we can expect to run into diminishing returns. At this point, the best way to increase our research productivity is to invest in other techniques, so moving in an orthogonal direction along ray B.[1]

We said that one of the reasons why we need to maintain a plurality of research approaches is to maintain an essential dialogue with adjacent fields and professions. Economists do not have a monopoly of wisdom about economics, because many other people develop a vernacular understanding of economics from their everyday experience. This dialogue is essential if we are as academics to do what every business has to do: bring together the results of divided labour into a complete finished product. But it is also essential if we are to ensure that we have the data we need, and if we are to maintain a virtuous circle between applied research and data collection by outside agencies.

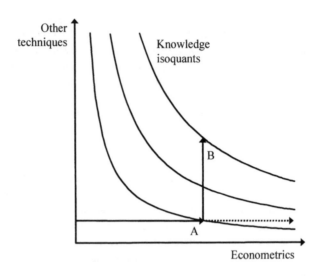

Figure 10.1   Diminishing returns

We likened economic research to exploration and composition, and suggested that both of these activities require the researcher to look at a question from all angles and perspectives. We suggested that plurality is important because it can sometimes generate interesting paradoxes, and these play an essential role in learning – a point we return to in Chapter 23. We noted that the literature on creativity saw an essential role for bisociation – where the creative thinker develops an understanding of a phenomenon from two or more habitually distinct perspectives. Finally, we noted that excessive specialisation does not generally lead to wisdom.

Now let us turn to 'what'? What do we seek by using a plurality of research techniques? Here I find myself taking what may seem an unusual point of view. Those scholars in the methodology of social scientists who advocate triangulation – in the *modern* sense, and not in the original sense of Frisius (see Chapter 4) – recommend it as a way to check that research findings are robust. From this point of view, if two techniques give the same results, then that is good news: we have reliable research findings. But if they give different results, then that is bad news: we have a problem.

I agree with the first part of this, but disagree with the second. The apparent paradox that arises when two different research techniques give contradictory results is not really a problem. It is an opportunity to learn!

This observation turns out to have an exceptionally important implication for the design and selection of research methods. If we seek compatibility between different research techniques and their findings, then there is often a tendency to stress the similarities between the different methods and to play down the differences between them. But if, on the other hand, we delight in plurality because of the many distinct perspectives it can give us, then we may be less interested in the similarities than the differences. Indeed, in selecting and designing our research methods, we may wish to stress the differences between the different techniques and play down the similarities. In short, the priorities are reversed when we actively seek paradoxes!

THE WEAKNESS IS ALSO THE STRENGTH

In writing this book, I have constantly been tempted to claim that the features which give a research technique its greatest strengths are the very same features that give the technique its greatest weaknesses. This may sound a bit paradoxical, and it may be an exaggeration. But there is actually a very strong justification for this remark, and it captures an essential insight into the reasons for plurality in research methods.

We use different techniques to solve different types of research problems, and these techniques are *horizontally differentiated*, in the language of industrial economics. Using one of the conventions of economic theory in industrial economics, we can for convenience envisage these techniques arrayed around a circle, as shown in Figure 10.2.

The different research techniques are represented by the points on the circumference of the circle (A, Z, etc.) The multi-faceted research phenomenon which we wish to illuminate is the hexagon in the middle of the circle. To illuminate each facet we need a collection of different techniques. The best research method to illuminate facet α, for example, is a technique (A) located on the upper half of the circle, perpendicularly above the mid-point of facet α.

It is well known in the economics of product differentiation that we cannot put horizontally differentiated products into any unambiguous order of preference. In the present context, the characteristics that make technique A the *most* suitable to illuminate facet α also make A the *least* suitable technique to illuminate facet ω. In this sense, we can say that the features which give a research technique its greatest strengths are the very same features that give the technique is greatest weaknesses.

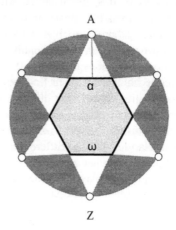

Figure 10.2   Diverse techniques illuminate different facets

The reader may find it helpful to use the golfing analogy again (as introduced in Chapter 1). The 'putter' is designed for the task of holing short putts. It would be silly for a golfer to criticise the 'putter' on the grounds that it is not a good club to get the ball out of a deep bunker. Equally it would be silly for the golfer to criticise the 'sand wedge' on the grounds that it is not a good club to hole a three foot putt. The characteristics that make the putter good for one task make it quite unsuitable for the other. The same applies (in reverse) to the 'sand wedge'.

Plurality is a special strength when the techniques are very different. In that case, we can reasonably expect that the strengths of one technique will compensate for the weaknesses of another – and vice versa. Moreover, with highly differentiated techniques, we have a greater chance of 'catching' a paradox, if that is what we want to do. But if our research techniques are not differentiated, then we may find that the strengths of one technique do not compensate for the weaknesses of another.

For example, the strengths of econometrics are these: it is analytical, rigorous and quantitative; the outputs are reasonably precise (or at least we know the margin of error); estimates based on large data sets do not suffer from sampling error; and because econometrics analyses data on actual behaviour, it does not generally suffer from the more obvious sorts of respondent bias. On the other hand, the weaknesses of econometrics are these: it is comparatively shallow in that relationships between variables are treated as a 'black box'; it is selective, because almost any econometric analysis can only examine the effects of a sub-set of possible explanatory factors; there can be serious problems with the signal-to-noise ratio (as we saw in Chapter 6); the structure of relationships is more or less assumed in advance rather than revealed by the analysis; it is not especially good at identifying structural change; it is not adaptable to ill-shaped data; many variables are hard to quantify as required for econometric analysis; and it is not an especially good integrative technique.

By contrast, for some of the qualitative techniques described below, the strengths and weaknesses are almost the mirror image of those for econometrics. So, for example, where econometrics is strong, case studies are weak. Case studies can lack rigour, they are often non-quantitative, they are descriptive rather than analytic, and a handful of case studies only adds up to a rather small sample. On the other hand, where econometrics is weak, case studies are strong. The case study can reveal the workings of a specific part of the economy in some depth; a good case is inclusive rather than selective; the structure is revealed rather than assumed, and structural change can be identified; and most of all, the case study is an integrative technique, capable of adaptation to data in all shapes and sizes.

No technique can qualify as a universal solvent for all economic research questions. Each has its place. Rather than getting embroiled in sterile debate about the relative merits of these techniques as universal techniques, it is much better to understand their different strengths and weaknesses, and therefore how they can complement each other.

NOTES

1. Of course, if the marginal cost of econometric analysis falls towards zero while other research techniques are relatively expensive, then the economist will carry out more econometric work – even if the returns are vanishingly small. This was the point made by Friedman (1991) – see Chapters 1 and 5.

11. Applied econometrics

This book is written primarily for the economist, so I don't think it is necessary to give more than a very brief account of econometric technique because almost all readers will know this well already. For that reason, my aim in this chapter is to see how far we can get using econometrics to tackle a particular problem in applied economics, and to see where we come to a halt.

In Chapter 5, we summarised what the critics of econometrics have said is wrong with it. In view of that, it may seem redundant to be devoting a chapter to the strengths of econometrics as an applied tool. Not so. Much of the criticism summarised in Chapter 5 is really directed at the idea that econometrics could ever be – in the language of this book – a universal solvent that could solve all applied economic problems on its own. By now, it should be clear to the reader that neither econometrics nor any other technique could ever be that universal solvent. Therefore, the purpose of this chapter – as of the others that follow in Part IV – is to make it clear what are the strengths and weaknesses of this tool.

We find that econometrics has some strengths that make it stand apart as a tool of applied economics.   But we shall also find that it has some weaknesses, and these are not shared by all the other methods of applied economics.

DESCRIPTION OF THE TECHNIQUE

To summarise the essentials of econometrics in a few pages seems an absurdly ambitious quest. But we need to have an elementary description of the essence of the technique if we are to compare it with all the others. I believe that what follows, though a vast simplification, does capture that essence.

The beauty of econometrics is that it holds out the hope of quantifying the relationship between variables without fieldwork, without the need for a detailed exploration of the causal link. If the world wants to know how changes in the price of petrol affect petrol consumption in aggregate, then econometrics should be able to deliver. It does not require detailed analysis of individual behaviour and decision-making processes. It does not require a detailed analysis of what travel is discretionary, what alternative travel options are available on any route, and at the margin how car-owners may switch to more fuel efficient machines as fuel prices rise. It does not require an understanding of the multi-faceted consumption activity involved in driving a car. We don't need to visit any drivers and talk to them. All we need to do is explore the statistical relationship between aggregate petrol consumption, petrol prices and other relevant variables. We may need a sufficient time series to capture the dynamics. We may have difficulty in isolating and measuring all other relevant variable. But econometrics can even cope with random omitted variables (disturbance terms) and can tell us what sort of bias will follow if we omit relevant variables (according to the correlation between omitted and included).

We drew the analogy in Chapter 4 between econometrics and surveying. Econometrics offers the prospect of mapping relationships between variables without visiting these relationships in detail. It is surely impossible for any community of researchers to visit all phenomena in detail (that would seem to call for a community of researchers as large as the community of subjects they study). Accordingly, we must have a technique for mapping relationships at a distance, and econometrics offers that possibility. This is one of its obvious attractions.

All econometrics proceeds from three assumptions. First, if we are interested to explore the relationship between a set of variables, we are able to split these into two groups, endogenous (y) and exogenous ($\mathbf{X}$).[1] Second, that we know (or at any rate feel reasonably confident to assume) that the relationship between y and $\mathbf{X}$ can be summarised by:

$$g(y, \mathbf{X}; \beta) = u \tag{11.1}$$

where u is a random error or disturbance term.

Third, we know (or at any rate feel reasonably confident to assume) what is the distribution of u, and can describe this in the density function $f(u)$.

From these three assumptions, all the rest can be made to follow. The function

$$f[g(y, \mathbf{X}; \beta)] = h(y, \mathbf{X}; \beta) \tag{11.2}$$

can be interpreted in two ways. It defines the *probability* of observing specific values of the endogenous variable(s) y, conditional on particular values of the exogenous variables $\mathbf{X}$ and parameters β. Or, it defines the *likelihood* that the true values of the true parameters are given by β, conditional on the observed data $\mathbf{X}$ and y.

Econometric estimation by maximum likelihood is the art and (mostly) science of estimating the most likely value of β consistent with observed data **X** and *y* – conditional on these two preliminary assumptions about $f(.)$ and $g(.)$.

From this description it doesn't sound too hard – conceptually at least. It doesn't sound as though too much could go wrong. Econometricians have been extraordinarily clever at devising methods of estimation for different assumptions about $f(.)$ and $g(.)$.

Moreover, econometrics has been very clever at devising two broad categories of diagnostic tests:

- for a given $g(.)$, tests of whether the assumed $f(.)$ is consistent with the data. (An example of this would be tests of normality of regression residuals, tests of heteroskedasticity, autocorrelation and so on).
- for a given $f(.)$, tests of whether the assumed $g(.)$ is consistent with the data (an example would be the Lagrange Multiplier specification test).

Indeed, at a deep level, these two are inter-related, because the act of imposing a false specification on an econometric model – that is, a false assumption about $g(.)$ – will tend to cause actual model errors to violate the assumptions in $f(.)$.[2]

These methods are, moreover, very rigorous. Assumed forms for $f(.)$ and $g(.)$ either do or do not pass such tests. If they do not, there is something wrong with the specification and we should reject the model and correct the mis-specification.

The beauty and appeal of econometrics is clear:

- It allows us to summarise economic relationships without 'being there'
- It is very elegant
- It is rigorous and objective

It is easy to see why econometrics looked such a promising prospect in the 1930s and why the Econometric Society placed the technique at the centre of the project to quantify the economy and economic relationships.

However, as we have already seen in Chapters 5 and 6, econometrics has attracted a fair degree of criticism, from outside economics, from inside economics but outside econometrics, and even from inside econometrics. There is no need to repeat this here. But we shall venture one general observation.

In my opinion, almost all the problems of econometrics arise because we typically know rather little about $f(.)$ and even less about $g(.)$. We tend to make some standard assumptions about $f(.)$ (such as normality). And we adopt one of two broad strategies with respect to $g(.)$. Either:

(1)   we make a very restrictive assumption (for example linearity);
(2)   we make a very unrestrictive assumption (a very flexible functional form).

With the former strategy, we can generally make quite good progress in obtaining reliable estimates of β – conditional on the restrictive assumed form of $g(.)$. But the concern must be this: have we 'discovered' the form of the relationship between y and X? Or is what we have largely a consequence of our assumptions?

With the latter strategy, it is common to find that economic data can only make limited progress in discriminating between different variants within a particular flexible functional form. Or, to say the same thing another way, parameters in an estimated flexible functional form have high standard errors and wide confidence intervals. So it is hard to get any precision in our parameter estimates. (In fact, this understates the problem. We argued in Chapter 6 that non-sampling uncertainty is generally more serious than uncertainties due to small sample sizes.)

And some would say that this leads us back to strategy (1): the only way to get such precision is by finding some other grounds (other than in the data) on which to impose particular restrictions on a flexible form. Strategy (1) is a fairly arbitrary way to do this: 'impose linearity', 'set this to zero', 'omit these variables', 'assume X_1 and X_2 have the same effect', and so on. We would like to do better, but econometrics alone doesn't take us very far. We need other approaches to reducing the parameter space. Such approaches might come from theory – but that is fairly unusual.

A slightly clumsy statement of a well-known and highly respected empirical research strategy in econometrics is this: 'intended over-parameterisation with data-based simplification'. This is the idea that we start with a general model with a large number of parameters, and then seek to impose such simplifying restrictions as are consistent with the data. But simplification that is purely data-based does not take us very far. We need other grounds for simplification. The original aim of the Econometric Society was to use the triad of economic theory, mathematical economics and econometrics to put more structure into our analysis. But, for the most part, that has not worked either.

We sometimes extract 'privileged' hypotheses ($b = 0$) and test these. If they cannot be rejected, then we impose them. But this is really a very peculiar strategy. Why is that hypothesis privileged? Do we really believe it? My view, based on casual observation of many applied econometric studies over many years, is that we often impose 'privileged' hypotheses for no good reason at all. The only argument for these privileged hypotheses is that they are mathematically convenient within the particular parameterisation we have chosen.

APPLIED DEMAND ANALYSIS

As an example of applied econometrics at work, I want to pick out one area which summarises many of the strengths and weaknesses of econometrics in one. That is applied demand analysis.

One of the objectives of advances in the econometrics of applied demand analysis has been to use the theory of consumer behaviour to shape estimated demand functions. The idea is that estimated demand functions should be consistent with theory and use the best insights of theory in order to estimate unknown parameters as efficiently as possible.

A pioneering study in this tradition was by Stone (1954a, 1954b). Although several subsequent studies have applied more sophisticated theory and technique to superior data, Stone's study still stands out as one of the great attempts to measure actual demand elasticities. In what follows, I shall compare the character of results obtained by Stone with those obtained in later studies using more flexible functional forms, and reflect on what we can learn from this comparison.

All of these use a revealed preference approach to measuring demand. It is worth reminding ourselves why economists have had such a strong preference for this approach.[3] The aim of revealed preference is to use data on observed market behaviour to make inferences about preferences. Some sociologists, of course, have argued that observed behaviour doesn't necessarily reveal anything much about preferences.[4] This difference between the economist's and sociologist's perspectives is beautifully summarised by Duesenberry (1960, p. 233): 'economics is all about choices, while sociology is about why people have no choices'.[5]

Why is revealed preference the preferred technique in applied demand analysis? Why don't economists make more use of methods such as stated preference analysis, used by marketers and others? There are several reasons for this, but the two most important are these.

First, applied economists tend to believe that when consumers are asked to explain their behaviour they are liable to give a somewhat distorted response. This distortion may happen for a number of reasons. There may be an element of randomness in any answer. When asked how they would respond to a particular event, respondents may feel they are giving hypothetical answers to hypothetical questions. The answer given at one moment may differ from the answer given at another moment. More serious, perhaps, is the possibility of strategic respondent bias. The respondent may deliberately slant his/her answer because of the use which (s)he thinks will be made of that answer. Suppose, for example, a survey asks rail travellers about their attitude to rail services, and suppose that part of the survey is about fares. The respondent might reasonably surmise that the researcher's objective is to test how sensitive the traveller would be to fare increases. It is clear that (part of) the purpose of the survey is to explore the scope to increase fares. Regardless of what his/her true price elasticity is, the respondent does not want to see fares increase. In that case, it is quite likely that the respondent will slant his/her answer so as to discourage the rail company from increasing fares. The best way to do this is to imply that demand is highly sensitive to price, which in reality it may not be. This issue of respondent bias is a serious one, for sure, though marketers seem to believe that the risks from this are less than the problems encountered in the indirect inference required for revealed preference analysis.

The second reason why economists are sceptical about consumer 'accounts' lies in the foundations of economics. As we have described above, the founding fathers of the Econometric Society argued that the future of economics as a science depended on the triad of theory, mathematics and statistics applied to numerical data. Scientific demand analysis would proceed along the same lines. 'Soft' methods of demand analysis, including case studies and stated preference, do not fit so well with this vision. In short, revealed preference was the preferred empirical approach because it was consistent with the Econometric Society vision.

There are three non-trivial problems with revealed preference, however. The first problem has been noted already. It is not generally agreed that consumption behaviour actually reveals anything much about preferences. The sociologist would say that consumption patterns are highly constrained by social norms. The economist is not usually too concerned about this aspect. For sure, the consumer's choices are constrained, and do not represent pure preferences. But in most circumstances, there are still some degrees of freedom, and the consumer still has some discretion.

The second critique of revealed preference is that, like any other method of indirect inference, it has to make inferences about one parameter from a pattern of correlation amongst several variables. This is the problem of the signal-to-noise ratio described in Chapter 6.

The third critique is perhaps the most serious of all. The technique of revealed preference assumes that all data used in estimation are reflections of the same preference function. But this may be a strong assumption. The data may come from different years, or they may represent the behaviour of a changing aggregate. In either case, the assumption of constant preferences may not be warranted. Moreover, the assumption of fixed tastes has tended to divert economists' attention away from the rather important questions about why tastes change.

STONE'S MAJOR STUDY (1954)

Stone's (1954a, 1954b) study of consumer behaviour in the UK is one of the great works of applied econometrics. Despite limited data, Stone made major advances in estimating price and income elasticities for a wide variety of consumer goods. Throughout, he consistently used economic theory to guide his applied econometric method. While subsequent studies have had access to better and more voluminous data and have refined the econometric techniques used, even now few compare with Stone's study. Stone's study makes major advances in estimating price and income elasticities for a wide variety of consumer goods. Much subsequent work, by contrast, has been more preoccupied with technical matters, and it is not clear that they have added all that much to the original objective of applied demand analysis – to determine what factors influence demand and to what degree.

Stone developed the Linear Expenditure System (LES) – the first approach to estimating a system of demand equations. As Deaton (1987) says, the LES is a very efficient or parsimonious representation: a system for n goods requires only $2n - 1$ parameters. In Stone's case, he has a six commodity system, so the LES model requires only 11 parameters. This parsimony was essential for Stone's work as he only had a short time series from which to estimate his model. But this parsimony must have a price. As Deaton (1987) argues, the LES is rather restrictive. In general, it cannot model inferior goods, nor can it model complementary goods. The LES also makes a strong implicit assumption about the marginal propensity to consume a good: it has to be the same regardless of total expenditure, and as Deaton points out, this is not the case in many cross-section studies of household budgets. In short, the LES is not ideal. But it worked, and offered some plausible empirical price and income elasticities that are still taken seriously (despite the flaws of the LES).

Deaton (1987) notes that much work on demand analysis after Stone used exactly the same modelling approach but with better algorithms, faster computers and better and different data sets. In view of all the progress in computation and data collection since Stone's study, we might expect that his work has long since been surpassed by bigger and better studies. After all, as Huxley (1963) reminds us, scientific studies are essentially instrumental. Old scientific studies will be displaced by better new scientific studies. And yet it is not so in this case: Stone is not displaced, not even with the improvements in data and computation. Why does Stone's study still continue to be so highly regarded?

The main reason is that he applies econometric method with a primary objective to produce credible parameter estimates. That was his purpose in the study. And it is – or should be – the parameter estimates that we are in it for. By contrast, many subsequent studies have been more preoccupied with theoretical and technical matters, and they have arguably lost sight of the economic parameters which drive our interest in the first place. My reading of more modern work on complete systems of demand equations finds much on technical matters, but little discussion of the empirical plausibility of parameter estimates.

Indeed, I detect in some quarters some nostalgia for Stone's study. Nostalgia in the history of thought generally means that people are unhappy with where the discipline is now, and think it took a wrong turning. They retrace their steps to a time with which they are happy, and ask: what went wrong thereafter? We have already noted, in Chapter 5, Stone's (1978) remarks that applied econometrics seems in some ways to have regressed rather than progressed.

FLEXIBLE FUNCTIONAL FORMS

It is instructive to compare the character of the results obtained by Stone with the character of results obtained in later studies that used flexible functional forms. There were at least three leading examples of this latter sort of work: the *Rotterdam System* of Barten (1964, 1969) and Theil (1965, 1975), the *Translog* utility function of Christensen et al. (1975), and the *Almost Ideal Demand System* of Deaton and Muellbauer (1980). Of these three, the third is in a sense the most advanced because it is a flexible functional form consistent with theory – meaning that it observes the aggregation, homogeneity, symmetry and negativity conditions of economic theory.

These later studies were great achievements. The authors had to solve some demanding technical challenges to estimate these models. Moreover, the Deaton and Muellbauer study represented as good an attempt as one can find to integrate the economic theory of demand into econometric practice. But were they successful by the Frisch (1970) criterion? Did they have relevance for 'concrete realities'? Did they enhance our empirical knowledge of the income and price elasticities of demand?

I think the answer has to be, 'no'. Careful perusal of the parameter matrices in these large scale 'complete system' demand studies find unexpected (and even implausible) parameter estimates. The authors spend most of their energies discussing the technical issues in estimation, and rather little time in discussing their estimates. The reader is left thinking that the research objective has moved on. We are no longer looking for empirical knowledge about price and income elasticities. Instead, such studies are primarily concerned with tests for homogeneity and symmetry, and what we are to make of the rejection of such null hypotheses.

Indeed, Deaton makes a fascinating observation about this. He notes that informal empirical studies of demand have a long history, and use a pragmatic approach. This pays little attention to formal theory, but focuses instead on trying to find empirical regularities. Deaton (1987, p. 600) endorses the pragmatic approach for practical research and observes that some of the major developments in the econometrics of demand analysis are not very relevant to such practical work. [6]

In view of the remarks I made above, this may seem surprising. The idealistic interpretation of what we can gain by bringing theory to bear on applied econometric technique is better econometric measurement. Not today, perhaps, but eventually. But I agree with Deaton that for the most part, advances in the econometrics of applied demand analysis since Stone have not really been relevant to the practical matter of estimating price elasticities, but instead have been directed at testing theory.

Is this how it should be? In my view, 'no'. Applied econometrics, in the tradition of Jevons and Frisch, was supposed to be about the superior measurement of important economic parameters. But the experience in applied demand analysis is an excellent illustration of the path that econometrics has actually tended to follow. The pioneers attempt to estimate parameters, but subsequent advances in methods, algorithms and data do not necessarily do very much to improve the quality of parameter estimates, and as a result econometricians turn their attention to more esoteric, and less practical, questions.

Deaton (1987) draws some important conclusions about where econometric studies of demand have reached. The flexible functional form will yield demand functions that can have any set of price and expenditure elasticities. This is important for empirical work because we can then be sure that estimated elasticities are freely measured, and are not the result of our model assumptions. Deaton notes that the LES was too restrictive, and estimated elasticities are not independent of one another. We could say, therefore, that the LES doesn't *measure* all the price and income elasticities, but computes them using a combination of assumption and measurement.

Deaton argues that the flexible functional form was an important step forward in methodology, but he notes that while the LES is probably too restrictive, the flexible functional forms ask too much of the data (Deaton, 1987, p. 602). By that he means that the flexible function form puts too little structure on the econometric problem, and as a result we obtain large standard errors, a lack of robustness in parameter estimates – both of these are standard symptoms when we try to estimate a model with an unmanageable number of parameters. Deaton argues that these problems are especially relevant to the measurement of price elasticities, because these are generally estimated from time-series data, and different price indices tend to be highly collinear in time series. These are essentially the same observations that I made in Chapter 6, when I showed that the (partial) signal-to-noise ratio was especially low in these systems of demand equations.

Deaton (1987, p. 602) comes to a rather pessimistic conclusion that despite all the advances in demand analysis, there is still no real consensus on the empirical values of price elasticities. While estimates obtained from the LES look plausible in themselves, we have to remember that they are not so much estimates as a mixture of assumption and estimate. But, at the same time, estimates obtained from flexible functional forms do not look very reliable, because the model asks too much of limited data, and the data cannot give a reliable answer.

Econometric demand analysis is a major achievement. Let there be no doubt about that. But it has not answered the original question: How exactly does demand react to changes in price? Unable to answer that, econometricians have turned their attention to more esoteric technical questions that they can answer. But the original question still remains, and the applied economist needs an answer to it. Let's try to find it another way. It's time to consider experimental economics, surveys and interviews – and indeed other techniques.

NOTES

1.   We only require weak exogeneity. That is, we do not require that X is exogenous in an absolute sense. All we require is that in the relationship between y and X, the direction of causation runs from X to y, and not vice versa. Whatever it is that influences X, it is not y, nor anything influenced by y.
2.   For example, the act of imposing a false parameter restriction on a time series model will commonly introduce autocorrelation. Intuitively speaking, a false parameter restriction is rather like excluding an important variable, and if that important variable is autocorrelated, then the errors from the estimated model with the false parameter restriction will also be autocorrelated.
3.   The discussion that follows is based on Swann (2002a).
4.   As Warde (2002) makes clear, revealed preference is not a view with which sociologists have much sympathy.
5.   Here quoted from Becker (1996, p. 17).
6.   Another great study of consumer demand in this pragmatic tradition is by Houthakker and Taylor (1970).

12. Experimental economics

After the United States passed the Eighteenth Amendment, enacting Prohibition, President Herbert Hoover described this as a 'great social and economic experiment'.[1] Economists and other social scientists may influence the decision to hold such a 'great experiment', their analysis may help to assess how the experiment has performed, and indeed they can interpret what we learn about the workings of the economy and society from such an experiment. But ultimately, the decision to carry out an experiment, the design of the experiment and the control of other factors that may influence the outcome of the experiment do not lie in the hands of the economist. The reasons for that are clear: the experiment could be a huge Pandora's Box.[2] The consequences and risks of such experiments are so great, with such widespread implications for law and order, that only the most prominent politicians are empowered to sanction experiments of this sort, and a vote in Congress or an Act of Parliament is required.

Experimental economics, as the term is used today, is concerned with experiments on an altogether more modest scale. These are experiments carried out in the classroom, usually with students as the subjects. The stakes are not very high, though prize money (and sometimes class grades) may be involved. There are ethical issues in experimental design, but for the most part, such experiments do not have implications for law and order – occasionally perhaps in the classroom, but rarely beyond the campus. The economist is empowered to carry out such experiments without an Act of Parliament or a vote in Congress. Again, the reasons are clear: the consequences and risks of such experiments are generally modest. Some critics still suggest that because the experiment is not 'for real', then neither is the behaviour elicited, and hence such experiments tell us little about 'real behaviour in the real world'. Those who use experimental economics as a research technique, however, dismiss that view as being much too pessimistic. The aim of this chapter is to assess what applied economists can expect to learn from modern experimental economics, and what they cannot expect to learn.

First, let us put the modern experiment in context by comparing it to the 'great social and economic experiment' of prohibition. Then, we shall ask whether economics is really an experimental science – in the sense that economists themselves sanction the experiments. Since the answer to that is plainly 'yes', at some level anyway, then we show that a more useful debate revolves around four supplementary questions: What sorts of experiments? What sorts of laboratories and subjects? Do the results from laboratory experiments carry over to the field? And what can applied economics learn from experimental economics?

PROHIBITION AS AN EXPERIMENT

The experiment I refer to here is the national prohibition of manufacture, sale or transportation of alcohol enacted in the USA between 1919 and 1933.[3] This is not the only, nor indeed the first, such experiment with prohibition. It has also been used in Canada, China, Finland, Iceland, India, Japan, Norway, Russia and Sweden. Nor, indeed, was it the first such experiment in the USA, because a series of state prohibition laws appeared from the 1840s onwards. But in most cases, these experiments have not lasted for long, and countries that have imposed such bans have soon repealed them. The most notable exceptions are those Muslim countries which have maintained a national prohibition. Sometimes the motivation for such prohibition was religious: temperance was a virtue and alcohol consumption a vice. Sometimes the motivation was pragmatic: a concern to limit the damage from alcoholism, with all its social and economic consequences.

The pressures leading up to the national prohibition in the USA included antipathy to the growth of heavy drinking in city bars, the prevalence of corruption in the saloons, the attitudes of an evangelical Protestant middle class, the industrial employer's concern to prevent accidents and increase productivity, and the domination of state legislatures by rural interests. The Prohibition Amendment was ratified in 1919, and a National Prohibition Act, known as the Volstead Act, was passed later in 1919 – providing guidelines for the enforcement of Prohibition.

Did prohibition work? Not very well. Despite legislation, illicit manufacture and sale of alcohol continued on quite a large scale. Prohibition was generally enforced where the population was sympathetic to it (for example in rural areas and small towns), but not where they were not (especially in large cities). Prohibition led to increased prices for alcohol, and the cost of prohibition fell more heavily on the working classes than the middle or upper class.

Even more problematic were the side-effects. Prohibition was a huge Pandora's box – generating all kinds of undesirable and unanticipated adverse effects. Most notable amongst these was the fact that prohibition created a new kind of criminal, the *bootlegger*. The growth of bootlegging was accompanied by a succession of gang wars and murders – one of the most notorious being the 1929 *St Valentine's Day Massacre* in Chicago.

Support for prohibition faded during the 1920s, because of the increase in criminal activity, continued illicit production and sale, a split in the prohibition movement between the evangelicals and the moderates, and frustration with the restrictions on individual freedom. In the 1932 Presidential Election, the Democratic Party's platform included a proposal for repeal, and following F.D. Roosevelt's victory in that election, Congress in 1933 proposed the Twenty-first Amendment to the Constitution to repeal the Eighteenth. Repeal followed later in 1933, although a few states retained state-wide prohibition for a while longer.

Did we learn from the experiment? The answer must surely be 'yes'. For if the experiment had had no unexpected consequences, it would surely have continued for longer. The experiment had lots of unexpected and undesirable consequences, but for sure we have learnt from these.

What have we learnt? We have learnt a lot about the way that such prohibitions are usually circumvented by the emergence of black markets, and we have learnt about the operation of these. We have learnt about the emergence of gang warfare for monopoly control of a particular illicit business. Indeed, it was suggested that by the time of the 1929 massacre in Chicago, the market was approaching monopoly and hence crime would start to tail off. We learnt about the emergence of the *Speakeasy* (an illicit liquor shop), and the unfortunate fact that illicit distilleries produced poisonous substitutes (containing methanol as well as ethanol). In short, we have learnt a lot.

In particular, we have learnt that the great social and economic experiment can open up a great Pandora's box. It is highly risky. On the other hand, we learn all kinds of unexpected things that we probably could not have learnt any other way!

This is perhaps an extreme example. Governments regularly try more modest economic experiments, for example in macroeconomic management. Here, perhaps, the stakes are not quite so high – though the cost of UK exit from the ERM was high enough. But even here, though economists may guide and recommend,[4] the ultimate responsibility for design and control of the experiment is in the hands of the politician.

Moreover, governments do not have a monopoly on such real market experiments. Entrepreneurs especially and companies more generally are constantly carrying out experiments with markets. Moreover, academics may sometimes carry out such experiments by joining the ranks of entrepreneurs and spinning off new start-up companies to commercialise their research ideas. However, the discussion of experimental economics that follows will focus on a narrower type of experiment: the experiment sanctioned by and carried out by academic economists purely for research purposes.

IS ECONOMICS AN EXPERIMENTAL SCIENCE?

Until relatively recently, many economists and non-economists would have said that economics was a non-experimental science. Tinbergen (1951, p. 7), in motivating his pioneering textbook on econometrics, said that it is rarely possible to experiment in economics. He conceded that 'nature experiments with the economy' by variations in weather and harvests, and that governments sometimes experiment with the economy when they seek to control the business cycle. But for the most part, he considered that most economic relationships cannot be determined by experiment.

The fact that it is non-experimental does not debar it from being a science – no more so that the non-experimental nature of astronomy and meteorology exclude these disciplines from the category of science. And that perception, of course, is one of the reasons why economists latched onto econometrics with such enthusiasm in the 1930s and 1940s.

Such a view was still prevalent in the 1980s. Friedman and Sunder (1994, p. 1) note that the 12th edition of a leading textbook of economics (Samuelson and Nordhaus, 1985, p. 8), was still arguing that economists could not really perform controlled experiments. But by the time Samuelson and Nordhaus (1989, p. 6) produced their 13th edition of that text, four years later, they conceded that such experiments are possible, if difficult.

Experimental economists believe that experiments are possible in economics, and more to the point, economists themselves can carry out such experiments – just as the experimental chemist or biologist. Experimental economists argue that disciplines become experimental when innovative researchers devise relevant experiments. This took a long time in economics, but experiments are now commonplace in game theory, finance, public choice and many other micro fields.

Actually, in my opinion, this apparent difference in opinion really just boils down to a difference in definitions. We should not just ask, 'Can economists do experiments?' They can and they do! We need also to ask four supplementary questions, and then we can reconcile the earlier views expressed by Tinbergen, Samuelson and Nordhaus, on the one hand, and the views of modern experimental economists on the other.

- What sorts of experiments can economists do?
- In what sorts of laboratory can economists do experiments, and with what subjects?

- Do the experiments carried out in the class laboratory reveal the same sorts of economic laws or principles as we would find if we could experiment in the market laboratory?
- What can applied economists learn from these experiments?

Economists certainly can and do carry out experiments where the laboratory is the classroom. Moreover, in that environment, the good experimental economist can control for many or even most (but possibly not all) other important factors. In that sense, these are controlled experiments as well.

However, these were not the sorts of experiment that Tinbergen, Samuelson and Nordhaus were writing about – nor, more to the point, was this the sort of 'laboratory' they were writing of. They were thinking of a market or an economy as a 'laboratory', and for sure, it is rare that the economist can perform an experiment using a national economy as a laboratory. As we have said before, if experiments are carried out in such a grand laboratory, politicians or business people – not economists – control the experiment. Moreover, it is unlikely that any but the most powerful of political systems could control all the other important factors that might influence their experiment.   So these are rarely, if ever, controlled experiments.

In short, the difference between Tinbergen, Samuelson and Nordhaus on the one hand, and experimental economists on the other, is simply that the former are talking about the market economy as the 'laboratory', while the latter are talking about the classroom as a 'laboratory'.

Instead of asking, therefore, whether economists can do experiments, we should be asking a different question. Do the experiments carried out in the class laboratory reveal the same sorts of economic laws or principles as we would find if we could experiment in the *market laboratory*?   This is sometimes described as the question of *parallelism*: can we assume that results from a small laboratory (classroom) would carry over into a larger laboratory (market economy)?   Or are results in the former a poor guide to the latter, because life in the class laboratory is not for real, while life in the market laboratory is indeed for real?

THE ADVANTAGES OF EXPERIMENTS

Compare the idea of experimental economics (using a controlled experiment) with the application of econometrics (using uncontrolled happenstance data). We saw in the last chapter and Chapters 5 and 6 some of the practical problems that arise in applied econometrics. Chapter 6 wrote, in particular, about the problem of the signal-to-noise ratio. This problem is very common in econometrics because of the non-experimental character of the data, and the coincidence of multicollinearity in a set of regressors and noisy data. This is especially relevant when the effects of *focus variables* (explanatory variables of interest) are tangled together with the effects of some *nuisance variables* (influential variables which are not of direct interest to the researcher). In this case, the *independent* signal in a focus variable (independent of the nuisance variables) has a small variance – and in particular, this variance is small relative to the noise in the data.

Contrast this with the ideal of a controlled experiment, where the independent signal in the variable of interest can be as large as we like. First, the experimenter can alter that variable at will, so the signal in the variable can be as large as we like. Second, there need be no issue of collinearity between multiple causal variables, because in a controlled experiment other causal variables (besides those of immediate interest) can be kept constant. There need be no nuisance variables. As a result, there need never be a signal-to-noise problem in experimental economics. To put it informally: there need never be a problem of disentangling multiply correlated influences.

Experimental economists would add that there are further advantages from the use of experimental economics. Some economic theory has a very fine structure that cannot really be tested using the rather crude data that we tend to have to work with in applied economics. For example, some theory applies to disaggregated choices by the individual consumer, but we are obliged to test it with crude aggregate data – and it may not apply to aggregate data in a predictable way. With experimental methods, by contrast, we can in principle devise an experiment to test a particular theory, and so collect data that are entirely apposite to the theory in question. We shall see in this chapter that probably the greatest strength of experimental economics is its capacity to test economic theory.

WHAT SORT OF EXPERIMENT?

We have already said that the experimental economics of today differs from the 'great social and economic experiment' in terms of the laboratory in which the experiment takes place. But there is also a difference between the style of many experiments used in experimental economics and the style of the marketplace experiment. There is a logic to this difference, but it may seem a little strange to applied economists and other applied researchers from some empirical traditions.

A key element to much experimental economics is that the economically relevant preferences of the experimental subjects should be *induced* rather than innate (or acquired). Friedman and Sunder (1994, pp. 12–13) explain that the idea of induced value theory is to motivate experimental subjects to have specific preferences and characteristics, so that the original or innate preferences and characteristics of these subjects no longer matter.[5]

Some applied economists find this strange at first.   Why should an experimenter wish to replace innate characteristics with induced (and pre-specified) characteristics?   Surely by doing this, we lose the opportunity to tease out information on the unobservable innate characteristics that we want to know about, and instead can only expect to recover the characteristics which are programmed into the subjects. What do we learn from that?

What we learn is something different.   It is similar to what we learn in role-playing games – where each participant is given a role to play that may relate to his/her personal character, or may be something very different indeed.   We do not tease out much about personal characteristics, because these have been overwritten by induced characteristics.   But we can learn a lot about the character of group interaction.

But even so, why use induced rather than innate (or acquired) preferences? The main reason for this is that it is harder to elicit innate preferences than it is to induce preferences.   Davis and Holt (1993, p. 18) explain that experimentalists have tried to develop a variety of elaborate schemes to elicit preferences, but on the whole they have been much less successful with these than with the inducement of preferences.

Friedman and Sunder (1994, pp. 10–12) further explain the rationale for this approach. They ask (p. 10) whether an experiment should seek to mimic reality or mimic formal models, and come to the sensible answer, 'neither'! They argue that it is futile to try to create in the laboratory a model that tries to capture all the complexities of the real world. Instead, the objective in experimental design should be to try to learn something useful.   The right criterion by which to judge the success of a laboratory experiment, in their view, is by its impact on understanding. Truth to reality or consistency with a formal model are not the right criteria (Friedman and Sunder, 1994, p. 12).

It seems to me that there is plenty of sense in this, but the applied researcher needs to be clear about the implications of this philosophy for the applicability of experimental economics in his field.   When used in this fashion, experimental economics is not about 'what are empirical preferences?'   Rather, it is about another question: 'if preferences were like this, then what group interactions follow?'

How does this compare with other experiments in other fields? A striking difference with animal experimentation is clear. The subjects in a classroom experiment with induced preferences are told the 'rules of the game' either verbally, or on paper, in advance of the game. They are told what their induced preferences should be.   Contrast this with experimental animal psychology, where it is hard to see how much experimental subjects can be 'told' about what their induced preferences should be. In the area of animal experimentation, a more common aim is to elicit innate (or possibly acquired) preferences.[6]

WHAT SORT OF LABORATORY AND SUBJECT?

A second difference between the 'great social and economic experiment' and the experiments of experimental economics is that the former take place in the real marketplace, while the latter mostly take place in the classroom with students. Does this matter? There are two issues here. One is what we can expect classroom results to tell us about the real world. This is the question of parallelism, and is discussed in the next section. The second is, what are the implications of using students rather than experienced business people as experimental subjects? This section focuses on this second question.

From my reading of experimental economics – and I confess it is a superficial, though not a cavalier reading of the field – experimentalists find the experienced business person a problematic subject for experiment. For an applied researcher familiar with other traditions, this seems a bit strange. Even stranger is the idea that the experimenter will learn more from an experiment carried out using undergraduate students as subjects than experienced business people.

I am, of course, well aware of why experimentalists prefer undergraduates as subjects. Partly this is because of the most important economic influence of all – price! But a more important reason is the idea that undergraduate students are more malleable. If, as described in the last section, experiments are designed around the assumption of induced (rather than innate) preferences, then it is easier to induce such preferences in undergraduates. They are more impressionistic and most do not yet have a powerful (and contradictory) mental model which the experimenter must displace.

It is instructive to see what practical guides to experimental economics say about the relative suitability of different students. As I said, undergraduates are seen as ideal, and MBA students are also acceptable. The arguments in their favour are that the researcher has ready access to the subject pool, easy recruitment, subjects with a low opportunity cost to their time, a steep learning curve and a lack of exposure to 'confounding external information' (Friedman and Sunder, 1994, p. 39).

By contrast, doctoral students are not seen as ideal experimental subjects. Friedman and Sunder (1994, pp. 39–40) argue that this is because the experimenter may 'lose dominance with doctoral students'. In experiments, doctoral students tend to react by drawing on their knowledge of relevant theory and lose sight of the incentives that the experimenter wishes them to concentrate on.

It is also very interesting to read what experimental researchers say about the prospects of using business people or other professionals in experimental studies of this sort. Burns (1985) designed and implemented an experimental wool market auction using students, on the one hand, and professional wool buyers on the other. Participants were encouraged to maximize their profits. Burns (1985, p. 152) observed the buyers tended to react to familiar cues and incentives from their earlier work experience and not to incentives designed into the experiment.   Friedman and Sunder (1994, p. 41) describe unpublished work by Anderson and Sunder which found a similar result. Although the experimenters gave a very careful explanation of the rules of the game in the experimental market, the traders still continued to trade by the rules with which they were familiar, and tended to ignore what they were told.

In short, when the objective of experimental economics is to observe reactions to experimental conditions and objectives, it is not a good idea to choose as subjects people who have extensive prior experience which is not compatible with the experimental design. The professional wool buyers were apparently used to the challenge of identifying quality differentials among the different sale lots, but this feature did not appear in the experimental auction, and this confused the professionals.   The students, by contrast, were unencumbered by incompatible prior experience. Anyone who has taught economics in a business school – and especially to executive programmes (post-MBA) – will understand and to some degree sympathise with the experimentalist's predicament.

However, the applied economist who believes in the essential role of integrating formal and vernacular in economics may find this a very peculiar perspective indeed. For such an applied economist, it is exactly this sort of innate (or acquired) behaviour that one wishes to elicit. The writer of a case study would, ninety-nine times out of a hundred, be more interested in the opportunity to interview an experienced business person than an undergraduate. The idea that experimental economics works when it uses undergraduates with no specific vernacular economic knowledge, but doesn't work when it uses business people with a large amount of vernacular knowledge, makes one wonder to what extent experimental economics is really an applied technique.

Some might be tempted to say that if experimental economics finds this behaviour on the part of experienced traders a problem, then so much the worse for experimental economics.   But that is to miss the point. Experimental researchers have found that their experiments work best when preferences are induced, and that attempts to elicit real innate preferences by experiment are much less successful.   In view of that intellectual honesty, other applied economists must have a clear understanding of why experimental economists favour undergraduates as experimental subjects. The objective of the experiment is not to elicit the informal mental models built up over years of experience. Definitely not. The objective is to induce pre-specified preferences and characteristics, and then observe group interactions.

It is not perhaps a great compliment to 'economic man' (or to economics) that experimental economists find they can learn more about him from experiments on pre-programmed undergraduates than on 'economic man' himself. However, within experimental method as it stands now, that is the constraint. The proper reaction to experimental economics is not therefore to criticise its peculiar taste in experimental subjects, but to understand it on its own terms. Those terms are that it is (at present) a technique with limited domain as a tool of applied economics, and not applicable to quite a lot of the applied activities that economists seek to carry out.

PARALLELISM: IS IT REASONABLE?

What can experimental results from the laboratory tell us about what would obtain if an experiment could be carried out in the real world? Critics of experimental economics have argued, 'not much', because the type of experiment and the type of laboratory is so different from the real world.

As the experimental economists point out, however, this question is not unique to economics. It applies in the natural sciences and engineering too. A prototype semiconductor may work perfectly in the laboratory but be very fickle in the field. A car may work perfectly in a garage but break down quickly when on the road. And it applies in companies that use market research experiments to assess consumer attitudes to a new product. Market research trials may suggest that a product has a promising future in the market, but some unfortunate companies can find that the actual market outcome is much less rosy. Or vice versa.[7]

The problem of carrying experimental results from a small laboratory to a larger (or real life) laboratory is present in very many contexts – and yet this does not mean that small laboratory experiments are of no value. If we are prepared to make the leap of faith involved, then experimental results are certainly of value, but must be interpreted with caution. In my view, this is exactly how we should interpret results in experimental economics.

Experimentalists refer to the 'parallelism precept' due to Vernon Smith (1982, p. 936). This is the assumption that economic propositions that have been tested and found to hold in experimental laboratories will also apply to non-laboratory economies. But Friedman and Sunder (1994, p. 16) also present a much stronger version of parallelism, according to which the burden of refutation lies with the sceptic. It is for the sceptic to say why experimental laboratory results should not be expected to apply in the outside world.

How does the parallelism precept look to applied economists from other traditions? At first sight, it has something in common with a null hypothesis of *no difference* in an econometric study. For example, consider a model that is estimated with data on two or more industries or regions (or whatever). A common null hypothesis used by those who would pool data from different industries or regions is that there is no difference between the model parameters for observations from different industries or regions. A privileged null hypothesis of no difference may seem unreasonable to some applied economists, but it is a very common practice to privilege such a null hypothesis. Then, in hypothesis testing, we continue to accept the null hypothesis on a provisional basis until we have evidence that firmly rejects the null. In that sense, the burden of disproof is to find data that reject the hypothesis.

In many ways, this is the same as the parallelism precept. According to that, the experimental economists continue to accept the assumption of no difference between laboratory and field unless any conclusive evidence is found to the contrary. There is a difference in degree, however. In econometrics, no one has a great deal of faith in the privileged null hypothesis of no difference until it has been subjected to at least some tests, and those tests fail to reject the null hypothesis. In experimental economics, it seems, we are asked to put our faith in the parallelism precept, even if it has never really been put to the test – perhaps because there is no way of knowing whether the results found in the laboratory do actually apply in the field. From that point of view, the parallelism precept seems a strong assumption.

However, one thing is clear: as long as there is some obligation to try to test the parallelism precept, then experimental economics (in the sense described in this chapter) cannot aspire to being a universal solvent. Tests of the parallelism precept require data from the real market as opposed to the classroom, and that calls for something beyond the confines of modern experimental economics.

Experimental economists believe that while laboratory experiments may be very simple compared to real market behaviour, the experiments are still real in the sense that real people participate for real and substantial profits and follow real rules in doing so. As a result, experimental economists reject the idea that experiments applied to students tell us little about experiments carried out on business people. Experimentalists maintain the parallelism precept: *results from experiments with students are similar to the results we would get in real market situations with business people.*

However, it is salutary to remind ourselves of the observations made in the last section to the effect that business people are unsuitable experimental subjects because they do not obey the rules of the game, while students are well-behaved in that respect. But this observation seems to be a negation of the parallelism precept: *results from experiments with business people are not the same as the results we get from experiments with students.*

I think there are some good grounds for being sceptical about parallelism, in the same way that we would be sceptical that model parameters estimated from data for the semiconductor industry would apply identically to the textile industry. However, this is definitely not the same as saying that we can learn nothing from experimental results in the laboratory. We can learn from this, as we can learn from every other method described in this book. But we must just be careful not to claim too much.

WHAT CAN WE LEARN?

As we have argued above, what one thinks of any technique of applied economics depends critically on what one thinks is the scope of applied economics. If applied economics is only about testing economic theory, then experimental economics looks pretty good. Experimental economics is a fine 'test' of economic theory. However, as we argued before, testing theory is only one of the things that an applied economist tries to do – and in my opinion at least, it is probably one of the least important of the activities in which the applied economist is engaged.

We argued in the previous chapter that applied econometrics is more often used for the purpose of calibration than testing theory per se. How does experimental economics look as a technique for calibration of empirical parameters? Not very good. As we have stressed before, experimental economists tend to carry out experiments using induced preferences in experimental subjects (rather than their innate preferences). As a result, we cannot expect such experiments to tell us much about innate preferences – except to the extent that experimental subjects rebel against the experiment.

What help is experimental economics in the other activities of applied economist? It is not much help to us in establishing lists of possibly relevant variables, it is not useful for working out long-term implications and it doesn't look particularly useful as an integrating device. The fact that experiments using experienced business people as experimental subjects have not been very successful suggest that it is not the ideal language in which to converse with vernacular economists. However, experimental economics can play a very useful pedagogic role; MBA students like participating in such experiments, and say that they find it a useful technique for developing economic intuition.

Experimental economics does, however, use a language that is well understood in other disciplines, and has been instrumental in promoting dialogue between economics and experimental psychology, for example. It is, moreover, one of the best channels of communication between economic theorists and applied economics; by contrast, theorists tend (rightly or wrongly) to pay rather little attention to applied econometric results. If the only contribution of experimental economics were to re-open the dialogue between economic theory and applied economics that has been more or less dormant since the 1960s, then it would have served a very valuable purpose.

CONCLUSION

Many economists and non-economists have asked, 'is economics really an experimental science?'. We have argued in this chapter that this is the wrong question. Economics is undoubtedly experimental: the evidence for that is that experimental economists do indeed carry out experiments! But these experiments have some limitations, as do the laboratories in which they take place, and the selection of experimental subjects proceeds in an opposite way to (say) the selection of subjects for interview. These limitations do not mean that economic experiments are of no use. What they do mean is that economic experiments can only help us with a small sub-set of the activities that the genuinely applied economist needs to get involved in. The issue then is not whether experimental economics is really experimental, but whether this is really a technique of applied economics – or more a technique of economic theory.

If experimental economics – as currently practised – is more a technique for economic theorists to test their theories than for applied economists to elicit information about 'the way the world works', then why is it so popular? Once again, it enjoys the vestiges of formality that we have grown to love in econometrics. It does not suffer from the untidy vernacular informality of the techniques described below, and we can publish it in the leading economics journals in a way that we cannot publish the rest. However, it is probably fair to say that experimental economics is even less well suited than econometrics to be a universal solvent – though, in fairness, I have never seen any experimental economist claim so much for their subject as econometricians have claimed for theirs.

NOTES

1. *Oxford Dictionary of Quotations* (1953, p. 254).
2. After Prometheus upset Zeus by stealing fire from him, and taking it back to earth, Zeus sent the beautiful Pandora to earth, carrying a box. Prometheus was suspicious and shunned her, but his brother Epimetheus was enchanted by her, and married her, whereupon Pandora opened her box, and all the evils that would afflict the world flew out and could not be recovered. The only thing left in the box was hope.
3. This section draws on the entry on 'Prohibition' in *Encyclopaedia Britannica* (2002).
4. For example, Milton Friedman had great influence on the Thatcher Government's experiments with macroeconomic policy. Economists were also very influential in designing the auction for the 3G mobile licences (Binmore and Klemperer, 2002). Plott (1987) describes some policy applications of experimental methods.
5. Friedman and Sunder (1994, p. 13) state that three conditions are sufficient to induce agents' characteristics: (a) monotonicity: more reward is always better; (b) salience: the relationship between action and reward is defined by rules which the subject understands; (c) dominance: changes in subjects' utility come primarily from changes in reward.
6. Despite this difference, some believe that animal experimentation can yield important insights into human economic behaviour. See, for example, the fascinating paper by Kagel (1987).
7. Sony did market research on the market potential of the Walkman, which suggested there was little demand for the product. Akio Morita, founder of Sony, had a hunch that the market research was wrong, and decided to go ahead anyway. This is perhaps the most quoted example of when market research has been negative while the actual outturn has been very positive.

13. Surveys and questionnaires

This chapter concerns economic surveys using questionnaires. For the most part, I am thinking of questionnaires completed by a respondent on paper, or perhaps online. Sometimes, the researcher may complete the questionnaire himself by making observations (for example in a traffic census), rather than by asking questions. Sometimes these questionnaires may be answered by telephone – or even face to face – and it is the researcher who fills out the paperwork. I am referring to the sort of questionnaire where the respondent has to tick boxes or give numerical answers. That is: most of the data collected are categorical or numerical. Apart, perhaps, from a few identifiers, the answers do not involve a substantial amount of text. I am not thinking of the in-depth face to face interview here – that is treated in Chapter 18.

Much of the data produced by national statistical bodies derives from this sort of questionnaire, and hence applied economists use secondary data of this sort all the time – frequently in conjunction with econometric analysis. But the focus in this chapter is not on the use of secondary data but the *collection of primary data*. What do we learn from conducting such a survey ourselves?

I am not going to say much here about the concept of a questionnaire. We have all filled out questionnaires, and are well aware of what they look like. I want to focus on what we learn by carrying out questionnaires, some of the problems with them, and an assessment of how critical these problems really are.

BENEFITS FROM QUESTIONNAIRES

One of the main things we learn is to what extent it is possible to describe an economic reality by a set of categorical and numeric data. As applied economists, this is very important because we are taught to believe that the economic world can and should be measured in numbers. Practice in the art and science of questionnaire design and application teaches us a lot about the extent to which the economic world can really be quantified and categorised.

By contrast, when we use secondary data collected by someone else (who we do not know and do not meet), then we have to take the data on its own terms. We cannot know how well the data represent reality. Sometimes econometricians seem to prefer it that way. It means that the econometrician does not have to feel responsible for the data, but can play the role of heroic technician who is trying to make sense of the world despite the poverty of the data.

We have written above about the *Lady Bracknell principle*: 'I do not approve of anything that tampers with natural ignorance'. When someone else gives us a data matrix with 1,000 observations and 50 variables, it is a beautiful thing to behold, so long as we don't look at it too closely. We may take the view that there is nothing we can do to improve the data, and that our ignorance of data defects means that it is reasonable to make two highly convenient assumptions. First, that the data contain no systematic bias. Second, that any measurement error is random and of indeterminate variance. With these assumptions, we can happily progress on an applied econometric voyage, using standard techniques. These standard techniques – and perhaps even the voyage itself – might not be justified if we know the true character of the data. But if we don't, then we can claim it is legitimate to press on.

Sometimes the econometric enthusiast, keen to show technical bravura or keen to try out some new algorithm, may not care to know about defects in the data, and indeed it can be a somewhat disillusioning experience to realise that elegant data are actually very fragile. But it is still an important lesson to know the quality of our data. Recall the lesson of Chapter 6: in complex econometric models, the (partial) signal in a regressor may be quite small, so noisy data matter. Moreover, it is only by trying out the questionnaire technique ourselves that we understand the shortcomings of such data but also the achievement of those who collect it.

A second important thing we learn from conducting questionnaire surveys ourselves is how to interrogate our own knowledge base. How can we explore our accumulated knowledge, theories and intuition to identify a list of relevant variables for our questionnaire? In fact, writing a questionnaire can be a powerful way to integrate diverse parts of our knowledge base. A questionnaire may start with the aim of testing a particular theory, but will grow to include questions that do not derive from theory but from other sources.

Equally, questionnaire design can be a useful way to quiz a wise counsel. How does she react to the questionnaire? Which questions work well, and which work badly? What is missing? What is superfluous? Seeking reactions to a draft questionnaire is a good way of starting such an informal discussion, with a wise counsel, and also a useful way to achieve closure. In the same way, a dialogue over questionnaire design can be a good way to communicate with the classroom, with people in the field, with vernacular economists, other disciplines and technicians.

Designing a questionnaire has a third benefit. It encourages us to think about collecting new types of data, by asking new questions which were not asked in prior surveys, and to integrate insights from different techniques that have not been recognised in previous surveys.

Moreover, questionnaire design gets us to think about how we might calibrate model parameters by direct measurement. Applied econometrics as a technique uses *indirect inference*: we make inferences about model parameters from correlations amongst explanatory and dependent variables. We do not attempt to measure the parameter directly. But, as we saw above, indirect inference runs into all kinds of problems with economic data. If it is possible to measure a parameter by *direct description* – and the survey questionnaire may offer that opportunity – then it is worth trying.

PROBLEMS WITH QUESTIONNAIRES

For all the learning benefits involved in questionnaire design, it is also true that the output from a questionnaire survey can be problematic. These issues are very well discussed in a number of specialist books on questionnaires and surveys (Aldridge and Levine, 2001; Foddy, 1993; May, 2001; Thomas, 2004). The critique of the questionnaire comes from five different directions. In fact, there is some overlap between these.

Spurious quantification

Silverman (2001, pp. 29–30) notes that a prevalent critique of the questionnaire method is that it can be a misguided attempt to achieve a spurious degree of quantification or categorisation. It is not good science to categorise and measure human activity on a cardinal numerical scale of reasonably low dimension, or in terms of a small number of categories, when in fact the underlying realities are neither naturally numerical, nor limited to a small number of categories. This critique insists that quantitative researchers use ad hoc methods of quantification, and claim a level of scientific objectivity that cannot be achieved.

This is related in turn to what is often called a humanistic critique of the questionnaire (Aldridge and Levine, 2001, pp. 12–14). This critique argues that the problem with surveys is not so much their failure to be scientific, but rather that the aim to be scientific is misconceived. The humanistic critique also argues that questionnaires are artificial, and as they are an intrusion into social life, so the research instruments are bound to distort the data. The humanistic critique also recognises that respondents can be self-conscious, they may show guile, they may be uncomfortable with the closed questions of the researcher, which are in any case driven by the agenda of the researcher and not the agenda of the respondent. All of these points recur below.

From these critical perspectives, quantitative measurement is not superior to qualitative description in the social world. It would be if the magnitudes to be measured were naturally numerical or categorical, because in that case the quality of our knowledge is marked by the quality of our quantitative measurements. Measurement error implies weak knowledge. But from these critical perspectives, the shortcoming with questionnaire data is that the underlying realities are not fundamentally numerical, but the questionnaire tries to force our descriptions into a categorical or numerical scale. This is an error of data description rather than an error due to weakness of measurement.

Unwise to assume and demand good will from respondents

The naïve questionnaire technique proceeds as if respondents can be counted on to show good will towards the interviewer, and answer an unlimited number of questions in a dispassionate, neutral and wholly honest way. Some critics of the questionnaire technique point out that this is unrealistically optimistic, for a variety of reasons.

As noted already, questionnaire surveys are an intrusion into social life, often unwelcome. It is wrong to assume automatic good will on the part of respondents. Moreover, those respondents who show apparent 'good will' towards interviewers may in fact be those who have their own agenda in participating in the process. Critics argue therefore that we need to think carefully about the social context of surveys (Aldridge and Levine, 2001, pp. 15ff).

When and why are people willing to help the surveyor? It may be altruism, a sense of good citizenship and a sense of 'do as you would be done by'. But it may equally be driven by a respondent's desire, 'let's talk about me'. It may also be driven by a conscious desire to influence the results of the survey for the respondent's own ulterior reasons (Aldridge and Levine, 2001, pp. 17–19). We discuss that sort of respondent bias below.

When and why are people unwilling to help the surveyor? It may reflect survey fatigue in the face of strong competition from market researchers and salespeople to find suitable respondents. It may reflect a resentment of the intrusiveness of 'cold calling', a dislike of form-filling and the stress of being pushed into a questionnaire straitjacket (see below). It may reflect a desire for privacy, a suspicion of the motives of those who conduct questionnaires or just an outright dislike of academics (Aldridge and Levine, 2001, pp. 19–21).[1]

As a result, the sub-set of willing respondents may be an interesting mix indeed. They are unlikely to be a random sample – or even less a stratified sample – from the set who are invited to respond.

Noise in questionnaire responses

Critics of the questionnaire technique point out, furthermore, that our problems do not end when we recruit respondents. Even the well-intentioned and cooperative respondent may give unreliable results. Foddy (1993, pp. 2–9) provides a comprehensive list of the problems that can emerge. First, there is not a close correlation between what respondents say they do and what they actually do. Second, the attitudes, beliefs, opinions, habits and interests of respondents are notoriously unstable – and their statements about these may be even more unstable! Indeed, it is not uncommon to find that the same question inserted twice at two different points in the questionnaire may elicit different answers! Third, respondents commonly misinterpret questions, and small changes in the wording of questions can lead to large changes in the answer. Fourth, answers are path dependent: responses to question 10 (say) depend on the character of and answers to questions 1–9.

Systematic respondent bias

If the well-intentioned respondent is not always reliable, the canny respondent can certainly throw a spanner in the works!

At first sight, we might hope that the answers given by well-informed respondents are superior to those given by well-intentioned but not well-informed respondents. This may be too optimistic, however. The well-informed respondent probably has some professional interest in the subject of enquiry, and may not be neutral about the outcome of your survey. This can lead to subtle forms of respondent bias: the respondent deliberately adjusts his/her response to bend the outcome of the survey in a direction that is favourable for his/her interests.

For sure, the well-intentioned but poorly informed respondent may give answers subject to a large variance, but these are probably not subject to a systematic bias. By contrast, the guileful and well-informed respondent may give answers that are less susceptible to random noise, but which are invariably subject to systematic bias.

What is systematic respondent bias, and what forms can it take? A respondent may deliberately give an inaccurate – or more diplomatically, 'a not entirely accurate' – answer for several reasons.

First, the respondent suspects that responses may be used by the surveyor to devise a strategy, and it is therefore in the respondent's interests to give a strategic answer. We discussed an example of this in Chapter 11 which illustrated why rail passengers may give a strategic answer to questions designed to elicit their price elasticity of demand. The respondent bias in that case is likely to overstate price elasticity of demand.

Second, the respondent may fear that his/her answers will be scrutinised by tax authorities or by forces of law and order. This may lead to subtle changes to answers, or refusal to give answers to some questions.

Third, some people who enjoy participating in questionnaire surveys (and there are such people) may want to please the interviewer. Answers may be unduly polite, interested and complimentary when the respondent has in truth no interest in the subject of survey. Or, equally, the respondent may wish to be less than polite to the surveyor – not because of any specific dislike of surveys, but because the surveyor is a convenient scapegoat for more general grievances. For example, while most of the anonymous student feedback forms we receive at the end of our courses are reasonably diplomatic, and some make criticisms which we have to admit (to ourselves, at least) are justified, a few are unduly critical and offensive. Again, the questionnaire becomes a convenient vehicle to express a more generalised collection of grievances and discontents.

Finally, some view the questionnaire as one of those rather tiresome tasks that must be done, but as quickly as possible and at minimum cost. Some in the farming community have told me that when they received questionnaires asking about the numbers of animals on their farm, their answers are at best a rough guess, or more likely a plausible fiction. In this case, it is easy to appreciate the criticism that the questionnaire response just gives the surveyor the sort of number she wants.

It is interesting to compare the perspectives of this section and the last section with the experimental economists' view of the questionnaire survey. In their invaluable summary of experimental economics, Friedman and Sunder (1994, p. 6) argue that although survey data are empirical their reliability is in doubt unless the responses are economically motivated. This is consistent with the view of the last section. Questionnaire responses are subject to high variance, especially if respondents are disinterested – that is, they have no economic motivation. But the critical perspective described in this section can lead to a different view. Systematic respondent bias may be more serious when respondents *are* economically motivated, for it is then that they have a strategic incentive to modify their answers to promote their own interests.

Questionnaire as straitjacket

The final critical perspective sees the questionnaire as, in effect, a straitjacket. The respondent is so constrained by the questionnaire format that (s)he cannot express any individuality. In this case, it is debatable whether the responses collected contain much 'data', or whether they are in essence the surveyor's own construction. Even if we doubt this rather extreme critique, there is no doubt that it has provoked a useful debate on the comparative advantages and disadvantages of open and closed questions. By 'open', I mean questions where the respondent can put the answer in his/her own words; by closed, I mean questions where the questionnaire only permits a limited number of categorical and/or numerical answers.

Foddy (1993, pp. 128ff.) lists at least five advantages of open questions over closed questions. First, these allow respondents to express themselves in their own words (assuming, of course, that they actually want to). Second, open questions neither suggest answers to respondents, nor limit the answers they can make. Moreover, they allow the respondent to indicate his/her level of knowledge about the topic, they allow the respondent to indicate what is salient, and to indicate strength and character of feeling. Third, open questions allow us to identify complex opinions, influences and frames of reference in greater depth. Fourth, some would argue that a survey using open questions is a necessary preliminary before we try to develop a questionnaire with closed questions, and a limited set of response options. Fifth, the problems of interpreting responses to closed questions are reduced – to some degree, at least. A good example of this problem is found in surveys of innovations. Suppose such a survey contains the question, 'did your company make any product innovations last year?' and permits only a binary answer ('yes'/'no'). The responses from such a survey make rather problematic data. Some respondents set the innovation hurdle very low, and count a packaging change as a product innovation. By contrast, some set the innovation hurdle much higher, and discount anything except the radical innovation.

But equally, Foddy (1993, pp. 128ff.) recognises a similar number of advantages of closed questions over open questions. First, while the open question can be taken in different directions by different respondents, the closed question leads respondents to answer the same question. This makes it easier for the researcher to compare answers in a systematic way. Second, the closed question produces less variable answers. This is, of course, the flip side to the 'straitjacket' problem, and it is debatable whether this reduced variety is a good thing or a bad thing. It makes the researcher's task easier but may suppress some genuine and interesting variety. Third, the closed question presents the respondent with the task of recognising the 'right' answer as opposed to recalling the 'right' answer. This makes the respondent's task easier, and we saw above that this may be an important consideration in many survey contexts. Fourth, the researcher is not faced with the problem of recording and coding responses to open questions, and hence the answers are easier to computerise and analyse. In short, the use of closed questions reduces transaction costs. The difference between open questions and closed questions is a bit like the difference between custom-designed products and standardised products. The production and transaction costs involved in making a few standardised product lines are much less than the production and transaction costs involved in custom design. But these standardised products lose the valuable variety available in custom design.

HOW SERIOUS ARE THESE PROBLEMS?

After reading the various critiques summarised above, and even more so after reading some of the references listed at the start of the last section, the reader may think that the structured questionnaire with closed questions is so problematic that it is not usable. It is definitely not my objective to give this impression, and indeed I don't agree with that impression. While the problems of the last section are to be taken seriously, it is rare that they completely invalidate a questionnaire survey. Moreover, I am convinced that some of the questionnaires that I have designed and used have told me things that I would not (and possibly could not) have learnt any other way.[2] Some of the critics are too critical.

Here we must dwell on one of the most vital lessons in measurement theory – as developed, for example, in physics. This argues that we should *neither overstate nor understate* the accuracy of a measurement. As Rabinovich (1993) argues, it is generally important that those who measure do not overstate the accuracy of their measurements – that seems obvious enough. We have seen in Chapter 6 that the accuracy of econometric results depends on the signal-to-noise ratio in our data. If noise is substantial relative to signal, econometric estimates will be highly inaccurate. It is no good hiding our heads in the sand and pretending data are perfect.

More surprising, perhaps, is Rabinovich's (1993) argument that it is also important that those who measure do not *understate* the accuracy of their measurements. Why is that?

The easiest way to see this is with a zoological example. (I apologise in advance for some mixing of metaphors here.) Imagine an animal with good, but not perfect, hearing and which is constantly alert to sounds that signal danger. This animal is a bit like the statistician testing a hypothesis. There are two hypotheses: null (no danger) and alternative (danger). The animal, like the statistician, can make two mistakes. One is the type I error: to reject a true null. The other is the type II error: to fail to reject a false null. In this example, it is the type II error that is critical – or perhaps I should say, *fatal*. If the null hypothesis is false, but the animal fails to reject it, then the animal becomes prey to the predator. By contrast, in this case, the type I error is a more minor problem. If the null is true, but the animal rejects it, then it takes flight unnecessarily, but lives to see another day.

In this context, those who understate the accuracy of their measurements are liable to make too many type II errors. The signal may suggest danger, but this is discounted as noise because the measurement technique is considered to be hopelessly inaccurate.

Moving from the zoological to applied economic research, we find something very similar. Suppose that we test an economic hypothesis using applied econometric work, and this econometric evidence supports the hypothesis. (More precisely, the econometrics does not reject the null hypothesis.) Suppose then that another researcher provides evidence from a questionnaire survey that seems to contradict this hypothesis. The applied econometrician who has little regard for surveys may argue that this contradictory 'evidence' is so inaccurate that it need not disturb the comfortable endorsement provided by the econometric study. But this decision not to reject the null may in fact be a type II error. In the same way as above, those who understate the accuracy of measurements are liable to make too many type II errors. They are too likely to disregard contradictory evidence on the grounds that it is noise, when in fact there is a genuine contradiction.

For that reason, it is very unwise to let the litany of problems listed above create the impression that the questionnaire is of no value. It can provide some very telling evidence that may not be available from any other source.

In particular, I believe that the idea of the questionnaire as straitjacket is seriously overplayed. Taken at its extreme, it implies that data produced from questionnaire responses are not 'data' about the respondent at all, but the construction of the surveyor. That would seem to suggest that, regardless of who fills in a questionnaire, there is little variation in the results obtained. Or, to put it another way, questionnaires cannot discriminate between respondents.

This seems to me a gross exaggeration. Consider the example of an insurance policy. The individual who wishes to insure a car, for example, has to fill out a questionnaire where many of the questions are closed, and only allow a limited number of response options. Is it really the case that such a questionnaire is incapable of discriminating between respondents? Surely not. From the insurance company's point of view, the whole point of getting people to fill in these questionnaires is so that they can discriminate between the good and bad risks, and avoid problems of adverse selection. If these questionnaires did not achieve this discrimination, then the insurance company would find it profitable to devise another means of discriminating between the risks. And if all the questions in the questionnaire conveyed no information of value to help in this discrimination, then the company would save itself the cost of processing the questionnaires. The fact that insurance policies are granted on the basis of a questionnaire response alone, suggests that such instruments can certainly measure accurately enough for the levels of risk involved.

It is worth noting also that insurance companies prefer the closed questionnaire to the unstructured interview with open questions. Why is this, if the latter provides much richer data? The answer seems obvious enough: transaction costs in processing questionnaires are modest compared to the transaction costs in conducting and coding unstructured interviews. In addition, the costs are mostly carried by the form-filler not the form processor, because it is quite time consuming to fill in such a form, but not very time-consuming to process it once complete. Moreover, the closed question approach ensures that the key questions have to be answered, while the evasive interviewee could use the freedom of the unstructured interview to skirt around tiresome questions like, 'how many road accidents have you had in the last five years?'.[3]

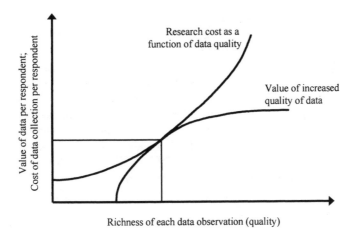

Figure 13.1   The optimum 'richness' of a survey

We could say that the questionnaire is a compromise. Figure 13.1 illustrates this. This diagram shows two functions: the value of data as a function of the richness of each data observation, and the cost of data collection as a function of richness. The first is concave and the second is convex. Why so? The shape of the value function implies that there are some essential pieces of information that must be gathered for each observation, but additional items beyond this are of limited additional value. The shape of the cost function implies that it becomes increasingly expensive to collect additional items of data, because respondent fatigue leads to lower response rates and a higher incidence of errors. The point of tangency illustrates the appropriate compromise.

Figure 13.2 then turns this into a trade-off between quantity and quality of data. The horizontal axis is the same as before (richness, or quality) while the vertical axis now shows the number of data observations that can be collected for a given research budget. The budget line shows the choices open to the researcher: a large number of shallow observations or a small number of rich observations? The indifference curve shows the trade-off between quality and quantity of data in the researcher's eyes. Again the point of tangency illustrates the appropriate compromise.

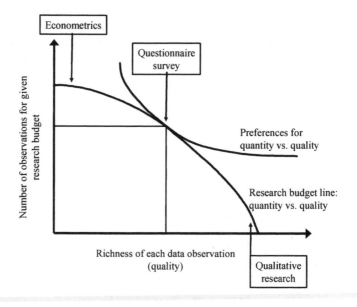

Figure 13.2   The trade-off between quantity and quality of data

The questionnaire is a compromise. It is unloved by qualitative researchers, who prefer in-depth and unstructured interviews – illustrated at the right-hand side of the diagram. It is unloved by economists who prefer to work with a smaller number of variables and as many observations as possible – illustrated at the left-hand side of the diagram. But it is the perfect choice for those in the middle.

CONCLUSION

We have argued in this chapter that the practice of designing a questionnaire and conducting a survey using that questionnaire are both important learning experiences – over and above what we learn from statistical analysis of someone else's questionnaire. We learn many things that we do not learn when we use data conveniently collected for us by government agencies, market researchers and so on. We have seen that answers to questionnaires are far from unproblematic, and may contain all sorts of noise and biases. But it is not helpful to say that the data are so problematic that the technique is no use. We have argued that it can be as dangerous, and sometimes *more* dangerous to understate the accuracy of measurements than to overstate the accuracy of measurement. We should neither treat the questionnaire data as perfect nor as rubbish.

The message of this book is to recognise that every technique has its shortcomings, but equally each technique has its own unique contribution to make. We should never ask which is best for all seasons, which technique is mostly right and which is mostly wrong. Rather, we should ask what we can learn from each technique that is different.

All techniques have their champions, and these tend to polarise debate about techniques. They argue that their technique is superior while others are inferior. This tends to encourage researchers from different traditions or different communities to specialise in one technique, and to neglect the others as unreliable. I have argued in this chapter that this tendency to play down techniques from other traditions and dismiss them as unreliable can lead to a high incidence of type II errors. We continue to believe false hypotheses because we disregard contradictory evidence when it comes from the wrong tradition.

I shall go further and say that this polarisation of debate about different techniques is one of the most damaging tendencies in all social science research. If advance in knowledge involves the testing of hypotheses and the rejection of false hypotheses, then the practice of disregarding rejections emanating from another tradition must slow down the advance of knowledge. A good researcher will use several techniques, at different times and for different purposes, even if (s)he only has mastery of a few. (S)he will do this as part of what we shall call, in Chapter 23, a paradox-seeking research strategy.

NOTES

1. In 1997, I was privileged to advise a House of Lords Select Committee about a report on the economics of innovation.   As part of my job, I was required to telephone several prominent industrialists to seek their views on questions raised during the Committee's deliberations.   It was amusing to contrast the responses I received in that capacity with the sort of responses we sometimes receive in our academic capacity.   The preface, 'I am ringing on behalf of the House of Lords Select Committee' produced an almost embarrassing deference and willingness to cooperate.   By contrast, the preface, 'I am a professor at the University of . . . ', often produces a less enthusiastic response!
2. Daniel Birke and I recently designed a questionnaire on mobile phone usage amongst the 250 members of a second year undergraduate class.   The responses from this indicated an extraordinary degree of implicit (if not explicit) coordination of operator choice amongst the different student communities in the class.   For example, almost without exception, the Chinese students in the class used Vodaphone as their mobile operator.   Subsequent informal enquiries suggested that this was sometimes the result of a conscious and economically informed decision to adopt the same operator as used by others in the same community.   At the time of the survey, on-net calls (for example, from one Vodaphone number to another Vodaphone number) were typically cheaper than off-net calls (for example, from a Vodaphone number to an Orange number). For this reason, if a community co-ordinates operator choice, then it is possible to reduce costs (Birke and Swann, 2005).
3. Of course, the insurance questionnaire becomes part of a contract between the customer and the company.   If the respondent makes false answers, this may invalidate the policy. This provides a strong incentive for the respondent to eschew the temptation of 'strategic respondent bias' and instead to give truthful answers.   The research questionnaire, by contrast, is rarely a contractual document, and the research has no comeback against the respondent who gives false answers.

14. Simulation

When I started in economic research in the late-1970s, simulation was not really regarded as a suitable technique for use by economists. With a few exceptions – such as the rigorous use of *Monte Carlo* methods in calculating small sample properties of estimators – simulation was seen at best as a poor mathematician's alternative to a proper analytical solution. It seemed that the good economists should resist the lure of simulation. In the intervening years, that attitude has changed for several reasons, which we discuss below.

Some, however, have expressed doubt as to whether simulation should really be regarded as a tool of *applied* economics. For example, Friedman and Sunder (1994, p. 5) argue that simulations do not in general yield experimental data. For that reason, simulation should be seen as a branch of theory and not a branch of applied economics. The first point here is quite right: if we build a computer model and simulate its behaviour under a variety of assumptions about parameter values, then the outcomes are hypothetical projections, not real empirical data. But, in my view, the second point is not right. Applied economists use simulation as a 'go between' to develop a better interface between theory and application. Simulation can tell us what sorts of parameter values must apply (if our theory is right) to generate the types of behaviour we observe in the empirical world.

I use simulation a lot, and have done so from an early stage. If I had been a better mathematician, and if I had not had a strong and early interest in the potential of personal computers, then I might have delved deeper into what could be solved analytically. But it has always seemed to me that simulation is invaluable when one cannot solve the maths, or does not have the inclination to struggle, or is more interested in the economic issues than the mathematics.

We shall first explore why there was early resistance to the use of simulation in economics, and why that has changed. We then address a most important and still unresolved puzzle about simulation. Is the key to the productive use of simulation in economics to insist on the purest scientific practice? Or is simulation most useful when it is used in a more ad hoc and impressionistic way? Controversially, perhaps, I shall argue the latter. We then give an example of the use of simulation to study the emergence of standards in the spreadsheet software market.

INITIAL SUSPICION OF SIMULATION

Some of the pioneering applications of simulation in social sciences were in economics (for example, Adelman and Adelman, 1959; Duesenberry et al., 1960; Orcutt et al., 1961; Phillips, 1957), or on the boundaries of economics and management (Bonini, 1963; Cyert and March, 1963). It is used by some econometricians to investigate small sample properties of estimators (see, for example, Malinvaud, 1980, p. S40), and in that context has the suggestive name, Monte Carlo methodology. But on the whole, economists have been rather suspicious of simulation. Sceptics see it as a technique in which you experiment with permutations of several parameters and generate a huge quantity of other numbers, and emerge none the wiser at the end.

It is interesting to contrast this attitude with attitudes prevailing in other disciplines. The technique is widely used in physics, chemistry and engineering, as well as in operations research and management science. One of the leading texts on simulation methods claims that simulation is one of the most widely used research techniques in operations research (Law and Kelton, 2000, p. 2). Referring to articles published in a leading operations research journal during the period 1970–92, Law and Kelton find that simulation was second only to mathematical programming amongst 13 leading techniques used in that journal.[1] Moreover, although sociologists have typically been less well disposed to mathematical analysis than economists, the technique of simulation is attracting quite a bit of interest in sociology. In fact, Gilbert and Troitzsch (1999, pp. 5–6) argue that this higher status of simulation in sociology than in economics may reflect a view amongst sociologists that social science theories are probably better formalised in simulation models than in mathematics.

Why is the position different in economics? Three points seem especially relevant here. First, the bad reception of simulation in economics stems in part from the use of these techniques in the early 1970s by Forrester (1971) and by the 'Club of Rome' (Meadows et al., 1972) to explore the limits to world economic growth. These applications were highly influential, and put these issues very prominently on the political and research agenda. On the other hand, these studies made some extravagant and rather alarming claims on the back of rather little evidence. The great Nobel prize-winning economist Solow (1974, p. 40) described these as 'Doomsday Models', and was highly critical of them – not least because the teams who carried out this work had deliberately excluded input from economists. It seems as if the very word *simulation* was badly tarnished by this episode, and no economist wanted to be seen using it for some time.

Second, Irma Adelman, one of the pioneers of the use of simulation in economics, observed that simulation models are better accepted in economics the closer they resemble an econometric model (Adelman, 1988, p. 341). She also observed that simulation is more acceptable to economists when it is used to explore models that are too complex for analytical solution. From these observations, Adelman distils the essentials of good simulation. All simulation involves a compromise between reality and transparency. As far as possible, the components of the model should be based on economic theory and parameters estimated by econometrics. But she recognises that when theory is lacking, the alternatives are either some ad hoc approach or an omitted variable – and neither of these options are appealing to the mainstream economist.

Third, as noted at the start, simulation has been viewed as a poor man's technique compared to analytical solutions. The proper economist defines his or her models in such a way that they are amenable to analytical solutions – for the analytical solution is the gold standard of mainstream economics. Those who use simulation are often regarded as slapdash because they do not bother to invest in working out analytical solutions. Or – even more serious – the decision to use simulation is a signal of low mathematical ability on the part of the user.

These three observations allow us to make the following generalisation about the status of simulation in mainstream economics. Simulation is more palatable to the mainstream the more similar it is to the mathematical and econometric formality with which mainstream economists . have felt comfortable. Simulation becomes less palatable to the mainstream when it seems very different in character from this mathematical and econometric formality.[2]

Controversially, perhaps, I take a different view from the mainstream. While I have great respect for the work of those who have made the most rigorous use of simulation in their work, I have personally found simulation most useful to me when it is very *different* in character from econometrics. I shall explain why below. I believe that the preoccupation with formality in simulation blunts its use as a tool in applied economics. This preoccupation is another instance of the primacy of technical bravura over understanding, and this has not been helpful to the development of our discipline.

Attitudes to simulation have changed somewhat since the mid- to late-1980s. I believe there are four main reasons for this. First, due to Moore's Law,[3] the gulf between the complexity of models that can be explored by simulation and those that can be solved analytically has grown very rapidly indeed. The analytical purist who thinks it improper to use simulation techniques finds that he must forego ever more tempting opportunities in order to retain his celibacy.

A second reason lies in the emergence of evolutionary economics and the growing interest in modelling the economy as a complex adaptive system –

after Holland (1992), Arthur (1989) and work at the Santa Fe Institute (described in Waldrop, 1994). This trend has meant that increasing numbers of economists want to explore models that stretch beyond the bounds of what can be handled analytically.

A third reason has been the powerful role of simulation as a teaching tool. For example, the Institute for Fiscal Studies has produced a simulation model – the *Virtual Economy* – for teaching purposes.[4]

The fourth reason is related to the first. The growth of computing power has made it possible to move beyond what we might call macro-simulation models to micro-simulation. Micro-simulation modelling makes use of large numbers of heterodox agents – following pioneering work by Orcutt (see the summary in Orcutt, 1988). Gilbert and Troitzsch (1999) describe how micro-simulation has blossomed even if other sorts of simulation have not. The work described by Farrell (1998) provides exciting examples of how the agent-based models which are possible in micro-simulation allow us to explore economic worlds that are quite outside the reach of purely analytical work.

One index of the changing attitude to simulation in economics can be found in the Centenary celebrations of the *Economic Journal*. Here it received a qualified blessing from one of the greatest economic theorists of the post-war period. When asked to speculate about developments in economic methods over the next hundred years, Hahn (1991, p. 47) suggested that simulations will replace theorems. Hahn argues that this is in part a result of the increasing interest in path dependence in economic modelling (following David, 1985; Arthur, 1989), where general theorems will be few and far between. Although he says that simulation based on good data is perfectly respectable, Hahn (1991, p. 47) sounds a little ambivalent about this future. He predicts that economics will become a 'softer' subject, and reckons that those who contributed to the advances of economic theory from the 1950s onwards will not find this new work appealing.

TWO DIFFERENT APPROACHES TO SIMULATION

We can usefully distinguish two very different approaches to simulation. I shall call them respectively the *orthodox* approach, in which simulation is used rigorously as an adjunct to econometrics, and the *unorthodox* approach, in which simulation is used in a more impressionistic way to explore anomalies and paradoxes.

Orthodox: simulation as an adjunct to econometrics

This approach stems from the observations made above, to the effect that economists find simulation most palatable when the style is similar to the rigorous mathematical and econometric tradition with which the mainstream feels comfortable. In this approach, therefore, the main preoccupation is to make simulation as rigorous as possible, and as similar as possible in orientation to econometrics. This is consistent with the idea that our aim in using multiple techniques is to get 'several' fixes on the same facet of a research problem – what is often called triangulation. To see the same facet, the contributory techniques should not be too far apart.

In this approach, the simulator's duty is to search the entire parameter space, making sufficient allowance for the stochastic character of the economic phenomenon, and then systematically to summarise the mass of simulations. Law and Kelton (2000) give us an excellent account of how to do this. As this orthodox stance is well described in the literature, I don't think it is necessary to justify it here.

Unorthodox: simulation as technique in search of paradoxes

The second approach is very different. This stems from the arguments in Chapter 10 that good applied economic research requires us to recognise that the objects of study are multi-faceted, and that to illuminate all these facets, we must employ a multiplicity of methods. From this point of view, the main purpose of plurality is not to get several 'fixes' on the same facet; rather it is to examine *different facets*. This distinction is very important. In this case, if our objective is to use econometrics to illuminate one facet and simulation to illuminate another, then we must set aside any extraneous professional pressures to make our simulation as similar as possible to econometrics. If anything, we need to be *contrarian*: how can we carry out our simulation in a different way?

In this approach, we shall of course want to see if the simulation model has validity, or consistency with data and/or 'stylised facts'. But equally, if not more so, the simulator's duty is to look for interesting anomalies and paradoxes. The simulation results help us to develop our intuition[5] and to answer the question: 'where should we look next?'. The simulation must be seen as part of a grander research process, and not as a self-contained process in its own right.

As this perspective is an unusual one, it will need further explanation and justification below.

Comparison of these two approaches

The first approach is familiar to most economists. And when I ask colleagues how they approach simulation, almost all refer to this approach, or something like it. By contrast, I expect the second approach will seem very strange to many readers.

Indeed, when I first started to use simulation as a doctoral student, my objective was to make it an adjunct to my applied econometrics. The objective was modest differentiation: to ensure that the interface between the two should be as close as possible to ensure compatibility. It was only after many years as an applied economist that I came to realise that this methodological strategy misses the point.

For sure, if our objective is to have a comfortable life, where our innovations do not upset our professional colleagues, then modest differentiation between techniques is surely the right way forward. But if our objective is to understand complex and multi-faceted problems in the real economy, then the character of the research problem demands more significant differentiation.

Some have told me that the second approach described here illustrates a thoroughly cavalier attitude to rigour in applied economic technique. There is perhaps some justice in this charge. But I would respond that if my approach is that of the *Cavalier*, then the orthodox approach is that of the *Roundhead*![6] True, the Cavalier may be somewhat careless or devil-may-care – and these are not desirable qualities in a researcher. But the Roundhead is a puritan and a rigid, unthinking observer of rules and orthodoxies – and these are even less desirable qualities in a researcher.

Is the way to make simulation *respectable* to make it more scientific? Perhaps. Is the way to make simulation *useful* to make it more scientific? I don't think so. The way to get the most from simulation is to concentrate on the aspects that are different from other well-established techniques. Do not try to make it more like econometrics; try to accentuate the differences.

CAVALIER SIMULATION: A JUSTIFICATION

As I said before, the orthodox approach has been well described and well defended in many comprehensive publications, but the unorthodox view has not, so I will say some further words by way of justification. Let me start with a simple illustration which is based on my own observation of countless seminar and conference presentations over many years.

When an economic theorist gives a 45 minute presentation, we often get 35–40 minutes of model and maths, and 5–10 minutes of empirical anecdote.

The anecdote is selected to motivate the theoretical model. The choice of anecdote may be a bit cavalier: from the totality of empirical examples, the theorist picks one that fits the model. The theorist does not do justice to the full details of the example, nor does he answer the charge that such an empirical example may be atypical. The exercise is just a concession to the empirical world, to motivate the paper to an empirical audience. What does mainstream economics think of such a presentation? In general, economics does not think that this is bad science.

Now imagine a presentation by an applied economist in which the proportions are reversed. We get 35–40 minutes of empirical detail, and 5–10 minutes of low level theorising. The theory is selected to motivate the empirical description. The choice of theoretical result may be a bit cavalier: from the totality of possible theoretical results, the empiricist picks a result that fits a particular economic phenomenon of interest. The empiricist does not do full justice to theory, and does not answer the charge that such a theoretical result may be atypical. The exercise is just a concession to the theoretical world, to motivate an empirical paper to a theoretical audience. Now what does mainstream economics think of such a presentation? In general, mainstream economics thinks that this is a disgrace, and sloppy in the extreme to single out one or two simulations for attention, without discussing the parameterisation in detail, the justification for the parameter values, how these were calibrated and so on.

Why is the reaction asymmetric? If we treat theory and application equally, there is no editorial justification for the asymmetry, as the two types of presentation are mirror images of each other. In each case we are part cavalier and part precise. The asymmetry implies to me a deep-seated imbalance between a high regard for theory and econometric technique and a low regard for the empirical.

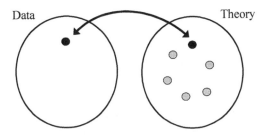

Figure 14.1   Precise about theory and cavalier about data

The theorist is precise about models and cavalier about examples. The theorist sets out the possible theoretical outcomes in some detail and then does a quick search of the data space to see if there is a story that conforms to a particular theoretical result. Figure 14.1 captures this.

By contrast, the empiricist is precise about examples, and cavalier about theory, going into some detail to explain the diversity of the empirical world, and then doing a quick search of the theoretical space for a theory which corresponds to one particular piece of data. Or if the theoretical space is summarised by a simulation model, the empiricist does a quick search of the parameter space to find a parameter set for which the predicted pattern corresponds to this observed data.

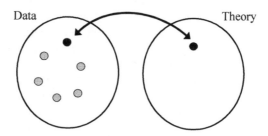

Figure 14.2　　Precise about data and cavalier about theory

So long as the cavalier simulator does not claim that a particular simulation is a leading theoretical result, then I see no harm in this second approach. It is no worse than the first. This is just an exercise to see what we have to do to a simulation model to generate a simulation which has some of the interesting, perhaps paradoxical, properties that emerge in the empirical evidence.

AN EXAMPLE OF IMPRESSIONISTIC SIMULATION

In this section, I shall take a brief look at the use of simulation in the context of a path-dependent world. In particular, I refer to a software standards race. This provides some useful insights into what simulation can achieve, when used in conjunction with other techniques. I definitely don't suggest that the approach taken or the resulting model should be taken as iconic examples of good practice. In any case, the definition of good practice is highly context specific. The key to the good use of simulation is not an internal definition but a contextual definition. It is not simply defined by reference to the elegance and rigour of the method itself. It is defined with reference to what simulation adds to the portfolio of applied research techniques we use to understand the economic problem. How can we use simulation (alongside the other techniques we use) to maximize its marginal contribution to the activities on the applied economist's desk?

Software standards race

I have constructed a large number of simulation models in my applied work. Here I shall focus on just one of them (Shurmer and Swann, 1995). I wouldn't claim that it is a particularly original or important study. In many ways, it was a very simple and crude simulation model. But I would claim that it was one of relatively few applied contributions, at that time, to an area that was (and still is) completely dominated by theory.

Our main objective in that study was to model the emergence of standards in the spreadsheet software market. The study grew out of a case study of the emergence of Lotus 1–2–3 as the de facto standard in spreadsheet software during the MS-DOS era. Clearly, things have changed in the Windows era, but those developments lay outside the scope of the study. What started as a case study turned into a simulation model. Indeed, to some degree the two were inseparable. The simulation model could not have been adequately developed without the richness of the case study findings to draw on. But equally, the case study would have been incomplete without the simulation model. The latter produced insights and paradoxes which demanded further work from the case study, and also suggested potentially important variables that needed to be measured, as far as that was possible.

Simulation plays a vital role because standards races exhibit extreme path dependence. This means that outcomes may be influenced by minor variations in (what appear to be) parameters of second order importance. Simulation was also an invaluable technique for our purposes because it offers a vehicle to integrate diverse fragments of empirical evidence and distinct theoretical building blocks. Analytic theory is not good at this. Indeed, many theorists apply a principle of *Occam's Razor* to their work: analytic models are kept as simple as possible in most dimensions, and all attention is focused on alterations to one or two parameters. When using analytic methods, this approach is understandable, if not indispensable. But many consider that Occam's Razor creates theory of limited empirical use. Econometric methods are not good at handling diverse fragments either: they demand neat matrices of data that are infrequently available in markets for new technologies.

In economics, therefore, we see an inadequate interface between theoretical models of standards and empirical studies that can really confront those theories. The models of de facto standards by Farrell and Saloner (1985) and Katz and Shapiro (1985) offer very elegant summaries of the special effects of network externalities on market equilibria. But they tend to offer 'knife edge' solutions between one standard and another, while empirically we often observe multiple standards – at least for a while.[7]

Coming from the other end of the spectrum, some excellent case studies of standards offer support for the basic structure developed by theoretical economics, but don't have a fine enough structure to refute any of these theories (David, 1985; Gabel, ed., 1987; Gabel, 1991; Grindley, 1995; and others surveyed in David and Greenstein, 1990). Simulation models, being quantitative, do offer a 'gateway' that allows the researcher to confront models with evidence in an altogether more demanding way.

Some from the IT standardisation community have not found their encounters with economic analysis of standardisation very helpful (Cargill, 1989, pp. 7–8). There is evidence, however, that cross fertilisation between social scientists (including economists) and standards professionals can be rather productive (Berg and Schumny, 1990; Gabel, ed., 1987; Evans et al., 1993). I have found that simulation models of this sort were very helpful in sustaining that dialogue – an essential item on the applied economist's desk, in my view.

In common with the leading theoretical models of standards races, the simulation models take it that users are concerned with both the intrinsic features of a product and also with the network of supporting products surrounding it. Our model offers several extensions to the basic theoretical model. The first is that we can deal with many more products and periods: the spreadsheet software case models analyse the dynamics of market share of 15 packages over 32 quarterly periods from 1981 to 1988. The second is that we allow for a wide diversity of user types, from the 'techies' (sophisticated and self contained users who are most concerned about intrinsic features) to the 'networkers' (whose prime concern is to use the product at the centre of a grid of software applications).

We collected secondary data on spreadsheet software packages and the spreadsheet market from a variety of trade and trade press sources. In addition, we conducted a small number of interviews with industry experts to supplement these secondary data. Often the interviews provided useful fragments rather than helping to fill out our data matrix. The data would not have been good enough or complete enough for an econometric study, but were adequate for this purpose.

The data related to a comparison of the intrinsic features of different spreadsheet software packages, and to market shares and installed user bases for particular packages. It soon became apparent during this data collection that those commentators reviewing software developments consider that intrinsic features are not necessarily as important as the extrinsic network of supporting products and services that are compatible with any one package. Indeed, this was not a surprise, given the potential role for network externalities in the underlying theoretical models. Indeed, in these models, a lead in network externalities is often enough to ensure that a product remains 'the standard' even in the face of competition from a much more sophisticated system.

One working hypothesis that appeared throughout the trade press was that while the leading product (in terms of market share) was 'the best' at an early stage, it was not necessarily the best from a technical point of view later on in the standards race, but offered the largest network of supporting products, user guides, training courses, add-ons and add-ins, and so on. Our data confirmed the latter network rather clearly. This observation, however, raises the question of whether the direction of causation is mainly from network externality to market leadership, or conversely from market leadership to externalities. Theoretical analysis would tend to say both. A product with a lead in network externalities will attract more new users, and the supplier of externalities will exploit this growing user base by producing a wider range of add ons, and the like.

Our data collection suggested that the existence of 'gateways' (partial compatibility links between different products, or especially between different generations of the same product) were very important. The literature on market defined standards had recognised this (see David and Greenstein, 1990), but had not built them explicitly into theoretical models. It is not difficult to modify a simulation model to take account of a complex mosaic of partial gateways between different competing products and upgrades, and it was clear that in certain circumstances the existence and capacity of the gateway could be decisive (within the model) in influencing the outcome of the standards race.

Anyone collecting data, moreover, cannot help but be struck by the occurrence of pre-announcements. These are where producers announce their plans to introduce a new product (or a new upgrade) in advance of the time when the product is actually available. The reason for doing this is (in part) to encourage users to delay adopting one of the existing packages in anticipation of your forthcoming product introduction. This phenomenon had been analysed in the theoretical economics literature (see again the survey by David and Greenstein, 1990), and this analysis showed how timely pre-announcement activity could help to reinforce a product's position as an industry standard. However, this simulation exercise (based on our estimated pre-announcement dates) was able to give some indication of how influential these pre-announcements could be in practice.

Most theoretical analysis of pre-announcements suggested that from the point of view of encouraging users to defer purchases, pre-announcements could not be made too soon – even though there could be quite different reasons for caution in making pre-announcements (commercial secrecy, uncertainty, advertising standards considerations). This simulation framework showed quite soon that this property of simple two-product analytical models is misleading when we move to an environment with multiple competing packages. The reason is that pre-announcement as a strategy depends on deterring users from adopting any system, and premature pre-announcement can perversely lead to a bandwagon behind the wrong product. We suspect that this perverse finding would not have appeared except in a modelling framework that used a simulation model to incorporate diverse pieces of information about this market.

Simulation models are reasonably adaptable at taking account of interesting sociological and ethnographic insights. The first was to recognise that users might primarily be concerned about the installed base of users within their own community – rather than globally – and this indicated a segmentation of the user spectrum. One way to do this was to segment the spectrum of users ranked according to the relative values they place on intrinsic and extrinsic features. This generated some very interesting insights about the emergence of different standards in different communities.

The second was to recognise that the representation and understanding of what packages can do is technically underdetermined, and therefore negotiated. This can be incorporated into the model – by recognising a random element in the assessment of intrinsic (and extrinsic) features. The incorporation generates a wider multiplicity of possible outcomes than would otherwise occur, and that result has the right character to it, even if the model does not add anything more to the basic insight.

Lessons learned

What did we learn from this study? Three main things. First, this is a useful way to model and understand practical examples of a standards race. The value of an individual case study can be enhanced substantially if it contributes to the construction of a simulation model. Second, we have learnt that simulation as a technique provides an important capability that is not offered by econometrics or analytical economic theory: it allows us to integrate different theoretical building blocks with diverse fragments of data to build a richer empirical model, while still retaining a quantitative character. Moreover, the modelling technique shows how a large number of socio-economic factors can shape the technology standards that result. And third, the model can also be inverted and used to assess the impact in terms of user benefits (and sometimes disadvantages) of having a unique standard. Indeed, we argue that the impact study and shaping study are interconnected. Firms in this market seem to use quite sophisticated strategies to shape and market their product in a way that gives it the best chance of winning the standards race. This was particularly evident with regard to gateways (partial and ad hoc compatibility links) and pre-announcement activity. Expected market impact becomes an input to standards strategy.

CONCLUSIONS

In the above, I have deliberately set out two more or less polar opposites. In the orthodox approach, simulation is an adjunct to econometrics, and the same mathematical and econometric rigour is required. In the unorthodox approach, simulation is an altogether more impressionistic technique, a device to explore anomalies and paradoxes, and to develop our intuition. Rigour is secondary.

Controversially perhaps, I myself find the latter the more useful. But I would readily concede that may simply be a reflection of the research questions that I address, and what I want simulation to add to the other techniques I use. There are certainly applications of simulation where a more orthodox approach would be essential. The most important message is this. The way in which we do simulation must be defined by the research problem in hand, and what we want simulation to contribute to the broad portfolio of research techniques we use (or should use) as applied economists. The style of simulation should not be defined by reference simply to intrinsic characteristics – such as elegance, rigour or comprehensive coverage.

NOTES

1. Pidd (1984) describes the use of simulation in management science.
2. We might add that simulation is more palatable when it is not called simulation! So for example, the Elsevier *Handbook of Computational Economics* (Amman et al., eds, 1996) contains much that could be called 'simulation', but prefers on the whole to avoid that word.
3. Moore's Law is the assertion that the complexity of semiconductor integrated circuits grows exponentially over time. First posited by Intel founder Gordon Moore in 1965, it has held pretty constant up to the present, but cannot continue indefinitely because of fundamental physical constraints.
4. http://www.bized.ac.uk/virtual/economy/model/
5. I am grateful to Paul David for this insight. Simulation can be a powerful tool to develop our intuition. Moreover, the observation seems to entail the implication that informal and non-rigorous intuition is a 'higher' activity than simulation.
6. The two opposing sides in the English Civil War (1642–49). The Cavaliers were Royalists, and the adjective came to describe their lifestyle and attitude: careless, devil-

may-care, negligent, incautious, rash, cursory, supercilious and superficial. The Roundheads (so-called because of their close cropped hair) were supporters of Parliament. They were puritans, or *precisians* – rigidly precise in the observance of rules or forms.

7. The model of Arthur (1989) is richer in this regard, as it allows for dual standards.

15. Engineering economics

This chapter[1] explores an approach to applied economics where the form of the economic model of a process – and indeed some of the parameters of that model – are derived from the physical and engineering fundamentals of the process. Amongst economists, this approach is often called *engineering economics*. We should point out that the same term, *engineering economics*, has also acquired another meaning amongst engineers: those economic and accounting principles useful to the engineer. In this chapter, I am only concerned with the first of these interpretations.

An important distinction is made between *analytical* approaches to engineering economics and *experimental* approaches. In the former, the production relationships (and even some of the parameters) are derived directly from well-established theory. In the latter, production relationships are derived from experiments in production. Either way, the engineering economics approach is still markedly different from applied econometric methods using indirect statistical inference. Engineering economics uses at least some engineering knowledge to shape production and cost functions. A purely econometric approach, by contrast, would select a general flexible functional form for the production or cost function, and then use statistical inference to give it a more compact form.

Engineering economics appeals to the hard (or harder) sciences to put structure on economic models in two ways: first, by deriving the functional form of economic relationships from physical laws; and second, by estimating key parameters of these relationships (such as cost parameters) from engineering data. Whereas applied econometrics uses indirect inference, engineering economics uses direct description, because: (i) prior theory gives a very precise indication of functional forms; and (ii) relevant parameters can be measured directly, by people who understand the process.

ORIGINS OF ENGINEERING ECONOMICS

Like many of the best ideas in economics, the idea of engineering economics (if not the name) can be traced back to some of the earliest writers on economics. Smith (1776/1904) describes the process of pin making in great detail, because it forms the basis of his discussion of the merits of the division of labour. This attention to detail is an essential part of the engineering economics approach, and one which marks it clearly apart from neoclassical production theory in which production is in a very abstract sense just a function of labour, raw materials and the services of capital and land.

The work of Charles Babbage (1835) provides very important foundations for engineering economics. Babbage built on Smith's work to provide economic principles of manufacturing technology, work organisation and the division of labour. He based this work on careful and exhaustive empirical study of production processes. He refined Smith's concept of the division of labour to recognise an often-quoted Babbage Principle (1835, pp. 175–6).

The founding of the Econometric Society brought a mathematisation of economics that might have advanced the conjunction of engineering process details with mathematical economic models. But, in practice, with a few striking exceptions (see Swann, 2002b, for a summary), it did not. Rather, the greater part of applied econometric work was concerned with the use of multiple regression analysis to estimate production functions. One shining exception was the work of Leontief and associates. Leontief's massive edited volume, *Studies in the Structure of the American Economy* (1953), contains a number of studies that take an engineering economics approach to the determination of production relationships. Leontief clearly found these very useful in his large-scale input–output studies. One of these is a classic in the empirical measurement of production relationships (Chenery, 1953). The Chenery study achieves far more in revealing the true character of production relationships than has been achieved in most econometric studies.

Despite this, and although there are a variety of other important studies of this type (reviewed in Swann, 2002b), the field of engineering economics remains very underdeveloped. Moreover, it is a field in which most professional economists receive no training. Why is this? It is a complex issue. In part, it reflects the view we have discussed throughout this book. Mainstream economics has tended to assume that econometrics is a universal solvent applicable to any problem in applied economics. But there is more to it than that. Chenery's study (and also the example of semiconductor cost functions described below) requires understanding of physical and engineering principles beyond the grasp of many economists, and moreover is probably fairly labour intensive. By contrast, applied econometrics seemed to offer a standard toolkit that could be applied to almost any economic problem without the need for much (any?) understanding of the underlying physical and engineering principles.

ENGINEERING ECONOMICS AT WORK

The best way to understand what engineering economics is, and what it can achieve, is to look at an example. One of the most striking examples of the power of this technique is the estimation of semiconductor cost functions from underlying engineering data. From a basic grasp of the physics of semiconductors, the details of the engineering processes used and some probability theory, we can write down a fairly precise description of the relationship between cost per chip and the number of components per chip. This function can be calibrated with engineering data. Here we just summarise the basic argument and how it is used to derive a quantitative economic model. For further details, the author is referred to Swann (1986), and especially the references therein.

The example derives a cost function for the production of integrated circuits in general, or microprocessors in particular. It is based on the state of the art in microprocessor design in the mid-1980s (reflecting the date at which the underlying research was carried out). Clearly the state of the art has moved forward substantially during that time, from the Intel 8086 microprocessor to the Intel Pentium microprocessor. Nevertheless, the basic physics and engineering principles still apply – but at a greater degree of miniaturisation and a greater capacity of components per chip.

Some fundamental relationships between technology parameters

The driving force behind developments in microelectronics has been the extraordinary rate of progress in cramming more active components into a single chip. As summarised by Moore's Law, the number of components per chip has grown exponentially since the first integrated circuits were produced in the early 1960s. At the start of this period, the rate of progress was a doubling in capacity every year. In the 1980s and 1990s, the proportional rate of growth has slowed somewhat to a doubling every 18 months or two years, but in absolute terms this still represents a staggering rate of advance.

This trend can be broken down into two parts. One is that chips have simply got larger, so that even at a constant dimension per component, the capacity of a chip increases. But the second, and most important factor is that the achievable density (in components per square millimetre) has continued to increase. This continuing advance in miniaturisation, in turn, derives from two sources: designers have become better at devising chip layouts so that a greater share of the chip surface is taken up with active components rather than 'wiring' or dead space; in addition, the space required to achieve a single component has continued to decline.

As we see below, this continuing miniaturisation has made it possible for chip manufacturers to produce ever more powerful microprocessors. But miniaturisation has also been the driving force behind many of the other key trends in microelectronics over the last 35 years: cost reductions, faster processing speeds, lower power dissipation and greater reliability. The reason is that there are some intrinsic relationships between these different technology parameters which derive from basic semiconductor physics.

Most of the components on a microprocessor are transistors. Transistors are what give the microprocessor its processing power. The transistors in a microprocessor act essentially as digital switches, and the key to the power of the processor is that they act quickly. The speed at which a transistor can operate depends on the speed at which it can discharge its output node capacitance, and this in turn depends on the size of these capacitances. The sizes of these node capacitances are proportional to the sizes of the elementary devices on the chip, and to the interconnecting line (or 'wiring') lengths. If the capacitances are reduced, then this implies a faster transistor, and hence a faster microprocessor. And, in addition, the smaller the node capacitance, the less energy is dissipated each time it is discharged, and so for a given processor speed, the smaller the power dissipation.

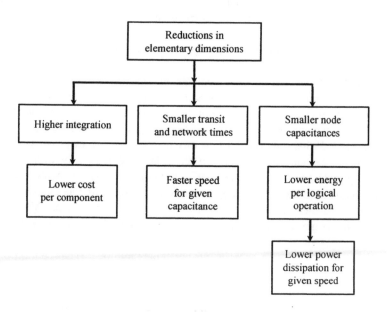

Source: Based on Swann (1986, p. 53)

Figure 15.1   Relationships between semiconductor parameters

Miniaturisation, then, leads to greater speeds (shorter paths), lower node capacitances (and hence a lower power-delay product) and higher component density – which, as we see below, reduces costs. Figure 15.1 summarises the inter-relationships between these parameters. The key lesson here is that reductions in elementary dimensions lead to improvements in almost all other technology parameters – perhaps within some limits. These relations stem from the basic physics of semiconductor devices, but as we shall see below some other relationships can be derived from the engineering principles and processes of microprocessor manufacture.

The manufacture of integrated circuits and cost function

The essence of the manufacture of integrated circuits has remained the same for many years, although the details of the process and degree of miniaturisation achieved have changed very markedly. The main technique used (in the mid-1980s) was the planar process combined with photolithography. The planar process builds circuits by growing a stack of cross-sectional layers of silicon dioxide on a slice of pure silicon. From the early days, photolithography has been used to imprint the right patterns onto these layers, though new alternatives are appearing.

For each layer, the process is much the same, and the cycle is repeated several times. Each cycle may contain two sorts of step: a masking step, where a photographic image is etched into the surface; and a diffusion or ion-implantation step, where the right sort of impurities are introduced into the silicon to make it act as a semiconductor. The precise number of cycles depends on the nature of the circuit and the particular variant of the technology being used. The last stage involves building a layer of aluminium on the surface and etching out the connecting paths.

Each photolithographic mask will contain not just one circuit but a large number, because a slice of silicon will actually have printed on to it several hundred self-contained circuits. Each of these circuits will be tested individually, and a large number of them will actually fail – for reasons that will become clear later.

The marginal cost of processing a slice of silicon can be written:

$$SC = p_s + c_1 m + c_2 d + T \qquad (15.1)$$

where p_s is the price of a slice of silicon, m is the number of masking steps, d is the number of diffusion or ion implantation steps, T is the cost of a bulk test per wafer, and where c_1 and c_2 are, respectively, the marginal costs per masking and per diffusion or implantation step.

As stated before, only a proportion of the circuits on the slice will work properly. There are at least three reasons why a chip may fail: first, the silicon slice may contain unwanted impurities; second, the masks are not aligned properly, which would tend to ruin an entire wafer; third, random photographic defects in the mask (such as dust particles) introduce defects. The last of these is by far the most important in practice.

Suppose that in a very small unit area of the mask there is either one defect with a (very small) probability f, or no defects with probability $1 - f$. Suppose too that the occurrence of defects in adjacent units are independent events. Finally, for a particular circuit corresponding to a particular area of the mask to work, there must not be any defects on any of the masks. Then we can derive a yield function as follows.[2] Suppose that the chip area (in these small units) is A. Then the probability that one of the masks will have no faults anywhere in the area corresponding to that chip is $(1 - f)^A$. For m masks, the probability of no defects on any of the masks in the area corresponding to that chip is $(1 - f)^{mA}$. For very small f, this can be approximated as follows:

$$Yield = e^{-mfA} \qquad (15.2)$$

This means that the yield of working chips falls exponentially with the expected number of defects per chip (fA) multiplied by the number of mask steps. And since cost is inversely related to yield, it is apparent that the cost of a working chip rises exponentially as a function of mfA.

Let the area of the silicon slice be S. Then, since the number of circuits that can be fitted onto one mask is to a first approximation[3] given by S/A, we can compute the expected marginal cost of a working chip to be:

$$CC = [p_s + c_1 m + c_2 d + T] \cdot \frac{A}{S} \cdot e^{mfA} + P \qquad (15.3)$$

where P is the cost of packaging a working chip. In what follows, it is useful to rewrite this as a function of the number of components per chip, N, rather than chip area A. To do this, simply write $A\theta = N$ where θ is the achievable density of components per unit area. Then equation (15.3) can be rewritten:

$$CC = [p_s + c_1 m + c_2 d + T] \cdot \frac{N}{\theta S} \cdot e^{mfN/\theta} + P \qquad (15.4)$$

Figure 15.2 illustrates this cost per working chip as a function of N. This graph is based on the following parameter values which are based on engineering data relevant at the time of the original study (Swann, 1986): $f =$

0.025 mm^{-2}, SC = \$0.0068 mm^{-2}, m = 10, P = 0.45, θ = 1,000 mm^{-2}. It shows how for chips with up to about 5,000 components, the cost is constant at the fixed packaging cost per chip of P = 0.45. The cost per working chip only starts to increase above that when the yield drops below 100 per cent – at around 10,000 components. After that, cost per working chip rises very rapidly.

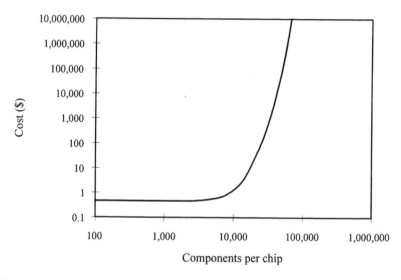

Figure 15.2   Cost per working chip

Given this cost relationship, it would be possible to start to calculate optimum chip sizes. But the precise character of this optimum will depend on the value attached to capacity – and hence the functionality of the chip. One interesting benchmark is the following calculation. Suppose that the designer wishes to put together a collection of chips that between them contain a given number of components. What is the best way to distribute these components across the collection of chips so as to minimise the total cost?

To answer this, we define CC/N as the cost per component, and we study the relationship between CC/N and the number of components per chip. This is easily derived from equation (15.4), and is summarised in Figure 15.3 – for the same set of parameter values as before.

This shows that the cost per 10,000 components reaches a minimum when the number of components per chip is just below 10,000. If chips contain a smaller number of components, then this is inefficient because unnecessary packaging costs are incurred.   If chips contain a larger number of components, then costs rise rapidly because yield declines.

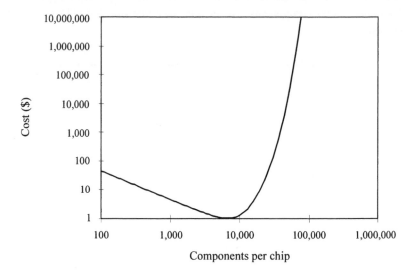

Source: Based on Swann (2002b, p. 10)

Figure 15.3   Cost per 10,000 components

Historical trends

These cost functions can be used to chart the implications of technological change in microprocessor production for the costs of chip production.   As Swann (1986) notes, most of the parameters in equations (15.1) to (15.4) have been subject to change over the last 35–40 years of semiconductor production. But in what follows we shall simply examine the effects of changes in θ – the attainable density in terms of components per chip – and hold all other parameters constant. In practice, this rather underestimates the effect of technological change on the feasibility of producing large and powerful chips. For example, the probability of mask flaws (f) has steadily declined as production processes in clean rooms get better and better, and that pushes the curves in Figures 15.2 and.15.3 to the right.

Figure 15.4 extends Figure 15.3 by showing the relevant curves for a wide range of values of θ. As the attainable density of components per chip increases, the cost function for larger chips moves downward and to the right.

But in each case there is a clear minimum to *CC/N*, beyond which cost per component starts to rise rapidly.

Figure 15.4 illustrates part of the effect of Moore's Law. Each time the attainable density has increased by a factor of 10, the optimum chip size (in components per chip) also increases by a factor of 10 and, moreover, the cost per component falls by a factor of 10. We have not attempted here to put dates against these different curves. Moreover, as indicated above, Moore's Law is perhaps a little slower (in proportional terms) now than it was in the 1960s, so the time interval between the successive curves would be getting a little longer. It was perhaps 3–4 years between $\theta = 1$ and $\theta = 10$, but would be more like 6–7 years between $\theta = 10^4$ and $\theta = 10^5$.

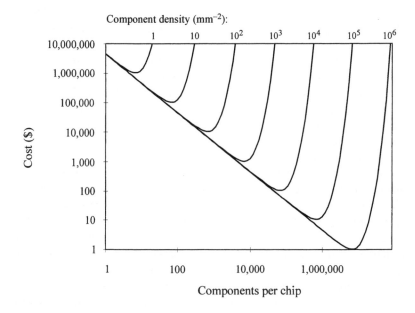

Source: Based on Swann (2002b, p. 11)

Figure 15.4   Miniaturisation and cost per component

STRENGTHS AND WEAKNESSES

This example does not attempt to show all the things an engineering economic approach can achieve, but it gives a good idea of the character of this approach. In this section, I shall try to draw out some of its strengths and weaknesses.

Strengths

One strength is that the technique makes credible use of direct description. This is typical of most engineering economic studies. The balance is definitely towards direct description of the process, and the relevant functional forms, rather than much indirect inference. In particular, the approach comes up with a remarkably precise indication of the relevant functional forms for cost relationships. These are far more precisely defined than would normally be possible with applied econometric work.

Another strength is that the physics and engineering literature on which this study is based is rigorous in its own terms. The application of these literatures to derive cost functions can be done with a degree of rigour comparable to that in applied econometrics. If there is a lack of rigour it relates to the question of whether these derived relationships are artificial or real – see below.

Another attraction, to the economist at least, is that the output of engineering economics studies is in some respects quite similar to that from an econometric study. It produces specific functional forms with parameter estimates – and indeed we may be more confident of the functional form here than we would be in conventional applied econometrics. In addition, the approach can provide – as we saw above – a relatively rich set of insights into fundamental relationships between technology parameters.

Another attractive feature of this approach is that the functional forms obtained above are not just black boxes. Their derivation lies in the physics of semiconductors and the engineering realities of the process. Admittedly, the above study relied mainly on secondary technical literature, and may have missed some of the richness of the process. But I think it is fair to say that the richness of understanding provided by this approach far exceeds what could have been obtained by an econometric approach to estimating cost functions.

The semiconductor example gave a good illustration of how well the engineering economic approach could map out the economic implications of technological change. But this was really modelling the change of selected parameters, rather than structural change. Now in the semiconductor case, arguably, our understanding of the basic physics is stable, and structural change resulting from that is unlikely – though not impossible. But the engineering process is not stable, and it is fair to say that the literature-based approach described above will only pick up structural changes with some lag.

Weaknesses

There are a few weaknesses, or at least limitations, to the use of engineering economics. The above example is, by economic standards, a fairly *micro* study. It relates to the cost function for producing one technology in one industry. However, some engineering studies could expect to be somewhat more macro than that. Nevertheless, I do not think that an engineering economic approach could ever be suitable for a truly macroeconomic study.

The engineering economics approach cannot offer the same degree of ubiquity as the econometric approach to estimating production functions. The example described above generated a cost function that is specific to a particular technology in a particular industry. It is not as general as an econometric approach to estimating cost functions, which might be applicable to a wide range of technologies in different industries. And neither does it offer any firm-specific insights – for example, why one semiconductor firm's cost function might give it a cost or quality advantage over another.

It is not as selective as an experimental economics approach, which might only look at one or two factors, or some simple statistical studies which do not attend to the multi-dimensional character of most socio-economic relationships. Nevertheless, it is not completely inclusive – as the best sort of case study should aim to be. The example described above covers a selection of the factors that will influence a semiconductor firm's cost function. But clearly it is not all-inclusive. It tells us little about why the output of semiconductor plants could sometimes be subject to periods of abnormally low yields.

Compared to some of the techniques that will be discussed below, engineering economics does not rank as one of the best integrators. As a communication tool, it has the advantage of credibility in that models and parameters are derived from the hard sciences. Its shortcoming is that it does not speak the language of ordinary people, while some of the other techniques described in this book are more user-friendly.

The engineering economics approach can only be applied to a restricted domain of problems. On the production side, it is most obviously relevant to science-based industries – so that some basic principles from physics, or another hard science – offer some leverage in understanding the basic economics. Moreover, it is most relevant in a context where the engineering principles of the production process are stable and well documented. It is less relevant in a context where production is dependent on tacit knowledge or a high degree of creativity. Moreover, it is essentially limited to the supply side of an economy. It is hard to see many applications of an engineering approach to understanding the determinants of consumer demand.[4]

Perhaps the greatest problem with the engineering economic approach is that it describes an idealised production process, rather than a real one. We have already commented that the example described above said little about the idiosyncratic factors that might create some substantial cost or quality differences between different companies. With some other application of the engineering economic approach, such problems might be even more serious. Even so, it is unlikely that these problems will be as serious as they can be with certain types of experimental economic studies, or certain surveys and questionnaires.

CONCLUSION

In many ways, engineering economics looks like a winning technique. It offers the quantitative rigour sought by econometric techniques, but with a greater credibility, richness and precision. We have already commented that, surprising as it may seem, the field of engineering economics is not densely populated. One of the reasons is that it is a hybrid technique. To do such work requires an understanding of the physical, chemical and engineering issues involved, as well as the underlying economics. Moreover, where it exists, engineering economics tends to be located in engineering schools or business schools rather than economics departments.[5] Why? Part of the reason is that an economist located within an economics department would probably find little kudos or career advancement in developing research within engineering economics.

Dogan (1994) and Dogan and Pahre (1990) have discussed the phenomenon of the *hybrid discipline*. The hybrid scholar crosses the accepted boundaries of his/her home discipline and integrates concepts, theories, methods and results originating from other disciplines. Loosely speaking, the hybrid scholar is an *intellectual tourist* who travels from one country to another, with a view to returning home in due course. Dogan (1994) claims that much of the invention in each discipline depends largely on exchanges with other fields. If this is right, then *marginal scholars* play an especially important role in intellectual invention, even if they have an uncomfortable time of it (see below). Dogan and Pahre (1990) coin the term, 'creative marginality', and suggest that progress in academic disciplines is concentrated at the periphery and not in the core. At the periphery, where there is cross-fertilisation with other disciplines, we find the most creative thinking.

One great attraction of engineering economics is that it is a forward-looking technique. As we saw in the semiconductor example, the precision with which the engineering economics model can be identified allows us to use it for extrapolation into the future – even in the face of rapid technological change. Frisch, possibly the greatest of the econometric pioneers, urged economists to turn their backs on what he called 'belated economics' (Frisch, 1956, p. 302). He argued that it is no good devoting our energies to theories, techniques and data that can only explain the happenings of the past. Rather, he argued that we should look forward to the analytical tools that we shall need in the future.

In my view, engineering economics is an essential tool on the desk of an applied industrial economist. It may also be an important tool for other applied microeconomists.

NOTES

1. This chapter draws heavily on Swann (2002b).
2. An alternative derivation is in terms of the Bose–Einstein statistics – see Feller (1957, p. 39).
3. This is a slight overestimate because of 'edge dropout': since the slice is circular, its periphery is unusable and this leads to a little wastage.
4. Optimising diet to achieve a required level of nutrition can be analysed using an engineering economics approach, even if the underlying principles here are biological rather than physical. Witt (2001) takes this approach further when he explores to what degree consumption can be understood as a biologically and genetically determined process.
5. In the USA, Canada and Italy, for example, the idea of engineering economics is a bit further developed than in the UK – but it is generally located within engineering schools.

16. Economic history and history of economic thought

I must approach this chapter with some humility. I am neither an economic historian nor an historian of economic thought. I cannot presume to write a chapter on why and how to study economic history and the history of thought. There are so many aspects to this, and I only understand a few of them. What I can do, however, is write a short essay on why applied economists will find that regular explorations into economic history and the history of economic thought help to improve their work as applied economists. In this chapter, I set myself that rather limited task. In my view, there are at least seven reasons that need discussion here. The first four refer mainly to economic history. The last three relate mainly to the history of economic thought. There was a case for splitting these into separate chapters, but as this chapter is quite brief anyway, I have not done that.

A LONG TIME TO WORK THINGS OUT

There is a joke (of sorts) which evolutionary economists tell against themselves.

Mainstream Economist:	'How has the French Revolution affected world economic growth?'
Evolutionary Economist:	'Too early to say.'

On the face of it this seems to make gentle fun of evolutionary economists, and our fledgling discipline. Apparently we are not yet able to work out the influence of an event – not even after 200 years or more. And yet, in a sense, there is nothing funny at all. We should not be surprised if some of the effects of a major historical revolution take a very long time to work their way through the economic system. It is only by following through a historical process over a long period that we can really hope to understand the process, and what affects what. Many economic histories choose to study a period of at least 100 years – and some much more than that.[1]

This generous time period is what sets historical studies apart from most of the other techniques described in this book. Econometricians rarely have access to 100 years of data. Or if they do, inconsistencies in the data series over time tend to constrain the econometrician to work with a shorter series. Case studies certainly do not tend to extend this long – and if they do, they tend to be retitled 'business histories' rather than 'case studies'.

This generous time dimension is important for at least two reasons. First, in the economist's language, we can expect large variations in explanatory variables over such a long period, and this helps us identify the effects of that variable. Suppose, for example, that we are interested in describing the effects of technological change on economic development. By taking a long historical perspective, we can look back to a world in which a particular technology did not exist, and hence obtain a much clearer perception of the full effects of technological change.

Second, again in the economist's language, study of a long time period allows us to identify the full dynamic effects of a change in an explanatory variable. If something changed in 1830, how long does it take to work through? And if an industry or country experiences an adverse period in its history, how long does it take to work this out of the system? Or to put it another way, how long is the shadow of this adverse period? For example, some have suggested that those coal mines in Britain whose 19th century owners treated their workforce especially badly still suffered from adverse labour relations at least 100 years later. Once trust is lost, it takes a long time to re-establish.

HISTORY MATTERS

Hicks (1979, p. xi) argued that 'as economics pushes on beyond "statics", it becomes less like science and more like history'. In this, as in much else, Hicks was ahead of the field. In the 1980s, the work of David (1985), Arthur (1989) and others started to draw our attention to the importance and pervasiveness of path-dependent processes in economics. Path-dependent models recognise *history matters* in economics.

To anyone outside economics, the idea that history matters seems so obvious that it hardly needs stating. But in static economic theory, history *doesn't really matter*. The equilibria of this theory are timeless, rather like the predictions of an experimental science. These scientific predictions do not depend on the date of the experiment (Hicks, 1979, p. 3). Neither do the characteristics of the static economic equilibria depend on the historical details of the path by which the equilibria are reached. From this point of view, it is not perhaps surprising that mainstream neoclassical analysis does not accord a particularly important place to economic history – because, in this static world, history doesn't matter.

In a path-dependent world, however, all that changes. The equilibrium reached may depend intimately on all kinds of (superficially trivial) historical details. So, for example, David (1985) and Liebowitz and Margolis (1990) debate the role of historical details in the emergence and resilience of the ergonomically sub-optimal QWERTY keyboard design. Some have suggested that the dominance of QWERTY owes much to a typing competition held in Cincinnati in 1888. In this contest, one Frank McGurrin of Salt Lake City (using touch-typing on a QWERTY keyboard) won a decisive victory over Louis Taub (using the hunt-and-peck method on a 72–key Caligraph machine). This, some claim, had a decisive effect in convincing observers that the Sholes–Remington (QWERTY) machine was technically the best. At the time, no one, reportedly, had the touch-typing skills of McGurrin, so a more evenly matched contest could not be arranged. Some argue that this historical detail was in fact an important factor in reinforcing the market position of the QWERTY layout.

Liebowitz and Margolis (1990) cast doubt on this interpretation. Their view is that QWERTY is not an example of lock-in to a sub-optimal technology resulting from arcane historical detail. Personally, I favour David's (1985) viewpoint, but my concern here is less with the specific case than with the general point. If we believe that processes are path dependent, then all kinds of historical details can play a role in explaining the outcome of economic processes.

If economists recognise that history matters in this way, then how should we do economic history? Should we follow the trend of cliometrics, where economic history becomes more like applied econometrics – but applied to historical (rather than current) data? No: on the contrary. Recall the observations by Hicks (1979) and Phelps Brown (1972), noted in Chapter 5, about the folly of anonymising data on which we have (or could have) relevant historical information. The slogan, *history matters*, refers to all the (apparently minor) details which would be lost when our focus is applied econometrics. We need an approach to economic history that preserves these details. The right way to do economic history is the same as the right way to do case studies (see the next chapter). Preserve all the obscure details, because in these may lie the essential clue with which to resolve the puzzle.

A VERY DIFFERENT DISCIPLINE

Think back to the discussion of Chapter 10. This argued that if we are to understand all facets of a multi-faceted problem, then we need to look at these from very different perspectives. It is rare to find an economic problem of which all aspects can be understood with the use of one technique only. Some of these different perspectives, if unfamiliar to us, give a completely different view from that with which we are familiar. Some of us feel uncomfortable with that. But this is how it must be.

I said at the start of this chapter that I am no historian – neither an economic historian nor an historian of thought. Earlier in my career, I found myself unable to get to grips with economic history because it was so different from the mathematical models in which I had been trained. Now I see that this difference is indeed the greatest strength of plurality in research methods, even if it presents a major challenge.

For the applied economist, economic history connects us to another world. It connects us to a great web of questions and answers, anomalies, peculiarities. Historians ask questions that economists do not think of asking. Historians look at evidence that we would not look at. In many ways, historians have many different priorities to the average applied economist. Sometimes historians are scholarly when we are cavalier; sometimes, by contrast, historians are cavalier when we are scholarly. Sometimes historians lavish intense scholarly attention on points to which we would not give a moment's attention. But sometimes they seem to be cavalier about claiming simple causal connections when the economist would insist on a far more detailed mathematical and statistical analysis before any causal connection could be claimed.[2]

How do we react to this difference? One of the things that I sincerely regret about our specialised training as economists is that many schooled in this fashion cannot cope with this diversity. They react badly when such matter is substituted for more familiar methodologies. The more enlightened graduate from this school may be open to other techniques, such as economic history, so long as it can be made more like traditional applied econometrics. We can call this the 'make everything like econometrics' approach. This seems to be the trend in cliometrics, where economic history is really just like applied econometrics – but applied to historical data. But I have been arguing throughout this book that distinct techniques are most useful when they are very different. From this point of view, cliometrics is arguably the least interesting aspect of economic history.

I would like to conclude this section with an essential observation from Hicks's *Theory of Economic History* about the character of economic history (Hicks, 1969, p. 1). Hicks said that despite the popularity of a quantitative approach to economic history, economic historians were less likely than economists to see their field as a purely quantitative one. The most important reason for this is that as we look back into history, there is not such a clear distinction between economic life and the other aspects of life.[3] It is good that applied economists remind themselves of this fact on a regular basis, so that we appreciate the context in which our discipline sits.

NOTHING (MUCH) IS NEW

One of the most humbling lessons to be learnt from reading economic history is that nothing much is new. As an applied economist working (mainly) on the implications of innovation in high technology industries, I have found it tempting to think that some of the latest new technologies open up economic questions and puzzles that have never before been encountered. This sort of thinking underpins some of the more ambitious claims about the 'new economics'. But as we have learnt, 'new economics' is really little different from the old.

As a result, I frequently find that economic history can very quickly offer us insights into areas of economics that seem underdeveloped or confused. Let me give some examples which I have found especially useful.

Quality

As a doctoral student studying the staggering rates of product innovation in microelectronic components, it seemed to me that most of the economics I had learnt up to that time was not well adapted to analyse this empirical phenomenon. The leading method to be used in such cases – the hedonic method – sought to adjust price indices for quality change. In short, product innovation was to be taken out of the equation by this method, and then we could use 'quality adjusted' prices in standard economic analysis. But it seemed to me that the very term, 'quality adjusted' was too demeaning. Rather as 'seasonal adjusted' data gets rid of seasonal variations of little interest, the term 'quality adjusted' seemed to afford the same residual status to quality. My understanding of this market was that quality change should be centre stage – not a troublesome residual.

For me, the resolution to this cognitive dissonance between what economic theory told me to do and what the empirical example told me was important was through economic history. Was this phenomenon – the central role of quality in economic affairs – really a new phenomenon? Emphatically not! The history of the mediaeval wool trade provided powerful evidence, and left a magnificent legacy in the trail of 15th century 'wool' churches. The greatest riches in the wool trade came to those whose sheep produced the finest qualities of wool (Power, 1941). If raw productivity were the key, and quality counted for little, then we might expect that sheep reared in the coldest climates would create the greatest wealth. But, in fact, the areas of greatest wool wealth included those on limestone hills, where it was possible to rear the less hardy sheep in sound health, and which would produce the finest qualities of wool.

So important was quality in the wool trade that an early fourteenth century merchant (Pegolotti) published a guide to the prices and qualities of wool available from the main English monasteries. It could not make sense to try to understand the pattern of trade and wealth creation in this industry by creating 'quality adjusted' prices. If that is what the prevailing technique encourages us to do, then the prevailing technique is a bad tool for the applied economist.

Standards and measurement

The second example relates to two adjacent areas in which I have done quite a bit of research. While there is a massive literature on the emergence of de facto standards in standards races, there has never been so much of a literature on what standards do to promote economic development. In addition, the related field of the economics of measurement is still underdeveloped.

My reading of the literature on standards was that several important gaps existed, and it was not clear how to fill them. Again, I found that historical research on the role of weights and measures in the growth of trade in classical times gave some vital insights. These early standards were essential to the growth of trade from the earliest times.

Equally, the experience of Whitworth in using standards and precise measurement to develop interchangeable parts played an essential role in allowing the division of labour to promote productivity and growth. The economic histories I read did not provide an analytical model, but did identify the essential aspects of the phenomena (for example, Price, 1957; Skinner, 1954). They are best able to do this when freed from the constraint to achieve the same mathematical rigour as we expect in economics.

The right rate of innovation

In my special field, the economics of innovation, some economists are revisiting the idea that we are locked into a rate of technological change which is too fast for our own good. To some in the field that seems like a radical idea, for it is not clear why (and how) a market should support a rate of innovation faster than anyone wants. But anyone who takes time to re-read some of the key works about the industrial revolution, or some writings of the great 19th century political economists, will be reminded that this is hardly a new idea. Many of those who wrote about utopia saw an ideal world in which innovation and technology played an altogether more modest role (Carey, 1999). And the great polymath Lewis Mumford (1934, 1952) has given a compelling account of this thesis, which anticipates many of the key ideas now re-emerging in the economics of innovation.

Transportation infrastructures and geographic dispersion

Some writers have suggested in recent years that the advent of the Internet, global communication networks and low costs of transportation is leading to a 'death of distance'.[4] Some go further and suggest that the corollary of this is that location will no longer be relevant to the success of a company, because all locations will have more or less equal access to the global market. For that reason, the current tendency whereby activity is clustered together into a small number of centres will change, and economic activity will become more dispersed.

In my opinion, amongst others, this assumed corollary is mistaken. The effect will actually work in the other direction. Clusters emerge and grow stronger when the scope of the market expands and when economies of scale and economies of agglomeration are important. The technological change referred to in the last paragraph does make it easier for the small village store to sell to the city. But it also makes it easier for the large urban retailer to sell to the village. It is as if they are placed side by side. Experience shows that when a giant retailer locates next to the small store, the latter does not tend to survive, unless it is clearly differentiated. In short, it is my belief that development of the Internet and transport infrastructure will not lead to a wider dispersion of economic activity, but will actually reinforce the concentration.

While I am no expert in transport history, it seems to me that several episodes in that history support my 'contrary' interpretation. The emergence of Manchester as a centre for the cotton industry at the start of the industrial revolution followed the growth of transportation networks. Independent producers in the same industry clustered together in the same location to take advantage of economies of agglomeration and economies of scale, and transported their output far and wide. A similar phenomenon was noted with rail networks in 19th century France: far from redistributing economic activity to the regions, such rail networks tended to pull all activity into the centre. And it is humbling to remember that Adam Smith, amongst all his other achievements, developed a clear explanation of why the growth of canal networks would have effects of this sort (Smith 1776/1904, Volume I, p. 148).

Clusters and division of labour

If we open up a personal computer today (2005), we find components from many different countries.[5] The computer industry exhibits a huge degree of specialisation, and massive economies of scale. A very small number of firms may account for a huge proportion of the world production of a particular component, which they sell globally. But most firms can only achieve global competitiveness by focusing on a very narrow range of specialised components. The globally competitive companies are all located in clusters, but these are spread across a large number of different countries. To assemble a computer today at lowest cost typically involves sourcing components from perhaps 20 different countries. The final producer, whose brand name is on the box, may do little more than assemble a few standard cards and add a power supply and the necessary peripherals.

Is this a new phenomenon? Not really. Although the economies of scale involved are much smaller, and the trade is national rather than global, we find a similar phenomenon in the history of mechanical clocks and watches. This industry was one of the most striking examples of how accurate measurement and standardised parts were used to support a very advanced division of labour. As a result of this division of labour, producers could achieve economies of scale and increase productivity. Symonds (1947) quotes a fascinating account (from 1747) that gives a rich description of what was found.[6] The person who was called the 'watch-maker' hardly made any of the components contained in the watch. Instead each component was made by a producer who specialised in the production of that component, and that component only. The 'watch-maker' did little more than some final assembly and then put his name on the watch.

THE ECONOMICS OF A DIFFERENT ERA

My last three observations are about my reasons for including the history of economic thought on the applied economist's desk. Some historians of economic thought have become rather dejected at the way mainstream economics tends to disregard the history of our discipline. Blaug (2001) gives a good summary of this. But as Blaug shows, the reason for this is not hard to understand. As he points out, the sciences do not bother much about their histories. If an old scientific perspective is still valid and useful, then it will be retained within the current state of the art. But if it is surpassed, then it will be forgotten. Blaug cites the wisdom of two great minds who capture this very succinctly. Whitehead (1929, p. 162) argued that 'A science which hesitates to forget its founders is lost', while J.B. Say considered that 'The more perfect the science, the shorter its history'.[7]

Huxley (1963, p. 35) argued that scientific writing is purely instrumental. If a work isn't useful, and a later work surpasses it, then the earlier work 'will go the way of all earlier scientific writings and be forgotten'. There is no place for sentimentality in science. Huxley (1963, p. 35) contrasts this with art and literature: 'Chaucer was not made obsolete by Shakespeare'.

If economics is a real science, then economists should not be sentimental about the history of thought either. The title of an article by Boulding (1971) captures this sentiment with characteristic irony: 'After Samuelson, who needs Adam Smith?' It seems to me that there are three reasons why we still need Adam Smith, and I deal with these in these last three sections of this chapter.

The first reason relates to a fundamental difference between economics as a subject matter and the physical sciences. The physical world of today is in most important respects the same as that of 100 or 200 years ago, so, as Hicks (1979, p. 3) argued, scientific predictions do not depend on the date of the experiment. By contrast, the economy of today is different in some important respects from the economy of the 18th and 19th centuries.

We should not be surprised therefore if the economic perspectives required to understand the past are different from the perspectives required to understand the present. Some old economic perspectives fall into disuse because they refer to a different era, and not because later theories surpass them as an explanation of the past. In saying this, I do not mean that every item of old literature is a neglected gem, any more than all writings of today are gems. But I do mean that some masterpieces from the history of thought are not displaced by modern masterpieces – because they refer to different phenomena. In a sense, then, economics occupies an intermediate position in Huxley's spectrum from science to literature. Writing in economics is instrumental, as in science, but the subject matter changes, so new writing does not replace the best old writings when these different works refer to different eras.

This is in a way the same argument that we encountered in Chapter 8. There we argued that efficient problem solving in economics requires the specific knowledge of time and place. We expect that vernacular knowledge and mental models will vary from place to place, and so too we should expect them to vary from time to time. So long as we think there is something to be learnt from history, from the study of a different era, then we must preserve – and from time to time, revisit – the best of the history of thought relating to that era. If we do not, then we will miss something very important.

A REMEDY TO THE WRONG TURNING

The second reason why, as Boulding put it, we still need Adam Smith is that the history of thought is the best remedy to the various types of intellectual *wrong turning* or *dead end*. Many of those applied economists who turn to the history of economic thought – and here I refer to general applied economists rather than specialists in the history of thought – do so because they feel that their part of the discipline has taken a wrong turning. We have followed a particular path, and while it may not be a dead end per se, it is not leading in the direction we want. Where did we go wrong? The history of thought is an indispensable way to retrace our steps. We go back to a point which, as far as we can tell, was on the right tracks, and then look for a different way forward.

Let me give an example. As a doctoral student I became aware that trying to estimate complex econometric models with unreliable data was a pretty hazardous process. It seemed to me that a combination of multicollinear variables and measurement error was a pretty toxic mix, and one could not expect to achieve reliable parameter estimates in such a situation. I cast around for advice, but found that modern textbooks and modern practice made little of this. My solution to this puzzle was to return to the work of Frisch (1934) on confluence analysis, because this seemed to be one of the few works that took this very real problem seriously.

I recall mentioning to one of the professors that I was reading Frisch (1934) and his reaction was one of complete dismay. He said that Frisch 'went out with the ark', and I was wasting my time in reading this.

In one sense, he was right: Frisch's work was essentially forgotten by most econometricians. But was it forgotten because it had been displaced by a later, better work? Not really. Not until the work of Kalman (1982a, 1982b) and Klepper and Leamer (1984) did econometrics seriously revisit the Frisch approach. Was it forgotten because the problem he sought to deal with was no longer a problem – or had never been a problem in the first place? Emphatically not! No, Frisch's work on confluence analysis had been forgotten because econometricians were no longer thinking about that problem. Just that.

In another sense, the professor was wrong. Frisch's confluence analysis was not, and still is not, a curiosity of history. The real curiosity is the way the subsequent development of econometrics since Frisch has given so little attention to his concerns. For, as Maddala correctly observed (see the end of Chapter 6), applied economists constantly face the problems of measurement error. It is very curious that econometrics has by and large turned away from that most pressing concern. And it is even more curious that econometrics has largely ignored the warnings of Frisch in his later works (1948, 1956,

1963, 1970) to the effect that econometric estimation on its own could not fulfil the dream of Jevons and Frisch, to make theory useful by measuring the parameters of economic relationships.[8]

I might summarise this section by observing that the history of thought is useful because we cannot be sure that all the important ideas from the past are carried forward with the state of the art in our discipline. We take wrong turnings and encounter dead ends. Rather like the lab notebook which the scientist uses to record all the experiments he does, the history of thought is a record of all our turnings, right and wrong.

THE POLYMATH AND THE SAGE

The third reason why, as Boulding put it, we still need Adam Smith, is that he achieved an intellectual breadth within economics and beyond, that most of us cannot aspire to, given the intellectual division of labour of our age.

These polymaths, whether pioneers from inside economics (Smith, Malthus, Ricardo, Mill, Marx, Marshall) or sages from outside economics (Carlyle, Ruskin and others) saw things that are now lost to many of us. We need to re-read these great works to rediscover what we have lost. Smith saw all the interconnections between technical change, division of labour, specialisation, trade, geographical concentration and so on. Now these topics are located in several sub-sub-disciplines of our subject. It is rare for the modern economist – a narrow specialist in one sub-sub-discipline – to have an appreciation of the big picture in the same way as these 18th and 19th century sages. It is humbling to see how many 'new' modern ideas are anticipated in the work of these great minds.

For Smith, the division of labour was the key to economic growth. But an essential condition for this division of labour to create wealth must be that the different parts of the labour process are combined or brought together in a finished product or service. In the same way, we may be persuaded that division of intellectual labour is essential to scientific progress, but an essential condition for this division of labour to create wisdom is that the different parts are re-combined. The polymaths and sages of the 18th and 19th century could do this. Today, as we have said above, we find it very hard to re-combine our divided intellectual labour. This is a theme to which I return in Chapter 22.

NOTES

1. Some examples demonstrate the general point. Studies of the industrial revolution tend to cover at least 100 years. Deane (1965) covers 1750–1850; Mathias (1983) covers 1700–

1914; Landes (2003) covers 1750–1968. In histories of technology and economics, authors often cover a much longer sweep of history, but with a more specific focus. In their studies of the mechanical clock, Cipolla (1967) covers 1300–1700, while Landes (1983) covers at least 1450 to the present. The polymaths, like Mumford (1934), cover an even broader sweep – from 3000 BC to the present.

2. One example of this is the following. Hicks (1969, p. 55) states boldly that technical innovation tends to exacerbate the economic difficulties of 'depressed groups and depressed areas'. This simple statement is in fascinating contrast to the large complex of research which agonises over whether the process of innovation reinforces or offsets concentration in market power and in geography. Many economists would say that one simply cannot make such a bold and sweeping statement, and 10 years ago, that would have been my response. Now, I think Hicks's bold and simple statement contains a large element of truth.

3. Compare Mumford's (1961) observations about the original marketplace as an arena where people meet for all sorts of purposes, only one of which is for the exchange of goods.

4. The phrase is enshrined in the title of a book by Cairncross (1997).

5. In the early days of the PC (early 1980s), most components were made in the USA.

6. The original source is an article by Campbell in *The London Tradesman*, 1747.

7. Quoted by Barber (1997, p. 93).

8. One explanation which I encountered as a doctoral student was that Frisch had become disillusioned with econometrics – though the reasons for that were unclear – and for that reason his influence had waned. This seems to me an inadequate account of why Frisch said what he said. It is telling that the collection of papers in honour of the centenary of Frisch's birth (Ström, 1998), made little mention of his concerns about the journey on which econometrics was embarked.

17. Case studies

As a doctoral student, I prepared three very detailed case studies about the importance of technological advance for the diffusion of different applications of semiconductor electronics.[1] I spent a year or more gathering data from successive editions of leading trade journals, from trade shows, and from brief discussions and interviews with those in the industry who would talk to me. I assembled and collated a veritable mass of information. I was immensely proud of my achievement.

I recall showing a first draft of this *magnum opus* to one of my advisers. He did not like it at all. He said that: (1) he found it quite exasperating to read; (2) it seemed to him little more than a random collection of disconnected facts; (3) that points 1 and 2 taken together implied that this was therefore a bad case study. I was a bit crestfallen at this response. But some 25 years later, thinking back to this episode, I have to concede he was essentially right. Having struggled through similar documents prepared by my own students, I sympathise with his point 1. Moreover, he was definitely correct about point 2. But strange as it may seem, I think he was wrong about point 3.

A case study may be frustrating to read, it may contain what appear to be a mass of disconnected facts, but these two characteristics do not in themselves make it a bad case study. On the contrary, I shall argue in this chapter that some of the very best research case studies may seem like this. They may seem like this because it is the duty of the case study to gather together all the disconnected and unresolved fragments about a particular case. A case study that discards these oddities for editorial reasons is losing things that may in time turn out to be critical. Immediately, I may seem to be out of line with the great case study tradition in business schools, which has produced elegantly crafted and highly readable *teaching* cases. But, strange as it may seem, I believe that some of the very best *research* case studies may look very different.

Oscar Wilde is said to have remarked: 'When I approach a museum, I feel a headache coming on.' In my view, the case study is a bit like a vast museum.[2] Such a museum contains every kind of artefact, many of which might appear to be of no interest whatever to most people. The curators attempt to put these into a logical order, grouping by date, country or technology. But despite this, many items do not appear to fit into any particular pattern, and the visitor who tries to take it all in is quickly overwhelmed. No wonder Oscar Wilde felt a headache coming on as he approached the museum! But at some point, long after the items are all collected together, some individual will bring together a few disparate objects, study them in depth, and find the key to some long-standing puzzle. They can only do this so long as the museum preserves all the anomalies as well as the cherished items. A museum that preserves only the great works of art which fit into a now well-developed story is a most enjoyable place to visit. But the museum that also preserves all the oddities for posterity can play a greater role in the subsequent advancement of knowledge.

If we accept the idea of case study as museum, then we learn three important characteristics of the case study. First, we must not be ashamed to include a mass of disconnected facts. Second, if (to adapt Wilde), as we approach a case study, we feel a headache coming on, then so be it. Research is not always easy. And third, the essential role of the case study is to preserve for posterity all the fragments that are lost when we use other research methods.

In Chapter 10, we asked what is the point of using a plurality of techniques? My answer was that each technique does something different. From this perspective, the best way to use a particular technique is to maximize what we learn from that technique which we could not learn in any other way. Some readers may disagree: surely the purpose of using multiple techniques is that we hope each will endorse the other, and that gives greater credibility to our research findings? That is one purpose, for sure, but not the most important – in my view.

WHAT IS A CASE STUDY?

Several very useful books summarise the idea of a case study, and how it should be carried out – for example, Gillham (2000), Hamel et al. (1993), Travers (2001) and Yin (1994) amongst others. Thomas (2004) provides a very useful synthesis of how different writers have defined the case study. From these sources we can distil a list describing some of the essential characteristics of the case study:

- a primarily empirical enquiry
- a research design based on a single (or a few) case(s)
- intensive examination of that case
- thick description of all the minute details
- does not start out with a priori theoretical notion

- the researcher must keep an open mind
- multiple sources of evidence are used
- are different sorts of evidence mutually consistent?
- preserve inconsistent or anomalous data
- more variables of interest than data points
- investigate the case within its context
- the boundary between case and context is blurred

The case study researcher is likely to build up a large box file of heterogeneous materials. She is also likely to fill several notebooks with many arcane details, many possible leads, contradictory observations and so on. The whole collection is a delightful mess. As we shall argue throughout this chapter, this is as it should be.

Why do we use case studies? Thomas (2004) suggests that there are three main purposes in conducting a case study: *exploratory*, *explanatory* and *theory-testing*. We use the exploratory case study when we know little or nothing about the phenomenon of interest. The exploratory case study (rather like the metaphor – see Chapter 20) gets us started on a particular research track, and may form the basis for more substantial studies thereafter. The exploratory case study as a written document may be quite messy. But we should not judge the contribution of the exploratory case study solely by the case study documents that emerge from it, but rather by the sequence of greater studies which follow on from it.

The second purpose is to use the case study to explain. The case study is used to produce *grounded theory*. Because the case study is so rich in detail, any theory grounded in this detail may carry more conviction than a theory developed in the armchair. Moreover, this sort of case study is likely to look less messy, since the various components are crafted together into a theory. This use of the case study has, however, led to a critique that theory grounded in one example cannot assume general validity. We return to that below.

The third purpose is to use the case study to test a prior theory. Obviously, the case study cannot test a theory grounded in the same case: how could the case ever contradict the grounded theory? But, in principle, a single case can provide a test of a prior theory. Einstein famously said that no amount of experimentation could ever prove him right, but a single experiment could prove him wrong. In the social sciences, however, we have come to accept that our observations are less than perfect, and hence an apparent contradiction between case and theory may reflect errors in the case rather than flaws in the theory. In general, we require more than one contradictory observation to reject a theory.

Thomas (2004) suggests that the second and third uses of the case study are the most common in social sciences. From the perspective of this book, however, the use that interests me most is the first. There are many other ways of explaining and of building theory, and arguably some of these are superior to the use of a single case study to build a grounded theory. There are many other ways of testing a prior theory, and arguably again some of these are superior to the use of a single case study as a test. But there are not so many ways of starting a research exploration into the unknown, where we have no idea what is the key to understanding the phenomenon of interest. To me, that is the distinctive advantage of the case study, and is why every applied researcher should not just read case studies, but also, from time to time, perform their own case studies.

READABILITY IN THE CASE STUDY

In the introduction, I argued that some very good case studies might prove to be very heavy going for the reader – but this did not make them bad case studies. This argument needs further justification.

I am aware that specialists in case study research may resent the perspective described in this section. They rightly point out that if case studies are to be published, then they have to be readable. Yin (1994, p. 151) argues that readability is not inconsistent with excellence in the case study. Moreover, as noted before, my observation seems strange when we think of the great case study tradition in business schools. The many teaching case studies in the Harvard collection are elegantly crafted, highly readable and memorable. If they were not, then I don't think students or their professors would read them and use them with such enthusiasm. These excellent cases serve as role models for other teaching cases, and I certainly don't imply that these teaching cases are poor cases. Definitely not. My argument is simply that some of the very best research case studies may look very different.

For me, the role model for the research case study is quite different. It is something more like the observations of the fictional Belgian detective, Hercules Poirot, in Agatha Christie's crime stories. Poirot is a meticulous collector of facts. When called on to investigate a crime, he gathers every possible piece of information from every possible source. His assistant, Captain Hastings, and indeed the reader can get exasperated by the endless discussion of what seem to be inessential details. And yet the resolution of each case invariably depends on some apparently trivial detail. In the denouement, when Poirot demonstrates to general amazement that the most unexpected person is in fact the criminal, the vital clue in his proof is often an apparently irrelevant fragment that almost anyone else would have discarded. In Poirot's mind, however, these trivia more often than not hold the key. Take away just a few minor details, and the case collapses.

I believe this role model perfectly captures the essential character of a case study. In the eyes of the researcher who has prepared the case, every minutia and every anecdote is cherished, and each detail has its place. Each footnote is essential. Nothing should be taken away. The writer is immensely proud of what he has been able to put together. And yet, in the eyes of many readers, this case looks like a mess with no clear thread to it. It is an immensely frustrating document to read, and needs heavy editing to make it palatable. That is the essential paradox of the case study.

The master can produce a highly readable case without compromising its integrity. Lesser mortals will probably not be able to achieve both. If we are always concerned to ensure readability, above all else, then we would generally have to apply a fairly strict editorial policy. Those facts that fit in with the main story can stay; those that seem to bear no relation to the main story, or any sub-plot, must go. But the essential characteristic of the case study is that we do not (and probably cannot) know which are the essential facts until some time after it is written. What subsequently turns out to be the essential fact may not fit in with the story as it is told at the time of publication. The strict editorial policy may inadvertently weed out the most important parts of the case. If these facts are to escape the editor's cut, then we must accept that many cases will turn into complex, rambling documents that are hard to read. We have to accept that sometimes we must read case studies that give us a headache.

CRITIQUE OF THE CASE STUDY

The case study has been subjected to much criticism by those who feel that the unsystematic investigation of one (or a small number of cases) is not a proper method of study. Gillham (2000), Hamel et al. (1993), Thomas (2004) and Yin (1994) discuss some of these criticisms. Thomas argues that the debate about the value of the case study has revolved around two key issues: internal validity and external validity.

The issue of internal validity is concerned with whether case studies can produce rigorous data. Critics point to the unsystematic research methods, the ill-defined methods of data collection, the frequent opportunity for investigator bias and the difficulty of replication. These concerns may have some weight, but equivalent criticisms could be made of many other social research methods. 'He that is without sin among you, let him first cast a stone.'[3]

Some consider that the issue of external validity is more serious. This is the concern that a theory grounded in one example cannot assume general validity. At some level, this must be right: it is rare that we can generalise from a sample of one.[4] But does the fact that a case study cannot produce generalisations really mean it is of no use? Surely not. First, as Thomas (2004) argues, many case study researchers have no intention to generalise from their cases. Their objective, on the contrary, is *particularisation*: to understand the workings of a particular example in great depth. Given the paucity of our empirical understanding in most social sciences (economics is no exception), then a deep understanding of one example alone is still very valuable. Second, the purpose of the exploratory case study is to get us started on the research path and to suggest possibilities. The exploratory case study should not be judged a failure because it does not produce generalised results. For it is the role of subsequent studies, building on the exploratory case but using different techniques, to produce generalised results.

In Chapter 10, I argued that the features which give a research technique its greatest weaknesses are the very same features that give the technique its greatest strengths. The very narrow focus of a case study is a weakness because the results may be specific to one case only, but the very narrow focus is also a strength because we find out and preserve so much detail. It seems to me that it is silly to criticise the case study because it does not match the strengths of the large-scale survey. It is silly to criticise the case study because its research methods are ad hoc, and lack the structure of a well-designed questionnaire. And it is silly to criticise the case study because the items in the case file are not a neat collection of complete transcriptions of in-depth interviews. If those characteristics are vital, then use the techniques that provide those characteristics in abundance. Use the case study when its distinctive characteristics are the key to solving the research problem. Cultivate the weaknesses of the case study (as viewed by the critics) because these characteristics are probably the key to solving a different research problem!

AN EXAMPLE OF WHAT WE CAN LEARN

In a way, it is rather self-important of me to cite one of my own case studies as an example of what I have learnt from the case study method. But in another way, this is entirely consistent with the message of the book. We can learn a lot from reading case studies, and we can learn even more by carrying out our own case studies.

The case studies I shall discuss are, indeed, those I described at the start of this short chapter (a shortened version was published in Swann, 1986). In these, I documented in some detail the advances made in semiconductor electronics during the 1970s and early 1980s, and the ways in which these advances were leading to new applications of the technology. The best-known summary of this technological advance is called Moore's Law: the idea that the functionality of semiconductor components has grown and will continue to grow exponentially. A crude correlation suggested that the growth of new applications was proceeding hand in hand with technological advance, as summarised by Moore's Law.

One possible interpretation of this was that there was a strong latent demand to apply electronics in a variety of different applications, and that limitations in the technology were holding this back. If correct, this interpretation would imply that as Moore's Law unfolded over time, then so too would the number and range of applications of semiconductor electronics. However, it was quite clear to me that no causal connection could ever be established simply by observing a correlation of that sort. It was necessary to carry out very detailed case studies to explore the engineering mechanisms at work.

One case study looked at how far advances in semiconductor performance could explain the increased use of semiconductors for engine control in cars during the 1970s and early 1980s. This found that the main force behind this trend in the USA was the Carter administration's tight regulations for required fuel economy in cars. These regulations could not be met using conventional electromechanical devices, and it was necessary to use electronic controls to achieve them. But while the case study found that it was indeed the performance of semiconductors that was constraining the application of electronics in engine control, it was not the conventional performance measures described in Moore's Law. Rather, the constraint on getting semiconductors to work under the bonnet of a car was the potential unreliability of semiconductors in a hostile environment, and the difficulty of getting semiconductor devices to adapt to working with existing sensors and actuators (designed for the previous generation of electromechanical controls). In short, this was a partial endorsement for the interpretation described in the last paragraph, but not a complete endorsement.

The second case study looked at the use of electronics in telephone exchanges in the 1970s and early 1980s. Here we found that the replacement of mechanical and electromechanical exchanges by electronic exchanges was actually quite a slow process – in the UK at least. In part, this was because these were large-scale system changes: it was not efficient to make slower piecemeal changes. Moreover, when an electronic exchange was introduced, the semiconductor components at the heart of that new system would usually be some five to ten years behind the state of the art. The constraint on the development and diffusion of electronic exchanges was not so much the result of shortcomings in the underpinning semiconductor technology, but rather the result of a serious 'language barrier' between telephone engineers and semiconductor manufacturers, and in some cases because of government's reluctance to allow free trade in exchange equipment. Nevertheless, further advances in semiconductor technology have been exploited within telephone exchange equipment, but this was not the main constraint on diffusion.

The third case study looked at the use of semiconductors in electronic calculators in the 1960s and 1970s. This turned out to be a striking example of how developments in one technology (the calculator) progressed at the same rate as developments in the underpinning semiconductor technology. Indeed, some of the early attempts to produce single-chip calculators in the 1960s and early 1970s failed because the manufacturers were attempting to push semiconductor technology too far, too fast. The successful development of a practical pocket calculator also had to wait for developments in low-power CMOS (Complementary Metal Oxide Silicon) technology in the early 1970s. Moreover, speed of computation was an important constraint on the earliest scientific calculators. The Hewlett Packard engineers who created the HP-35 wanted a maximum computation time of one second for any function. This was only just achievable by the time the HP-35 was introduced in 1972. We could summarise the development and diffusion of electronic calculators as a fairly pure case of waiting for the technology to be good enough. The simple interpretation described earlier in this section is right, for this case study at least.

Taken together, the three case studies provide neither an unambiguous endorsement nor a clear rejection of my working hypothesis. In that sense, they may seem rather disappointing. But in my view, the most valuable thing to come out of the case studies was, in fact, a small fragment which I came across purely by chance, and which in a sense had no place in any of the stories, but which I kept hold of because it seemed puzzling and anomalous, but yet very interesting.

My detailed reading of the trade press during the period I studied, and the other sources I used, uncovered a vast amount of material on the imperative for companies to innovate. There were intense races to be first to market with a particular generation of semiconductor component. People wrote of the many potential applications that would follow as Moore's Law unfolded, and hence the explosive potential growth in demand. Yet in the middle of all this, I found a chance remark in an editorial of one of the leading trade newspapers, attributed to the president of one of the most innovative companies in the entire industry.[5] To paraphrase, he was asking in effect, 'what do we do with all this technological advance?'. That seemed surprising. If the head of one of the most innovative companies in the semiconductor industry didn't know what to do with this technological capability, then who else did, and in that case, why was his company investing so heavily in the development of those technologies?

I held onto this fragment during several redrafts of the case studies. In the end, I found that it was the key to developing a complete reinterpretation of all my material, and a complete revision of my main thesis. I summarised this as follows (Swann, 1986, p. 164): 'the market incentive for quality innovations may appear some time before the end-user is able to appreciate the true value of the innovation'.

CONCLUSION

Critics of the case study say that it is a non-rigorous technique producing results of low generality, and therefore of limited value. Proponents of the case study rebut this, and claim that much of the bad reputation of the case study is attributable to the rather rough and ready way in which some rather cavalier researchers have pursued their case studies.

In my opinion, both are missing the point. There is no sense in criticising the case study because it does not share the characteristics of other (more rigorous?) techniques. The whole point of the case study is that it has strengths which no other technique can match, and it can yield insights that we would probably not find in any other way. Equally, while it is probably true that some researchers have been pretty cavalier in their case study work, I don't think that necessarily negates the value of these. For the greatest strength of the case study is its unique ability to bring together a splendid miscellany of interesting fragments in a highly ad hoc way, and preserve these for posterity. As I have argued above, it is often these interesting fragments that make the greatest contribution in the long term, and not the neat, systematic analysis. If we want a technique that is neat and systematic, there are plenty of others to choose from.

NOTES

1.   A shortened version of these cases is available in Swann (1985a), and a much shortened version is published as Chapter 8 of Swann (1986).
2.   Porter (1983, p. xi) likens the case study to a 'laboratory' in which we can study competition. That is very interesting because the idea of a technique as a laboratory has surfaced in several chapters in this book. I like this analogy, but find the metaphor of a museum even more apposite.
3.   Christ's words to the crowd confronting a woman taken in adultery: John, Chapter 8, Verse 7.
4.   And yet, in everyday life, we frequently do generalise from a sample of one. We watch a few minutes of a television series, do not enjoy it, and decide we shall not watch any more of it. We go to a particular restaurant, have a bad meal, and decide we will not repeat the visit.
5.   Swann (1986, pp. 1ff.) describes the source and significance of this remark.

18. Interviews

It has been claimed that about 90 per cent of all social science investigations exploit interview data (Holstein and Gubrium, 1995, p. 1). This observation alone shows how different economics is from the rest of social science, for the corresponding figure for economics must be much less than 90 per cent. The interview is not generally recognised as one of the key applied techniques in economics, in the same way as applied econometrics. Are we economists missing a trick here? I think the answer to that must be, 'yes', and my objective in this chapter is to describe what we might learn from the interview that we cannot expect to learn – or not so well, at any rate – from other techniques of applied economics.

Why is the interview so useful? Because it allows the researcher to focus the debate directly on research questions of immediate interest. Few other research techniques offer that opportunity to customise the material gathered to precise questions. As Alan Thomas (2004, p. 150) has reminded us, social scientists are rather privileged in being able to ask direct questions of the objects they study. If a physicist could interview the particles (s)he studies, then surely (s)he would jump at the chance – even if treating the answers with caution.

In view of that, why are economists reluctant to give prominence to this technique? Partly, it is because interviews are time consuming and at the end we have the sort of data we tend not to like in economics: a large number of variables but a small number of observations. Partly, it is because economists tend to think of the interview as informal, impressionistic, qualitative rather than quantitative, and thus lacking in rigour. I shall argue in this chapter that neither of these is really a very good reason to neglect the interview as a technique to develop our understanding. And indeed, I suspect that we do in fact use something approximating to an interview a good deal more than we care to acknowledge, but we use it in a rather different way from many other social scientists.

Much of the discussion on the interview focuses primarily on what the interviewer learns from the interviewee. But we all know (from personal experience, at the very least) that the interviewee also learns something from the interviewer: something from the experience, and something from the specific questions. These backwash benefits are in practice very important.

In what follows, we shall see that in some interviews, we may on occasion lose sight of who is the interviewer and who is the interviewee – and there is nothing wrong with that in the appropriate context.

In what follows, we shall contrast three different approaches to the interview. In the first, the interviewer aims to ask clear and concise questions of the interviewee, and the latter responds with clear and concise answers. In the second, the interviewer gently coaxes the interviewee to open up and give a full account of subjective experiences. In the third, the interviewer and interviewee interact in a complex way, and at the end of that produce what is in effect a joint manifesto. For some authors, the first or second are preferred because they are less problematic as data, whereas the output of the third is a complex product of more than one mind. However, a recurrent theme in this chapter will be the idea that interviews may be most informative when they are also most complex. The clean and pure interview is perhaps less problematic, but is not an interview from which we can expect to learn so much.

THE PURE INTERVIEW

In his detailed discussion of how to interpret qualitative data, Silverman (2001) describes a positivist's approach to the interview. We shall call this a *pure interview*, but it is also a *structured* interview. Such an approach may or may not be possible in practice. Let us set aside that question for a couple of paragraphs, and first try to understand what the pure interview looks like.

In the positivist's approach, the ideal is a pure interview which aims to provide a mirror image of reality as it is assumed to exist in the real world. In this pure interview, the respondent is assumed to behave rather like a random access computer database. If questions are asked in a way the database can understand, then the database will dutifully extract and deliver the piece of data relevant to the question – and nothing else. There is dialogue, but it is limited and simple. The database is passive: it shows no guile, no evasiveness and is not easily fatigued. But equally, it shows no initiative and no imagination. It only tells you the answers to questions on your 'script'. This database is epistemologically passive.

The pure interview can be described in the following diagram. In this way, the pure interview can in principle provide a form of external testing. In the pure interview – if such a thing is possible – we ask standardised questions, using good interview practice, and in return obtain clean responses. These responses are not contaminated by variations in the questions we ask, by variations in the way we ask the questions, or indeed by variations in how the respondent chooses to answer our questions.

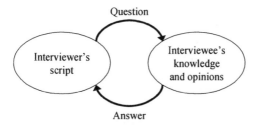

Figure 18.1   The pure interview

By now, some readers at least will be feeling distinctly restless. Two questions immediately suggest themselves. Is such a pure interview really possible? And is such a pure interview actually desirable?

In response to the first question, I think the only safe answer is that we don't know: probably it is not possible, but some interviews may get reasonably close. A large part of the critical literature on the interview says that such purity is unattainable. However standardised the questions and however well the interviewer follows best practice, the interview is ultimately a social interaction, and we cannot expect that the data elicited is uncontaminated by the context of that interaction. Indeed, if Bohr and Heisenberg were right to be concerned that observation in physics is not necessarily pure because the observer interacts with the observed, then we should certainly be cautious about that possibility here. Nevertheless, a large number of professional interviewers make a living from producing interview data where the degree of contamination is kept within acceptable limits.

To my mind, the second question is a much more interesting one. Even if a pure interview is possible, do we actually want to carry out such an interview? In my opinion, the appropriate short answer is, 'often not'. To explain this answer I need first to look at two other perspectives on the interview, and consider a number of related issues. Then I can return to this question below.

If we accept for now the possibility and desirability of a (near) pure interview, then what do we have to do to make sure it is done well? Thomas (2004, Chapter 9) gives a very useful summary guide to good practice in interviews, but here I shall focus on just two issues. What should be the interviewer's strategy in a pure interview? And what are the ideal personal characteristics for the pure interviewer?

We can answer the first question by summarising the key components of an interviewing strategy directed at maximising the purity of interview data and minimising contamination. Roethlisberger (1941, p. 93) lists the main priorities for such an interview:

- To listen and not to interrupt;
- Not to give advice or express opinions;
- To avoid leading questions;
- To refrain from making moral judgements;
- To avoid argument.

Holstein and Gubrium (1995, p. 38) and Thomas (2004, p. 152) elaborate on this. The following are some of the important items on their checklists:

- Read the questions exactly as written;
- Questions must be presented in the same order;
- The conditions in which questions are answered must be held constant;
- If an answer is incomplete, probe for elaboration in a neutral way;
- Answers should be recorded without interviewer discretion;
- Interviewer must treat the answers in a neutral manner.

Turning to the second question, what sort of person makes the best interviewer for the pure (or formulaic) interview? If our aim is to avoid contamination of interview data, then the ideal interviewer should have the following characteristics. It should be someone who is experienced in the art and science of interviewing. But (s)he should not have any specific knowledge of the research area to which the interview schedule relates. Why so? Because such a person is most likely to stick to the script. (S)he will not be tempted to modify questions according to context, will not be drawn into further unscripted dialogue with the respondent. By contrast, someone with any specific knowledge of the research area may be tempted to improvise, and whatever the merits of that, it is bound to compromise the purity of any research data.

This captures the paradox of the pure interview. It seems a rather strange idea that such a peculiar activity by such an ill-informed individual really leads to purity in data, but such a disinterested approach does indeed avoid contamination. However, it also makes us ask whether purity in interview data should really be our top priority. Can we really learn more from such a disinterested interview than from the active interview described below? We return to that later.

It is also interesting to note the commonality here with the question of the ideal experimental subject for experimental economics. In Chapter 12, we saw that the undergraduate was typically the ideal subject for a role-playing class experiment with induced preferences, while the experienced business professional was not an ideal subject for such an experiment because her/his responses reflected prior business experience rather than the specific circumstances of the experiment. It is as if the business professional's prior expertise gets in the way, and compromises the purity of the experiment, while the undergraduate has no such prior experience, and hence plays the required role with greater fidelity. Once again, we see a recurrence of what we called the Lady Bracknell principle (see Chapter 5).

THE EMOTIONAL INTERVIEW

Silverman (2001) talks of the emotionalist approach to the interview, where the unstructured, open-ended interview aims to elicit 'authentic accounts of subjective experience'. Metaphorically speaking, the interview is a little like tapping a tree to extract the sap. For example, the Canadian farmer taps the *Acer Saccharum* tree to yield the sweet-water sap which is evaporated to make maple syrup. It is a question of tapping in the right place and at the right time and then everything will flow out.

Implicit in this approach is the idea that within the interviewee there is a collection of experience, knowledge and feeling. This collection exists in its own right, and can be articulated by the respondent without a great deal of activity by the interviewer. The challenge for the interviewer is to start the flow, and then to sit back and listen. There may be an initial dialogue, but then the interview turns (for the most part) into a monologue. If the monologue dries up, then it is revived by occasional and gentle supplementary questions from the interviewer.

Figure 18.1 can also represent this sort of interview, but there are important differences. Compare the output of such an interview with the output from the pure interview. The pure interview aims to retrieve data from a random access database: the respondent would retrieve the relevant data, and nothing much else. In this emotional interview, it is more like retrieving data from a serial access source: the question prompts a complex flow of material relating to a whole collection of questions and not a concise, crisp answer to one question alone. It becomes a monologue rather than a dialogue.

While the data elicited here are obviously much more complex than those elicited using the pure interview, this approach may also aspire to deliver data that are uncontaminated by the interventions of the interviewer. Having said that, the critical literature on this approach to interviewing has cast doubt on whether the flow represents an 'authentic account of subjective experience' (Silverman, 2001), or is in whole or in part a repetition of 'popular tales'.

The interviewer's strategy is to tap the tree so that the sap runs out. The interviewer must ask some questions, of course, but they should be casual and conversational.

THE ACTIVE INTERVIEW

Holstein and Gubrium (1995) provide a coherent and compelling account of this third perspective on the interview. From this perspective, it is explicitly recognised from the start that any meaning elicited from an interview is inherently and unavoidably a *joint production* between interviewee and interviewer. It is highly unstructured. An extreme version of this position is the perspective of the radical social constructionist. From this viewpoint, there is no reality 'out there', all outputs from the interview are jointly produced, and the interview 'data' are not really data at all, because they are only valid in their original context, and meaningless outside that.

From this perspective it appears, at first sight, as if the interview is of limited value. After all, if it produces nothing that we can call *real data*, then what use is it? On closer inspection, this rather depressing conclusion is unnecessary. The output of the interview is not a set of clean answers to crisp questions. It is not pure maple syrup, but a compound. The output is not independent data, but is still full of meaning.

Moreover, it is highly possible that we may be able to learn more from this contaminated and compound data from the active interview, than from the clean data of a pure interview. How could that be? Consider Figure 18.1 above and then contrast it with Figure 18.2 below. In Figure 18.1, the process is a simple one. Each question of the script prompts an answer, and then (assuming the answer is complete) the interviewer moves on to the next question. The interviewer does not (must not) react to the answer, or that contaminates the data. It seems likely that such interviewing technique simply elicits what we might call *surface answers*. Because the answer is not challenged, the respondent can give an initial response (from the top of his/her head) and will not be challenged. There is no need for introspection on the part of the respondent to give a better or more thoughtful answer.

Contrast that with the active interview illustrated in Figure 18.2. Here the interviewer starts with a script, and perhaps the respondent can give initial answers that also come (so to speak) from a prepared 'script'. But in the active interview, the interviewer is allowed to improvise, to deviate from the script. So, for example, if an answer is unsatisfactory or implausible, the interviewer is allowed to challenge the answer. If an answer is counter-intuitive, the active interviewer can (and perhaps should) spend some time interrogating his/her intuition, to see if a supplementary question would be useful. Equally, when the interviewee is challenged (s)he may decide to quiz her/his own intuition, and see if a better answer is forthcoming. Moreover, the supplementary questions may again force the interviewee into further introspection.

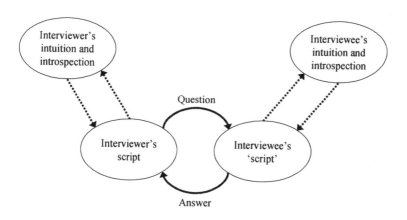

Figure 18.2   The active interview

Clearly this active approach breaks many of the rules of the pure interview. But it may make it possible to extract more knowledge from the interviewee's intuition – even if the form in which that gets articulated is inextricably bound up with the idiosyncratic (and non-replicable) way in which the interviewer improvised in the actual interview.

Arguably, there is not a great distance between the truly active interview and the brainstorming discussion with fellow academics. In general, we do not call the latter an interview as such, because we are not in search of interview data. Rather it is a conversation to help us develop our ideas and intuition: in such a conversation, we rarely stick to a predefined script, but improvise as the conversation unfolds. This is not because of a cavalier attitude: on the contrary, it is because we expect to get more from the conversation by improvising in that way.

What sort of strategy should the active interviewer follow? And what are the ideal personal characteristics of the active interviewer? The answers are wrapped up together. A trite (but not misleading answer) would be: the active interviewer can break most of the rules described above for the pure interviewer! This is because the active interviewer will obscure the line between interview and collaboration.

So, for example, Douglas described a strategy for creative interviewing, where the objective is to encourage '*a creative search for mutual understanding*' (Douglas, 1985, p. 25, emphasis in original). This reveals the totally different character from the pure interview. In the pure interview, the aim was to minimise interaction. By contrast, Douglas (1985, p. 25) emphasises the need for 'many strategies and tactics of interaction'. In the pure interview, the interviewer does not cultivate a relationship with the interviewee, beyond a superficial friendliness and politeness. By contrast, Douglas speaks of 'intimacy'.

A second example relates to the character of the interview as a social event. The pure interview is a fairly dull event. It is superficially polite, sanitised and without argument. Recall the advice from Roethlisberger, noted above, about the need for politeness on the part of the interviewer. And contrast this with the view, attributed to Sir Francis Crick, that real collaboration calls for candour and not politeness (Abra and Abra, 1999).

A third example relates to the clarity of the two roles in an interview. In the pure interview, the roles of interviewer and interviewee are strictly distinct. In the active interview, these roles are not so distinct – or may not be distinct at all, so one person could be interviewer at one time and interviewee (respondent) at another.

CONCLUSION

Which is the best of these three approaches to the interview? The reader who has worked his/her way through earlier chapters in this book will not be surprised at my answer: all of them! By that I mean that any applied economists worth their salt will run across different research problems that call for a different approach to the interview.

The pure interview is the right approach when the researcher needs to elicit the same sort of information from a large group of interviewees. Here data 'purity' and comparability are essential, and it is better if neither the interviewer nor the interviewee departs too far from the script. We have seen that 'pure' interviews may not actually yield data that are all that 'pure'. The data are conditioned by context and form of interview. But a consistent and pure interview technique is good for obtaining uncontaminated 'surface' data. It helps to use experienced interviewers, but ones who are not knowledgeable about the specific field – so they do not get actively involved in the interview. (This is a little like the observation in experimental economics that undergraduate students make better subjects for economic experiments than experienced business people.) In conclusion, we should add that the pure interview is intentionally a rather dull affair. It is unlikely to be a source of inspiration to interviewer or interviewee. It is unlikely to be an occasion for creative thought.

By contrast, the emotional interview is best if we wish to elicit responses that 'come from the heart'. This is the way to get at what the respondent really thinks – uncontaminated by our specific interview questions. In this approach, the interview can turn into a monologue rather than a dialogue. The outputs are unpredictable. The emotional interview may bring forth rich data, or just a lot of whingeing. In the first case, it can be inspirational for the interviewer; in the second, the interviewer must just take consolation in the fact that it is therapeutic for the interviewee.

The active interview is probably the best way to develop the deepest possible common understanding. It is a step in the direction of a collaboration, and sometimes the boundary between interview and informal discussion with a wise colleague is blurred. In this case, moreover, the distinction between interviewer and interviewee can be blurred too, but it remains very much a dialogue. All knowledge arising from the interview is a product of interaction, so it is nothing like the sort of 'pure' data we hope to obtain from the pure interview. The interview may be a source of inspiration. Sometimes it may lead to argument. We cannot remove this interactional ingredient – and we should not try to. Holstein and Gubrium (1995) say that all interviews are active. I don't necessarily go so far. But I would agree that it is often through the active interview that we learn the most.

The active interview can also be a powerful learning experience for interrogating our own intuition. Indeed, some interviewers (rather vain ones, perhaps) believe that the process of interview is valuable because it stimulates them to interrogate their own intuition. This is more valuable than anything the respondent says (data) as such. In that case, it is best if the respondent throws back questions, and the interviewer reflects on these, to interrogate his/her own intuition.

Despite the problematic side to the interview, as a technique, the qualitative researcher does not show any signs of abandoning the interview. And we still appoint people to lectureships and chairs on the basis of an interview, so we must believe the interview is full of content – even if it is problematic as pure data. I would venture to suggest that the more problematic it is as a source of pure data, the more interesting the interview. Is a scientific approach to the interview a good thing in its own right? Not if it reduces what we learn.

19. Common sense and intuition

Many people would say that the fact that something makes intuitive sense is not very strong scientific evidence in support of it. Kripke (1982), by contrast, has argued that intuitive acceptability is strong evidence in support. Indeed, Kripke (1982, p. 42) went as far as to say that 'I really don't know, in a way, what more conclusive evidence one can have about anything'.[1] This chapter considers the scientific importance of common sense and intuition.

Some years ago I attended a seminar where the presenter had estimated an econometric model of demand for durable goods. One of the parameters of his model described the rate at which durable goods depreciate in value. A rate of r per cent would imply that each year the durable good would decline in value by r per cent. The presenter told us that his best estimate for the value of that depreciation rate was greater than 100 per cent. This seemed rather a puzzle. A depreciation rate of 100 per cent would have meant that goods would depreciate immediately. A depreciation rate above 100 per cent would seem to imply not only that televisions fall apart immediately, but that as they do so they might cause the adjacent television sets in the showroom to fall apart too. By any common sense, let alone intuition or introspection, this seemed an implausible result. But the presenter was stuck: as he pointed out, whether we believe it or not, that is what the econometrics actually says. Econometrics has attained such an honoured position in our profession, that we may feel reluctant to dismiss its findings, even when they appear absurd.

As an applied researcher, I have done many pieces of contract research for government departments, public sector agencies and other organisations. Quite often such work is filtered by an advisory panel, who apply what they call a 'reality check'.[2] The panel consists of a group of non-academics and non-economists who have a good practical knowledge of the research area. We can see this as a test of the intuitive acceptability of the researcher's conclusions. What happens when a research finding fails the reality check? Sometimes the finding survives, and the advisory panel go away to think about whether the unexpected observation can be reconciled. Sometimes, the researcher goes away feeling frustrated that academic findings sometimes cut so little ice with practitioners. However, the fact is that in the business and policy world – whether we like it or not – common sense and intuition often carry a great deal more conviction than research findings.

What are we to make of common sense and intuition? The quotation from Kripke, cited at the start of the chapter, gives an unexpectedly strong endorsement to the value of intuition. At the other extreme, Albert Einstein famously described common sense as a 'collection of prejudices'.[3] Just because a scientific prediction or a piece of data defies common sense is not a good reason to dismiss the prediction or the data.

But whatever we make of common sense and intuition, we have sometimes to admit that they are in short supply. Lovins (1982, p. 28) recounts the tale of a woman who hires a carpenter to do a job, and shows him a rough sketch of what she wants. However, the carpenter follows the sketch too literally and produces a botched job. Exasperated, the woman asks him why he didn't use his common sense, and receives the reply: 'But common sense, Madam, is a gift of God; I have technical knowledge only'.

INTUITION IN BUSINESS, CHESS AND SCIENCE

Herbert Simon made a huge contribution to our understanding of the role of intuition in economic behaviour. More controversially, perhaps, he suggested that artificial intelligence could act as a framework for understanding the development of intuition.

Frantz (2003) gives a very useful survey of Simon's work on this. Frantz notes that Simon's interest in intuition developed from two sources. First, Simon was fascinated by Barnard's (1942) book, *The Functions of the Executive*. In the language of the present volume, Simon found Barnard's work a fascinating and profound piece of *vernacular* economics. Barnard gave many illustrations of the executive's use of intuition: for example, the good executive could study a complex balance sheet for a short while, and from that form an understanding of the company and its workings. Second, Simon came to interpret human intuition as subconscious pattern recognition after his work on 'thinking' machines. Simon argued that intuition is not independent of analysis. Indeed, the two interact to strengthen our decision-making process (Simon and Gilmartin, 1973, p. 33). By describing intuition as subconscious pattern recognition, Simon was in effect arguing that intuition was a rational way of making decisions, even if it did not involve conscious analysis (Simon, 1987).

As Frantz (2003) reminds us, one of the fields in which Simon demonstrated that intuition played a huge role was in chess. Simon observed that chess grandmasters decide on their moves so quickly (perhaps 5–10 seconds) that this could not be the result of conscious and detailed analysis (Simon, 1983, p. 25). However, these grandmasters would then spend a longer period of time checking that their initial hunch is in fact a good move.

When these grandmasters are asked how they manage to do this, they talk about 'intuition'. Simon (1982, p. 105) interpreted this as subconscious pattern recognition, drawing on a large memory bank of experience.

Simon argued that some kinds of human thinking progress in the same way as information-processing on a computer. Frantz (2003, p. 271) summarises this perspective very succinctly. Human thinking and information-processing programmes have three essential features in common. They both study evidence to find patterns; they both seek to memorise these patterns; and they use these patterns to draw inferences. Frantz stresses intuition does indeed involve analytical thinking, but as Simon (1997, p. 139) puts it, this sort of thinking helps us to make rapid decisions when we recognise familiar patterns. Intuition and analysis are always complementary.

Frantz (2003, p. 274) goes on to show how Simon recognised similar patterns amongst physical scientists. The more experienced scientists could solve scientific problems quicker, and by use of several short cuts. It is as if the expert's knowledge is like an encyclopaedia with a large index. The expert's problem-solving procedures show an 'appearance of intuition', while the novice's approach involves 'conscious and explicit analysis' (Simon, 1996, p. 136). Frantz (2003, p. 274) summarises this as follows: the expert's approach is more 'primitive', while the novice's approach is more 'algebraic'.

INTUITION AS AN EXPERIENCE-BASED MODEL

The idea of intuition as a mental model built up from a repeated practical experience helps to reinforce its position as a form of evidence that we need to take seriously. In its most general form, the mental model works like this. Let the vector $\mathbf{Z}$ describe a set of variables that summarise the state of the world. Let m describe a categorical variable, describing which of a set of possible outcomes obtains. Then intuition is a data-based model of the form:

$$m = f(\mathbf{Z}) \tag{19.1}$$

The function $f(.)$ here is not derived from a priori theoretical considerations, but rather from repeated experience. The agent experiences a sequence of states of the world $\mathbf{Z}_i$ and the outcomes in each state, m_i and using neural network procedures, or something similar, derives a data-based form for $f(.)$.[4] Each new experience which contradicts with the prediction leads to a revision of $f(.)$.

In some circumstances, this unique projection from each state of the world may be implausible. In that case, a more plausible interpretation of intuition is a probabilistic one:

$$\pi = g(\mathbf{Z}) \tag{19.2}$$

where π represents the probability of each possible outcome. Now, we have something more akin to a Bayesian model, where any experience can lead to an updating of prior probabilities in the light of experience.

From this point of view, any human intuition is the product of a personal *observatory*.[5] The data input passing through such an observatory may be far in excess of the data used for an econometric model. Perhaps the neural network model deriving and updating f (.) or $g(.)$ with experience is not entirely reliable – any more than an econometric model is reliable. Perhaps the model is not replicable [6] – in the way that a linear econometric model (at least) should be. Nevertheless, these models have their validity alongside other models.

A SIMPLE MODEL OF COMPUTER LEARNING

To see this process at work, it is useful to consider an example. As an undergraduate, I was set the challenge of developing a very simple model of computer learning. I suspect the basic idea will be familiar to many readers. The objective is to write a computer learning programme, where the computer learns how to distinguish different types of animals.

At the start, the computer assumes that all animals are dogs. It then starts to learn by questioning the user as follows (C is the computer; H is the human):

C: Think of an animal.
H: Yes.
C: Is it a dog?
H: No.
C: What is it then?
H: A cat.
C: Give me a question by which I can distinguish a cat from a dog.
H: Does it bark?
C: OK. So what is the answer for a dog?
H: Yes. A dog barks.
C: OK. And presumably a cat doesn't bark.
H: No it doesn't.
C: Thank you.

The computer has now learnt of the existence of a second animal, and a criterion or question it can use to distinguish between a dog and a cat. The next dialogue might go as follows:

C: Think of an animal.
H: Yes.
C: Does it bark?
H: No.
C: Is it a cat?
H: No.
C: What is it then?
H: A horse.
C: Give me a question by which I can distinguish a horse from a cat.
H: Does it go *miaow*?
C: OK. So what is the answer for a cat?
H: Yes. A cat goes *miaow*.
C: OK. And presumably a horse doesn't go *miaow*.
H: No it doesn't.
C: Thank you.

Now the computer has learnt of the existence of a third animal, and a second rule by which to distinguish different animals.

The process can continue indefinitely, as the computer builds up an ever more comprehensive knowledge of different animals and criteria by which to distinguish between them. The resulting structure of the computer's database may not be the optimal biological key, but nevertheless it has learnt quite a lot. And how has it learnt? It learns from the contradictions between theory and actuality.

Taking the last example above, the computer uses its criterion, 'does it bark?' When the answer to the question is 'no', the computer's intuition is that the animal must be a cat. But when told, 'no', it is not a cat, the computer acts creatively. Rather than stubborn denial or exhibiting a total lack of confidence in its intuition, the computer seeks to learn. It does not say, 'I don't believe that. It must be a cat if it doesn't bark'. Nor does it say, 'well if it doesn't bark and it isn't a cat, I've no idea what it is'. Rather, it tries to increase its understanding of a larger number of categories and a larger set of criteria with which to distinguish between these categories.

This is a very crude and simplistic model, perhaps, but it does illustrate the central point very well. We can learn from contradictions between intuition and actuality. To learn we must be confident enough in our intuitions to accord them some validity but not so stubborn that we cannot accept they are wrong or incomplete.

To illustrate this, consider the last example. The computer's starting intuition is:

Bark?	Prediction
Yes	Dog
No	Cat

In the last example the answers are: Bark? No; Cat? No. What is the computer to make of this? A computer with little faith in its original intuition would lose confidence and revise the above to the rather feeble intuition:

Bark?	Prediction
Yes	Dog
No	No idea

On the other hand, the excessively stubborn computer would persist in holding to its original intuition:

Bark?	Prediction
Yes	Dog
No	Must be a cat!

Regardless of the fact that this time the respondent tells the computer that the non-barking animal is not a cat, the stubborn computer maintains that it must be a cat, because there is no other option.

The learning computer can progress beyond these last two. Learning that the non-barking animal is not a cat, the computer is able to advance to the following understanding by expanding its repertoire:

Bark?	Miaow?	Prediction
Yes	—	Dog
No	Yes	Cat
No	No	Horse

A learning computer of this sort will eventually build up a detailed knowledge base – rather like a biological key. To learn like this, one thing is essential. We must be confident enough in our intuitions that we do not abandon them immediately in the face of some contradictory evidence, but equally we must not hold on to them stubbornly regardless of evidence to the contrary. We need to hold on to our earlier intuitions as valid but incomplete, and be creative about developing a deeper intuition out of every contradiction. The creative researcher with a well-developed intuition looks on contradiction not as an embarrassing problem, but as an opportunity to learn. In Chapter 23, we shall return to the idea of a paradox-seeking research strategy.

INTUITION AS A SCARCE RESOURCE

The concluding observations of Simon and Frantz, noted above, may persuade us that intuition is a higher faculty than technical proficiency. The chess grandmaster and the scientific expert rely on intuition while the novice takes a more 'algebraic' or consciously analytical approach. Surely the novice would mimic the master if (s)he could. The fact that (s)he doesn't suggests that (s)he can't. And for the expert, conscious analysis is at most a way of confirming that the intuitive hunch is correct. It is not his/her strongest asset.

This is not confined to chess and science. It is sometimes said of young musicians that they can show extraordinary technical competence but don't play as musically as older players. The older players, in their turn, may have lost some of the technical bravura and even play some wrong notes, but, despite that, play much more musically. This suggests that musicianship takes longer to develop than technical excellence. Two memorable examples were the pianists Schnabel and Cortot. It was said of Schnabel that he could hit wrong notes, and sometimes in the most unfortunate places, but his musicianship was staggering. And of Cortot, that he played many wrong notes, but his right ones were better than anybody else's.

And we find the same in economics. We often find that doctoral students show exceptional technical skill but lack the well-developed intuition of some older scholars. In their turn, older scholars may have lost some of their technical prowess but have developed a much richer intuition. Once again, it takes much longer to develop intuition than to develop technical excellence. Since the economics profession is steadily growing, and the young are technique rich while the old are intuition rich, then we should expect to find that well-developed intuition is a scarce resource in economics.

In view of that, it seems very perverse that the modern economics profession should accord a relatively high value to technical excellence (which is in plentiful supply) and a relatively low value to intuition (which is not). Waldrop (1994) made some fascinating observations about this in the context of the early days of the Santa Fe Institute. He described an early meeting where economists and physicists were comparing their approaches to their subjects. He notes that the physicists were 'awestruck and appalled' at the way in which economists made use of mathematics. Waldrop (1994, p. 140) quoted one (unnamed) physicist who reckoned that the economists 'were dazzling themselves with fancy mathematics' and that the economists would often have made better progress simply by using some common sense. In turn, the economists were puzzled at the comparatively casual approach of the physicists towards their maths. Kenneth Arrow observed that the physicists had a quite different style of research: 'a little rigorous thinking, a little intuition, a little back-of-the-envelope calculation' (Waldrop, 1994, p. 140).

My belief is that strong intuition will always be one of the most indispensable tools in the applied economist's armoury. And if I am right that economic intuition is a scarce commodity, then developing our intuition sounds like an exceptionally important priority. Part of the rationale for using a diversity of approaches, as described in this book, is that this is the best way to develop intuition. Using a multiplicity of research approaches is the best way to learn, because it is most likely to force us to challenge our intuition. As we saw above, the intuition is our capacity to perceive the truth of things without having to engage in deep thought, hard analysis or careful reasoning. When that is challenged, we do not feel comfortable. But, insofar as we can accept it, this is our best route to learning. This is the rationale for the paradox-seeking approach to research, described in Chapter 23 below.

APPLYING INTUITION

I conclude this observation with an example of how we should apply our intuition when we encounter 'crazy' econometric results. By this, I mean the sort of result described at the start of this chapter, where durable goods have an instantaneous rate of depreciation of well over 100 per cent. Or the demand equation which states that the price elasticity of demand for mobile phones is large and *positive*. Or the model of television viewing behaviour that predicts that the BBC1 audience share is maximised when BBC1 shows no programme at all.

Whether we admit to it or not, researchers are sometimes tempted to 'censor' crazy results – meaning that they simply do not report them. Sometimes, those who baulk at such censorship instead 'filter' what they say by admitting to their results but making it quite clear that these are 'implausible'.

Is it always bad to 'censor' or 'filter' counter-intuitive econometric results? Besides the obvious ethical issues, there are potential type I and type II errors here. If the perverse results were false, then it would be best that we filter them. Accepting perverse and false results is the type II error. But if the perverse results were nonetheless true, it would be best if we do not filter them. Filtering perverse but true results is the type I error that concerned Einstein (see start of this chapter).

Table 19.1   Type I and type II errors in using intuition

	Accept result	Filter/censor result
Perverse result but true	Correct decision ('some great truths defy common sense')	Type I error
Perverse result and false	Type II error	Correct decision ('common sense prevails')

Should we be more concerned about type I or type II errors here? The answer must depend on the use of our results. If we are consultants and large sums depend on the reliability of our results, then we should be very cautious indeed about the risk of type II errors. This is what the 'reality check' described above is trying to avoid. Consultants are arguably less concerned about type I errors. But if we are seeking to make scientific advances, then we should be just as concerned about type I errors, and maybe more so. We saw in this chapter that in a simple learning algorithm, the machine learns when it confronts a perverse result and tries to resolve it. What seem to be perverse results may in fact be the key to scientific advance. Don't let a 'collection of prejudices', as Einstein put it, get in the way of such advances.

CONCLUSION

Contrary to some views of intuition as a vague and unscientific type of knowledge, we have seen that intuition can provide good grounds for believing something. Human intuition is subconscious pattern recognition built from extensive experience. Experts often use intuition where novices use technique, and intuition takes longer to cultivate than technical excellence. As a result, deep intuition is much rarer than technical excellence.

I find that two streams in this book are converging on the same conclusion. In Chapter 8, we saw Hayek's argument that efficient economic decision-making requires the use of local vernacular knowledge by those 'on the spot'. In this chapter, we saw Simon's argument that experts make extensive use of this intuition, or vernacular knowledge, which is built up from the subconscious processing of local experience. Each economic agent builds up a mental model from repeated experience, where the signal-to-noise ratio is rather high. This vernacular knowledge can surely make a vital contribution to our economic understanding.

NOTES

1. Here quoted from Pust (2000, p. xiii).
2. Once this was described, less flatteringly, as a 'sanity check'. Sometimes, of course, the primary role of the advisory panel is to check that the researcher stays 'on message'.
3. Quoted in *Scientific American*, February 1976.
4. The literatures on artificial intelligence (see Finlay and Dix, 1996) and neural networks (De Wilde, 1997) both have learning models of this sort. See also Brunak and Lautrup (1990) and Dreyfus et al. (1986) about the connections between computing and intuition.
5. Some of my Italian colleagues use the term 'observatory' to describe a small-scale research unit. The term is a good one, for just as an astronomical observatory is a station for making a large number of localised observations, so too any one person's intuition can be seen in the same way. Every economic actor is an observatory.
6. By which I mean that different people experiencing the same data will derive different mental models, perhaps because the starting structure of their mental models was different.

20. Metaphor

It may seem strange to have a chapter on metaphor in a text on methods of applied economics. The economic puritan, indeed, may believe that metaphor has no place in economics. They would probably accept that metaphor may be allowed as an aid to communication and to make our work more appealing to some audiences, but would deny that the use of metaphor is good economics. But these are like Keynes's (1936) practical men, who think they are unaffected by intellectual influences, but are often in fact 'the slaves of some defunct economist'. To adapt Keynes, we might say that those economists who believe they are exempt from any metaphorical influences, are usually the slaves of some defunct *physicist*.

Following the work of Henderson (1982, 1994, 1995), McCloskey (1985, 1998), Mirowski (1988, 1989, 1994), Klamer and Leonard (1994), we know that such a puritanical view is untenable. Metaphors are used in economics all the time. Indeed, we could say that *any economic model is a metaphor*. And this is not unique to economics: as Harré (1986) argues, the use of metaphor is actually very common in all sciences. Metaphors are both useful and hazardous. Faced with a problem we do not understand, most of us make a first step towards a solution by likening the problem to something we do understand (Ashcraft, 1989, pp. 597–604). Moreover, metaphors are exceptionally useful as idea generators. But as Marshall (1898, p. 39) observed, 'analogies may help one into the saddle, but are encumbrances on a long journey'. If the use of metaphor is not to be too cumbersome, then we need to be careful that we do discard the unhelpful metaphors.

METAPHOR IS WIDELY USED IN ECONOMICS

It is salutary to remind ourselves that economists do in fact make extremely heavy use of metaphor. The following is just a sample.

Smith's invisible hand is arguably one of the oldest, best-known and persistent metaphors. Indeed, the idea of a market is also a metaphor: most of the organisations that economists currently call markets bear rather little resemblance to the open-air market which lends its name to such constructs.

A very common metaphor is to do with circular flow of income. This gives rise to the velocity of circulation. The idea of liquids is often used – namely in liquidity, pump priming and Dollar pool. Equally, the gas analogy is common: ballooning, bubble, inflation,[1] repressed inflation and deflation. A mechanical or physical analogy is common in macroeconomics: accelerator, closed economy, open economy, frictional unemployment, overshooting, targeting, leads and lags, built-in stabilisers, fine tuning, crowding out and stop–go. Psychological analogies such as slump, depression and money illusion occur on occasions.

Evolutionary economics draws on a wide range of biological metaphors: institutions as genes, growth, mutation, selection and adaptation. Evolutionary economists also draw on some metaphors from physical sciences – for example, critical mass. But one should not get the idea that metaphor is used outside the mainstream while the mainstream eschews such bad habits. The notion of equilibrium is a key metaphor, of course, in neoclassical economics. So also, atomistic competition, job market signalling and tatonnement. In economics, geometric metaphors are central: curves shift, the economy may move down the Phillips curve, and so on.

Game theory, indeed, is one of the richest hunting grounds for metaphors, with the prisoner's dilemma, battle of the sexes, fat cats, lean and hungry look, puppy dog ploy, horses, penguins, lemmings, lemons, cheap talk, zero-sum game, ultimatum game, centipede game and game of chicken.

Financial markets have their own menagerie: bulls, bears, stag, tiger economies, dragons, elephants, lion markets and puma markets. Financial operations involve a number of physical metaphors: back door (financial operation), crawling peg, dynamic peg, flexible or floating exchange rates and spot markets.

Industrial economists talk of: dumping, elasticity, infant industry, barriers to entry, venture capital, vertical integration, horizontal integration, wage drift, wage freeze, price wars, contestable markets, predatory pricing, hedonic functions, gravity models, shadow pricing, the winner's curse, fable of the bees, Robinson Crusoe and dinosaurs. A related category is the spatial metaphor, such as the product space and characteristics space.

Even econometrics and mathematical economics have their metaphors: the Monte Carlo method, turnpike theorems, dummy variables, catastrophe theory, chaos and martingales. Leamer (1987) has written about this.

In short, metaphors are all around us in economics. Let's not pretend that we could live without them!

ADVANTAGES AND RISKS OF METAPHOR

There seem to be two traditions with respect to the use of metaphor or analogy. Some classical (especially Greek) thinkers saw the metaphor as a useful device. By contrast, some neoclassical thinkers (notably, J.S. Mill) thought that the analogy could be deceptive and misleading. However, we should not think of these characteristics as mutually exclusive. Lakoff and Johnson (1980) argue that metaphors are useful and dangerous at the same time: you can't really have the first characteristic without the second.

Metaphor is useful because it gives us a start in understanding an unfamiliar phenomenon. We take a phenomenon that we do understand, and apply our model of that to a new phenomenon that we do not understand. In the face of an impenetrable problem, we have little alternative. Either we use metaphor, or else we probably cannot make any progress.

At the same time, metaphor is dangerous because it highlights similarities between phenomena and tends to overlook differences. That can be misleading.

The exchange between Alchian (1950, 1953) and Penrose (1952) has helped to clarify our thinking about the role of metaphor. Penrose (1952, p. 804) was concerned that a serious risk with the use of metaphor is that problems are framed in a very specific and sometimes idiosyncratic way, and this can obscure important aspects of the problem. Nevertheless, Penrose (1952, p. 807) conceded that the use of metaphor can add some colour to our analysis, and can help us to develop our understanding of the unknown by drawing on our existing knowledge. We can see already the dual characteristics identified by Lakoff and Johnson (1980).

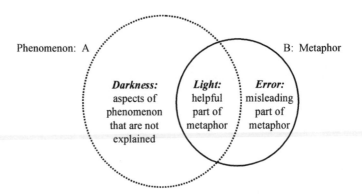

Figure 20.1   The metaphor

Figure 20.1 is helpful in capturing the purpose of metaphor. We try to illuminate phenomenon A, which we do not understand, by assuming it is like B, which we do understand. The circle A has a 'dotted' circumference, to mean that it is 'soft', or little understood. By contrast, the circle B has a solid circumference, to mean that it is 'solid', or well understood.

The metaphor is partly helpful, and partly not. It is helpful to the extent that it illuminates some aspects of the phenomenon A. This is the intersection between A and B (the Light in Figure 20.1). It may be unhelpful in two ways. First, it does not shed any light on some aspects of the phenomenon (the Darkness in Figure 20.1). Second, it may be misleading because it suggests several characteristics which are not part of the phenomenon B (the Error in Figure 20.1).

The helpfulness of a particular metaphor depends then on the ratio of light to (darkness plus error).[2] Clearly, some metaphors will be more helpful than others, and none of them is entirely free of hazards. But if in the absence of a metaphor one can understand nothing of the phenomenon A, then one must use some metaphor to make any progress at all.

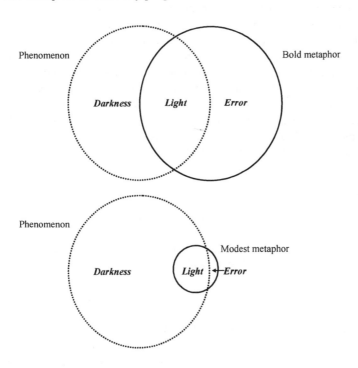

Figure 20.2   Bold and modest metaphors

It is now useful to make a further distinction between *bold metaphors* and *modest metaphors* (Figure 20.2). Bold metaphors are exciting but dangerous. They cover a wide area, and have a substantial overlap with phenomenon A but also a large area of error. Modest metaphors are less exciting, but also less likely to lead the researcher astray. These cover a small area, and in proportionate terms have a high overlap with phenomenon A, but only a small area of error.

If one were to ask a sociologist what (s)he thinks of economists' metaphors, (s)he would probably say that the problem for economics is that we have many bold metaphors, but are not good at throwing out the bad ones. Here it is helpful to recall the famous remark attributed to Linus Pauling: 'The way to get good ideas is to get lots of ideas, and throw the bad ones away'. It is fine to have lots of metaphors, bold ones even, but many of these will turn out to be stupid, so we must learn to throw away the bad ones. Other social sciences, perhaps, have a larger collection of modest metaphors, each of which perhaps sheds less light in absolute terms, but is less prone to lead the user astray.

The issue for this chapter is not so much whether we do use metaphor (we do), nor whether we should (we accept it is inevitable), nor whether it is potentially hazardous (it is). Rather, the issue for this chapter is how can we set about finding useful metaphors, and what can we expect to get from them.

We should not expect a metaphor imported from one discipline to work in another, any more than we would expect a technique imported from one industry to work in another. But, just as travel broadens the mind, so the researcher with a greater repertoire of metaphors from elsewhere will often be well placed to come up with a useful metaphor as a starting point.

Where do we search? Anywhere! Physical sciences, biological sciences, history, literature, art and music all have the advantage of a longer history than our own discipline. Physical and natural sciences, moreover, have the advantage that some of their subject matter (for example, a solid object) is probably less complex than our own subject matter, even if their standards of predictive accuracy are considerably greater. The humanities, by contrast, address subject matter that is a good deal more complex than our own (for example, the meaning of life), with attendant reduction in the degree of precision.

THE METAPHOR OF SONG REPERTOIRE

Rather than criticize any one particular economist's use of metaphor, I shall instead pick an example where there seems to be an interesting parallel between an area of industrial economics and an area of zoology, but where the metaphor has not yet (to my knowledge) been developed by either side. The example draws an analogy between the industrial economist's analysis of product proliferation as a barrier to entry, and the biologist's analysis of how variation in birdsong can deter rival males from entering a space. By coincidence, two of the key pioneering papers on these topics (respectively, Schmalensee, 1978, and Krebs et al., 1978) were published in the same year. But it does seem to be a coincidence, and neither field recognised the similarity of the other. We shall argue that there could have been, and probably still are, potential gains from trade between these two fields.

Writers on music have long recognised the remarkable inventive powers of some birds in their song. The blackbird, song thrush and meadowlark are amongst those innovators who continually invent new songs to add to their repertoire.

Until Howard's book on *Territory in Bird Life* (1920), however, the biological function of song was not fully understood. Howard noted that apart from call-notes (alarm, and so on), song was limited to males in the breeding season. This led him to assert that song was related to the defence of territory and to securing a mate.

The purpose of innovation in song was even less clear. Partly, it is thought to be a process of individuation: every bird seeks to create a unique song of its own. This is important because birds can recognise their neighbours as specific individuals (with a unique song) and not merely as one of the same species. If one bird is to live in peace with his neighbours, the bird needs to establish a unique identity, and then his neighbours will recognise who he is and accept his presence. If neighbours hear an unfamiliar sound from an adjacent territory, they assume that there must be an intruder, and in that case they are liable to become aggressive. In the same way, if a particular bird moves away or dies, the neighbours will recognise his absence, and will opportunistically (and quickly) try to expand their territories.

This explains individuality, but does not explain the role of what biologists call *repertoire*: that is, the unique collection of songs which the bird is capable of singing. Biologists believe that birds benefit from acquiring a diverse and complex repertoire of songs. Birds with larger repertoires are better at attracting mates (Catchpole, 1980), are better at deterring neighbouring males from trespassing on their territories (Krebs, 1977; Krebs et al., 1978), and are better able to defend larger and better quality territories (Howard, 1974; McGregor et al., 1981).

Of particular interest for our purposes here is Krebs's (1977) *Beau Geste*[3] hypothesis about the effect of repertoire on the male's ability to defend his territory. Krebs advanced the hypothesis that a bird prospecting for its own territory can judge the residential density of an area by the variety of song that can be heard. This is an important fact to establish because success in breeding is positively related to size of territory, and hence negatively related to density of population. The bird that hears only a narrow variety of songs will infer that density is low, and that is desirable. By contrast, the bird that hears a large variety of song will infer that density is high, which is undesirable.

The *Beau Geste* hypothesis states that a bird deliberately develops a wide repertoire of songs. This will have the effect of deceiving passing birds that an area is more densely populated than it actually is. That makes it less likely that new entrants will try to establish their own territories in the area. And, in this way, the bird with a large repertoire is thus saved the effort of defending territory in other ways.

In the economist's language, the *Beau Geste* hypothesis is that the bird uses song proliferation to deter entry. Interestingly, however, repertoire may also be an essential requirement for the new entrant. The bird that can draw from a large repertoire will find it easier to match a potential neighbour, and can therefore move into a territory with less resistance.

Later authors have cast doubt on the *Beau Geste* hypothesis, suggesting that some other motivations for repertoire may be more important:

- The size of repertoire is an advertisement of quality. A bird with a small repertoire is unattractive (to the female) and no threat to the rival. A bird with a large repertoire may be a sign of an older, larger, stronger bird; this is attractive to the female and a potential threat to the rival.
- A larger repertoire permits more effective communication with neighbours (that is, matching the song types of neighbours).
- To the female, the male's repertoire is an indicator of probable success in breeding. The bird with a small repertoire offers low breeding success because there are likely to be intruders in his territory. The bird with a larger repertoire may offer high breeding success as his territory will have fewer intruders.[4]

For our present purposes, the survival (or failure) of the *Beau Geste* hypothesis is not the issue. Our concern is simply whether it is a useful metaphor for a company's use of product proliferation as an entry-deterring strategy.

THE METAPHOR OF PRODUCT PROLIFERATION

To compare the beauty of birdsong to the details of breakfast cereal might seem a move from the sublime to the ridiculous. Nevertheless, we shall see that the analogy is actually quite close. The following summary of product proliferation is based on two pioneering papers by Schmalensee (1978) and Scherer (1979).

The case of breakfast cereals is often cited as an example of how product proliferation may have acted as a deterrent to entry. It is a well-known and widely discussed case because of the complaint pursued by the US Federal Trade Commission (FTC) against the four largest US manufacturers of ready-to-eat breakfast cereals between 1972 and 1981. The complaint was eventually dropped, but it helped to develop our understanding of when product proliferation is beneficial to consumers, and when it is not.

Product proliferation is the strategy whereby a manufacturer produces a large range of slightly differentiated products for a particular market. There is, of course, a strong case for some product variety to serve the diverse tastes of different consumers. It is possible, however, that beyond a certain point further product proliferation will add little to consumer well-being, but will make it harder for newcomers to enter the market. In that case, the benefits gained from increased variety are offset by the increases in price that may result from higher market concentration. The FTC complaint suggested that proliferating brands and differentiating similar products, along with intensive advertising, had resulted in high barriers to entry.

Scherer (1979) notes that the four-digit SIC industry defined as 'Cereal Preparations' is one of the most concentrated US manufacturing industries (at that level of aggregation). The three-firm concentration ratio has been 80 per cent or above for many decades. Market structure has also been pretty stable over time. The early entrants to the market were Quaker Oats, Post (later a part of General Foods), Kellogg, and from 1928, General Mills. Since the 1950s, Kellogg's market share has been about 45 per cent, with General Mills at about 20 per cent and General Foods at about 15 per cent. Few markets in the USA (or elsewhere) have shown such stability in market shares.

Does this high and stable level of concentration result from economies of scale? Shepherd (1990, p. 430) cites evidence that economies of scale in production are small, and that minimum efficient scale is equivalent to 5 per cent of total industry sales. This suggests that the level of concentration observed is well above what is needed to exploit production economies of scale. Rather, concentration seems to be the result of product proliferation, combined with advertising.

Proliferation

The industry's basic products and production technologies have changed little since 1910. The number of competing products actually marketed, however, has increased markedly. For many observers, the introduction of numerous new product variants was the most striking aspect of this case.

Scherer (1979) states that in 1957 the six largest manufacturers had between them a total of 38 brands in national distribution. By 1970, the figure was 67 brands. Shepherd (1990) states that by 1973 the figure was 80, and that many more have been introduced since then.

Many of the new brands failed to achieve viable market shares, and indeed of the 51 brands launched between 1958 and 1970, only five achieved market shares of 2 per cent or more. So most of these new products filled only small niches in the market, while many of the older brands showed considerable staying power. Only two pre-1958 brands were withdrawn from the national market during the 1960s. Moreover, the 29 brands that led the market in 1960 (with 83 per cent of industry sales) continued to account for 74 per cent of the market in 1970 – despite the proliferation of new competing brands.

If these new brands were relatively unsuccessful, why did the major firms continue to introduce them? There are several possible arguments, but one of the most compelling is as follows. The firm's incentive to proliferate brands is not simply to expand its sales. It is also to deter entry. If competing products can be thought of as points in a product space, then the more products there are, the more congested the space becomes. Just as a congested geographical space can be unattractive to enter,[5] so is a congested product space – essentially because in a congested space, firms can only expect to sell to a limited niche, and so the prospective sales from entry are small. If incumbent firms proliferate a sufficient number of slightly different cereals, then they can ensure that the only remaining niches are too small for the entrant to achieve the necessary break-even level of sales.

Proliferation is not used on its own. Advertising is also considered to be a very strong influence leading to the highly concentrated structure of this market. Scherer (1979) notes that amongst the 325 or so four-digit SIC industries for which advertising data are available, the 'Cereal Preparation' industry ranks second in terms of advertising outlays to sales. That speaks for itself. Advertising was thought to be especially effective in this market as it was frequently directed at young children, who are known to be highly impressionistic. Shepherd (1990, p. 430) argues that advertising in this market has probably served to harden the strong and stable concentration observed here.

Product proliferation can be a deterrent to entry. But can product proliferation also be part of an entry strategy? Yes it can. Kotler et al. (1986, pp. 106–7) have shown how Japanese companies, in particular, have used product proliferation as a highly successful entry strategy. A leading example of this was Japanese entry into the US market for motorcycles. In 1975, Honda offered a total of 26 models in the range 125cc to 750cc, Yamaha 29,

Kawasaki 22 and Suzuki 24. This compared with 11 models of Harley Davidson, 4 models of BMW and a total of 17 models from all the other non-US manufacturers of motorcycles (Kotler et al., 1986, pp. 106–7).

COMPARING THE TWO METAPHORS

As we said at the start of the discussion of this pair of examples, nobody (to our knowledge) used the birdsong metaphor to analyse the phenomenon of product proliferation, nor did anyone do the reverse.[6] But from what we have seen of each case, it seems clear enough that the economist with no solution to the puzzle of product proliferation could have learned much from the metaphor of song repertoire and entry deterrence described. Equally, the biologist without a solution to the puzzle of song repertoire could have learned much from the metaphor of product proliferation and entry deterrence.

Of course, the pioneering papers in these two fields were published at more or less the same time, so neither opportunity arose. But the point is that we have here two theories (both supported by some empirical evidence) with enough in common that one could provide a working model for the other. Unless this example is exceptional – and that seems most unlikely (how would I have stumbled on such a peculiarity) – then it is reasonable to expect that there will be others.

However, it is useful to compare these two models and identify the differences between them. Table 20.1 summarises some of the main features of each example, and the similarities and differences between them.

The first main difference is that the economic story has a role for customers, while the birdsong repertoire is not so much about customers as a joint-venture partner (the mate). The economic customers probably buy just one of the proliferation of products. The mate, by contrast, is impressed by the repertoire as a whole – and not so much as a music-lover, but as an indication of the credibility of their joint-venture partner.

Both stories have, of course, a role for rivals. But interestingly, the birdsong repertoire story discusses the effect of repertoire on entrants and neighbours (established competitors), while the discussion of product proliferation (as discussed here, at any rate) puts more emphasis on the first.

The economic story has an anti-trust authority to look after the interests of would-be entrants and overcharged consumers. Displaced birds have no such agency to protect their interests.

The functions of proliferation and repertoire have some elements in common but several differences. A naïve view is that proliferation is about matching products to diverse consumer needs. A more likely explanation in

Table 20.1   Comparison of two metaphors

Feature	Song repertoire	Product proliferation
'Customers'	Not really	Customers
'Joint venture partner'	Mates	Not really
'Rivals'	Entrants and neighbours	Entrants
'Competition policy'	None!	Anti-trust
Function of proliferation /repertoire	Attracting mate; Advertise quality; Communication; Deceive entrants.	Product for each customer; Segmentation; Deterring entrants.
Does proliferation have an attraction function?	Yes, maybe	Yes: custom product for each customer.
Does proliferation have a deterrent function?	Yes (*Beau Geste*)	Can do
Duration of entry barrier	Short?	Long?
Is proliferation an entry strategy?	Can be	Can be (Kotler et al.)
Is proliferation the only entry strategy to match incumbents' proliferation?	Yes: proliferation by incumbents calls for repertoire from entrants	Yes: proliferation deters single product entrants.
Proliferation customised when repertoire is an entry strategy?	Birds learn their repertoire from future neighbours.	Japanese motor cycle producers base their repertoire around incumbent offerings.
Deliberate deception?	Yes	Not necessarily – but there may be brand proliferation.
A single entry deterrence strategy?	No: *Beau Geste* works best in densely vegetated areas to enhance the deception	No: tends to be coupled with other signals (advertising).
Optimum diversity?	Yes: small repertoire is not a threat; large repertoire is an energy-consuming diversion.	Yes: proliferation for entry deterrence may be larger than for market segmentation.

many cases is that the use of product proliferation helps to segment markets. The other interpretation is that product proliferation helps to deter entry. Song repertoire is directed at prospective mates ('joint-venture partners') or entrants rather than customers. But it may also be relevant to neighbours – an aspect to the story that is not emphasised in the economic story.

The duration of entry barriers is a little unclear in the case of birdsong. The experiments by Krebs et al. (1978) used tape-recordings of birdsong to deter entrants, and these were pre-programmed and not responsive to the songs around them. As such, they were fairly unintelligent incumbents, and could not deter entrants for very long – though the tape-recorders with greater repertoire were more effective entry deterrents than tape-recorders with a single song. In the economic case, the barrier to entry can last for some time – in the absence of product innovation, which allows the entrant a new space into which to enter. (The deterrent worked in the case of breakfast cereal, since there was so little change in the basic technology of production, or in fundamental product characteristics).

In both cases, though for slightly different reasons, proliferation/wide repertoire can be part of an entry strategy – as well as an entry-deterring strategy. Moreover, in both cases, there is a suggestion that proliferation/wide repertoire is the only entry strategy in the presence of incumbents who use proliferation/wide repertoire. In both cases, we find that the entrant matches proliferation/repertoire to the precise proliferation/ repertoire used by the incumbent. Entrant birds learn their songs from would-be neighbours, and entrant companies devise their product range in the light of incumbent offerings. It is less clear whether incumbents fine tune the design of their proliferation/repertoire in the light of specific potential entrants.

In the case of birdsong, the *Beau Geste* hypothesis asserts that the incumbent intends to deceive potential entrants. In the economic case, proliferation need not deceive to work. There are, of course, sometimes proliferations of brands with common ownership but it seems more likely that this is designed to deceive customers rather than rivals.

In neither case is product proliferation used on its own as a single entry-deterring strategy. The bird combines repertoire with changes in perch – often singing different parts of its repertoire each time it changes location within its territory. Also, the *Beau Geste* hypothesis recognises that deception works best in densely vegetated areas with low visibility to enhance the deception. Product proliferation is a useful barrier to the single product entrant, but will not be such a deterrent to the proliferation entrant. The latter is better deterred by advertising or other selling expenses.

Finally, in both cases, there is a sense of optimum diversity in product range/repertoire. Industrial economics/marketing theory can (in principle) define an optimum degree of product proliferation to achieve maximum efficiency in market segmentation and second-degree price discrimination. Or, if proliferation is designed as a barrier to entry, an optimum degree of diversity can be described (though it is probably harder to define precisely). The story for birdsong also recognises an optimum repertoire. A repertoire that is too small does not impress the prospective mate and is no threat to rivals. A repertoire that is too large indicates a bird that spends too much energy singing, and not enough on the other strategies required to defend territory.

CONCLUSION: DARKNESS, LIGHT AND ERROR

Figure 20.3 provides the empirical counterpart of Figure 20.1. The left-hand circle refers to the 'product proliferation' case and the right-hand circle refers to the 'song repertoire' case. We find that there are some observations in the intersection: these are the elements of one case that apply reasonably well to the other case. But there are also several observations that do not lie in the intersection. These represent aspects of one case that do not help to illuminate the other case.

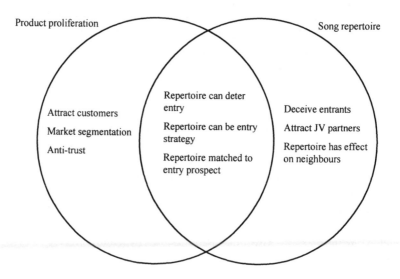

Figure 20.3   Darkness, light and error

The overall pattern is much as we would expect. Metaphor is useful and dangerous at the same time. If we use the story of song repertoires to illuminate the case of product proliferation as an entry deterrent, then we find some aspects of the metaphor that work, and some that are misleading. In addition, we find some aspects of the 'product proliferation' case that are not illuminated by anything in the 'song repertoire' metaphor. However, if we have no economic theory to use in trying to understand this 'product proliferation' case, it is clear that our chosen metaphor does shed some light. We could do a lot worse than use it as a starting point.

NOTES

1. In the 1970s, some spoke of 'galloping inflation' – a wonderfully mixed metaphor!
2. We can see something like a typical type I and type II distinction here – except that metaphors are not purely right or wrong, but part right and part wrong at the same time. To reject a metaphor as wrong is a type I error to the extent that it sheds 'light'. To accept a metaphor as right is a type II error to the extent that it contains 'error'.
3. This is so named after the Paramount Studios film, *Beau Geste* (1939). The metaphor refers to a scene in the film in which a lone French Legionnaire defends a fort by making it appear to be filled with an armed garrison of Legionnaires – except that every other Legionnaire is dead, but propped up at a parapet so that the distant observer still thinks the fort is well defended.
4. Interestingly, it is suggested that a very large repertoire may be taken to be an indicator of reduced probability of success in breeding, since the bird is preoccupied with singing, and that takes up a lot of energy.
5. There are, of course, circumstances in which densely populated spaces are attractive places to locate. We can see this from the fact that real-estate prices in crowded city centres show no sign of abating.
6. Swann and Taghavi (1992) used the concept of 'product territories' to describe the group of consumers (the segment in taste space) most likely to buy a particular product. A particularly interesting implication of this analogy is that the word 'territory' has such a similar meaning in both contexts.

21. Innovative economics: an essential miscellany

Frisch (1956, pp. 300–301) argued that the good economist must try to develop techniques that help us 'to look forward, to think out what will be the analytical tools that can be useful in the concrete situations that will prevail tomorrow'. How can we follow Frisch's advice? We cannot predict the future, so how can we know what tools we shall need in future? I think we have to follow the example of the wise builder who carries around all his/her regular tools and in addition a box of assorted oddments which may come in useful if some unexpected job arises. In exactly the same way, we need to carry around with us an essential miscellany of research techniques.

The last 10 chapters have examined what seem to me some of the most important approaches to studying applied economics. However, this is not an exhaustive list. Indeed, even if we were to increase the list to 20 techniques, that would not be exhaustive. I think we can go as far as to say, there will never be an exhaustive set of empirical research strategies. We shall always find new research problems that require us to devise new empirical research methods.

Why so? The reason is what Schumpeter told us: the economy is not static, and cannot be static. The object of study keeps changing. Three great forces, at least, fuel this change:[1] ongoing innovation, division of labour and reductions in transaction costs. Moreover, these three forces do not just change the character of the economy: they are liable, in some respects at least, to make it more complex. We find that: job descriptions become more specialised; production involves more complex trading arrangements across a larger group of companies, and over large distances; some products, at least, become more complex. If the economy is changing in character and especially if it is becoming more complex, then we may need new techniques to understand it.

We can use a slightly modified version of Figure 10.2 to illustrate this. In Figure 10.2, we saw that a variety of research techniques were required to illuminate each facet of a research problem. If the research problem changes, then we may expect that the right mix of research techniques will change. And if the problem becomes more complex, then it will develop facets that were not present in Figure 10.2. To illuminate these, it is quite possible that we will need different techniques.[2]

Figure 21.1 illustrates this. Here, the research object is similar to that in Figure 10.2, but slightly more complex in that it has a non-convexity. To illuminate this non-convexity, we need a specially defined research tool located at AB. Techniques A and B will do very little to illuminate this 'cavity', and indeed, the chosen technique must be just right.

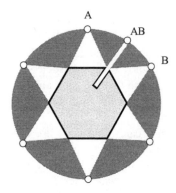

Figure 21.1   Special technique to illuminate complex facet

AN ESSENTIAL MISCELLANY

One of the most important research techniques is one that all of us use, though we may not necessarily think of it as a research technique. Everyday life is a research technique. By that I mean that we can encounter things in everyday life that illuminate the economic research questions we are thinking about. Almost everything has the potential to tell us something about how we should understand economics. However, I don't think the reverse applies: I don't think that everything in everyday life is amenable to economic analysis. We must be modest enough to concede that there is much more to life than economics.

One of the most celebrated examples of everyday life as part of a research technique is the following. Bronowski (1973, pp. 247ff.) describes Einstein's everyday journey by tram to the Swiss Patent Office in Bern, where he worked in the early twentieth century. Travelling on the tram, Einstein asked himself: 'What would the world look like if I rode on a beam of light?' Looking at a clock tower, he reasoned that if he rode away from the clock-face at the speed of light, then the time shown by the clock would stand still – and he would in effect be cut off from the passage of time.

Another celebrated example of everyday life as part of a research technique is the story of Archimedes. We all know that he ran through the streets, shouting 'Eureka', but sometimes forget why. When lowering himself into the bath, he saw by how much the level of the bath-water was raised, and this was the insight required to articulate his principle that a submerged object displaces an equal volume of water.

We have referred to the great econometric pioneer Ragnar Frisch at many points in this book. One of the less well-known facts about him was that he was a keen beekeeper. Some other academics I know are also keen on beekeeping, and they – following Mandeville (1723) – find in this a metaphor for the company, the economy or indeed society. However, let me make it plain that I do not recommend that the good applied economist needs to keep bees! Whatever one might learn from the pursuit, I myself am far too cowardly to start this hobby.

Even we lesser mortals can – and do – use everyday life as part of our research technique, and this should apply to economics just as to the physical science. I hesitate to use an example of my own to follow on from the previous three, but an excellent way to learn about industrial economics is to open up a personal computer and look at the origins of the components.[3] In this, we can find an illustration of the division of labour, globalisation, the life-cycle theory of trade and industrial clusters.

Several researchers have commented on how they find tourism an invaluable research technique. Partly, this is because we are looking at new places each with their own vernacular. Partly, it is because (with luck) we are at leisure when touring and have time to think. And partly, it is because we look at museums and other attractions that we would not have time to look at in a busy working week. Landes (1983, pp. xviii–xx) describes how his interest in the economic history of mechanical clocks stemmed from his explorations as a tourist and consumer. We have seen already (Chapter 16) that this is an economic history from which we can learn a great deal of economics. Indeed, it could be said that the clock was the most important machine of the industrial revolution. Marx noted that 'the whole theory of *production and regular motion* was developed through it' (his emphasis),[4] and Mumford (1934, p. 14) famously concluded that, 'the clock, not the steam-engine, is the key-machine of the modern industrial age'.

What we might call 'intellectual tourism' can also be a fertile ground for research ideas. In this approach, we take a tour around a related (or unrelated) field and see what we can find that may help us understand our own field. In a sense, this is just a search for metaphor: sometimes it is hazardous, for the reasons described in Chapter 20, but sometimes it can be hugely productive. Most famously, Darwin described how he read Malthus's book on population 'for leisure', and found in it all the necessary foundations of his theory of natural selection.

Another form of tourism, metaphorically speaking, is *surfing the net*. Some researchers treat this as a research technique in its own right (Jones, ed., 1999). It is not just a fast way to obtain access to a wide literature. By surfing the net we can find all kinds of interesting connections that have not, perhaps, been identified in earlier research. This is still an underdeveloped research technique.

Some find key economic insights in classic literature. Even if the greatest authors were not professional economists, it is quite common to find that from time to time they turned their acute powers of observation to economic matters, and when they did we can still learn much from them. Jackson (1996) gives many excellent examples of this. One of my favourite examples is the dialogue between Socrates and Critobulus, described in Xenophon's work, *The Economist*. Socrates starts by asking his companion Critobulus what he means by property, and whether it should include all a man's possessions. The unfortunate Critobulus paints himself further and further into a corner until Socrates concludes: 'Then the very same things are property to a man who knows how to use them, and not property to one who does not' (here quoted from Cook and Wedderburn, 1907, pp. 37–8).

Moving on from the classics, the committed – and perhaps I should say, obsessive – applied economist will find that much of the journalism we read or listen to on the radio fits into some economic framework. These tenacious journalists find out all kinds of things that we do not see – because they negotiate a quality of access to people, organisations and news stories that we cannot expect to match. We can learn from their observations, and by seeing how these illuminate or contradict our economic perspectives. Some journalists are also economists of distinction, and in their work find a very interesting perspective, containing the best of the journalist's and the economist's approach to understanding economics. Moreover, some leading business people have written fascinating books about their vision of how the economy works (for example, Barnard, 1942; Gates, 1999).

Benjamin Franklin described man as a tool-making animal. Moreover, we don't just take the tools about us and refine them, but we find and invent completely new tools. In the same way, we need to be innovative in our development of research tools and techniques. We must not doubt the capacity of an increasingly complex world to create phenomena which cannot be understood by conventional research tools. This is why, as Frisch said, we need to be forward-looking in our construction of research tools, and keep an essential miscellany of tools in our collection that can be used for unusual research problems.

NOTES

1. Another dynamic also leads to change in economic behaviour. This is a fundamental uncertainty principle in economics. When researchers carefully observe a phenomenon, the phenomenon may change as a consequence of the observation. A leading example of this in economics is Goodhart's Law of monetary aggregates: this asserts that when a monetary instrument is used for macroeconomic control, then it is no longer the appropriate instrument to control.
2. I note in passing that the analysis of fractals seems like a very promising way to analyse the increasing complexity of the research surface. To the extent that an ever increasing division of labour means that each active researcher must select an ever more specialised niche in which (s)he is competitive, then the complexity of the research surface becomes ever-more intricate. However, I have not attempted to develop the use of fractal geometry in this context.
3. In the same vein, Richard Whitley, the organisational sociologist, has told me that industrial economists would learn a lot if we spent more time visiting factories or companies – and I am sure he is right in that view.
4. Letter to Friedrich Engels, 1863, here quoted from Mumford (1967, p. 286).

PART V

The future in applied economics

22. Danger in the present trajectory

The division of intellectual labour has made us very clever, but it has not made us wise. Ernst Schumacher (1974, p. 26) argued that 'man is far too clever to be able to survive without wisdom'. In that case, the combination of cleverness and a lack of wisdom is a lethal cocktail. For our future peace and prosperity, we need to recover our wisdom – and spend less effort trying to be clever.

We can see this if we compare the economics of today with the economics of Adam Smith. In many ways, our economics of today is much cleverer than Smith's economics. We have theorems, numerical data, econometric methods of estimation and so on. But few if any economists today have Smith's wisdom. Few economists can work out how each and every part of the economy fits together to create an overall picture, and few understand how *everything relates to everything else*.[1]

Why has cleverness become the enemy of wisdom in academic work? The problem arises because while we use an intricate division of labour to increase our cleverness, we have lost the art of reassembling the fruits of this divided labour to create the complete picture that is needed for true wisdom. The division of labour increases our productivity – in research as elsewhere. But the greater the division of labour, the harder is this task of reassembly. Moreover, this reassembly requires healthy dialogue between adjacent fields and disciplines, but as discussed in earlier chapters, the quality of this dialogue between economics and adjacent fields has not kept up with the division of labour.

In the division of manufacturing labour, the manager takes great care to ensure that these discrete packages of labour are re-combined, so that a final product or service can be assembled and sold. Without that, the company cannot survive. This commercial re-combination of the fruits of divided labour may not be very harmonious, but it still happens, because it has to happen. In the world of intellectual labour, by contrast, such re-combination of divided labour is becoming ever more rare. A few polymaths manage to span several fields and disciplines. A few enlightened scholars travel around the intellectual world, and maintain a wide-reaching dialogue across many disciplines and fields. But these are the exceptions. In general, professional survival in the academic world demands that we maintain a fairly narrow disciplinary focus.

Ultimately, this non-dialogue between adjacent disciplines can become very dangerous. In the last chapter, I asserted some of the reasons why it is reasonable to assume that, in some respects at least, the world will continue to become more complex, and why the economic challenges that face us become ever more complex and multi-faceted. Politicians are increasingly aware that in a very complex and highly interconnected world, their actions can have unexpected side-effects some way away from the area where they have focused their attention. This is a familiar idea to students of chaos. We may prefer politicians who commit themselves to evidence-based policy, rather than whimsical policy. But academics can only follow through all the unexpected side-effects of a policy measure if we pull together the knowledge of many adjacent disciplines. But at the very time when complexity and interconnectedness are increasing, interdisciplinary dialogue becomes ever more difficult.

This is my interpretation of Schumacher's remarks. We know how to increase the cleverness of our disciplines, but have lost – and show no sign of recovering – the art of increasing our wisdom.

AN EXAMPLE OF THE DANGER

On 9 March 2004, the British Government gave permission for the first commercial planting of genetically modified (GM) crops in Britain. At the time, this was a controversial decision. In time it may turn out to be less controversial, either because we become less concerned about the possible risks, or because even though permission is given, little planting takes place because the economics does not stack up.

In announcing the decision to Parliament, the Minister for the Environment discussed the *scientific* case in favour and against (Hansard, 9 March 2004). But the Minister's statement made little reference to any other perspective on the case. Notably, apart from a brief mention of an inconclusive cost–benefit study by the Prime Minister's Strategy Unit, there is no reference to the *economic* or *social* case for or against.

Why is this? Is it really that this is a separable[2] scientific issue which can be considered in isolation from any economic and social issues? I doubt it very much! Alternatively, is it that the economics of the issue are very simple and clear cut? I doubt that too. After all, experience with the new high-yield varieties introduced in the Green Revolution showed that, however great the apparent scientific and agricultural advantages, there can be some highly adverse socio-economic effects – which scientists had not expected.

To make effective use of these new varieties, a farmer needed irrigated land, as well as the necessary energy inputs and fertiliser. Many small farmers did not have these pre-requisites. Larger farmers could afford these inputs, increasing productivity and reducing prices, which in turn impoverished (and in some cases bankrupted) small farmers. In short, the use of new varieties in the Green Revolution exacerbated problems of income inequality in ways that economists would readily understand, but which the scientists did not foresee. Similar issues, surely, arise in the context of GM crops, but such issues do not seem to have had much impact on government thinking.

In the government's mind, the decisive issues appear to have been *scientific*, and not social or economic. Why is this? In my view, this is exactly the sort of thing that happens when we fail to reassemble the intellectual division of labour. While language and standards within each discipline or sub-discipline are well developed, the interface between different disciplines (or even sub-disciplines) is not. Moreover, those who have tried to work at the interface find it a difficult environment. Faced with such difficulties, the government minister and civil servant conclude that it is just too difficult to take a holistic scientific and socio-economic view of such an issue, and instead, we must treat it as one or the other.

To my mind, this is regrettable. I have argued throughout this book that mainstream economics does not have much regard for vernacular economics – the economic ideas of non-professional economists. This low regard, the consequent poor quality of dialogue, and hence the intellectual isolation of economics have damaged our understanding, our standing and our credibility. But equally, some scientists are hard to please. If we economists 'dress up' our 'imprecise ideas' in formal scientific language, then this is met with some amusement. But if, instead, we talk informally about our discipline, in everyday language, then some scientists conclude that there is nothing much to our subject.

Depending on your perspective, GM crops offer a solution to famine, or GM crops are liable to exacerbate famine. Clever science has provided us with a very clever technology, but without wisdom we cannot tell which of these perspectives is the more reliable. Just as policy-makers are crying out for some wise advice, we can only offer cleverness, but not wisdom.[3]

NOTES

1. An idea often attributed to Lenin, but probably stated independently by many others.
2. The economic theory of separability is concerned with the conditions under which we can break a complex optimisation problem into several smaller problems, and achieve the same outcome by optimising each sub-problem on its own as we would have reached by solving all together.

3.   As we saw in Chapter 7, Ilich (1982, p. 74) describes Queen Isabella's wise response to
      the author of a new grammar of Castillian. In the same vein, Kohr (1982, p. xvi) describes
      the wise response of a Roman Emperor to the inventor of a mechanism to transport giant
      columns to the Capitol. The Emperor rewarded the inventor for his cleverness but
      dispensed with his services, remarking 'you must permit me also to let the man in the
      street earn his bread'.

23. Changing attitudes

The last chapter argued that cleverness is no substitute for wisdom in applied economics.   In his Foreword to Tinbergen's (1951) pioneering text on econometrics, Harold Somers (1951) noted that 'econometrics is no better than the econometrician'. No amount of cleverness in our econometrics will make up for a lack of wisdom in the applied economist. Frisch (1946, p. 4) made a similar observation, that it was easy to do more harm than good with econometrics, and therefore that only the most able people should be allowed to use econometric analysis.

Getting applied economics back on the right track is not about clever econometrics.   It is about trying to regain the wisdom of the pioneering economists.   To do that – and to avoid the dangers described in the last chapter – calls for a fundamental change in attitude.

In the earlier chapters of this book, I have described an approach to applied research which embodies this change in attitude. One aspect to this change in attitude is a different view of econometrics. We must accept that econometrics is not a universal solvent – and neither is any other technique. Good applied economics will always demand careful composition using a variety of techniques. Moreover, the point of using a plurality of techniques should not be just to seek an endorsement of what we find with our preferred method. It should be to illuminate different facets of each applied question, and to seek out different insights. We need to take a paradox-seeking attitude to research – a point we shall return to below.

A second aspect to this change in attitude is that we must take vernacular economics seriously, even if – indeed, especially if – it contradicts formal economics. We have to stop thinking of the vernacular as crude, anecdotal and unscientific. We need to think of it as local knowledge gained from wide experience, and which ordinary people often trust a great deal more than our sophisticated models.

BENEFITS FROM A CHANGE IN ATTITUDE

How will we benefit from this changed attitude to research? First, we can reduce the problems of restricted domain that we find at present. We have tended to seek out those research problems that can be solved using econometric methods, and tended to neglect those research problems that are not amenable to econometric analysis. This restricted domain is unfortunate. It doesn't do much good to our professional reputation if we select research questions according to whether or not they are soluble using a preferred technique and not according to their social and economic importance. I am aware, of course, of Medawar's (1982, p. 254) famous dictum that 'research is the art of the soluble'. Medawar's point was that we don't earn much credit from a brave but ultimately unsuccessful attempt to solve a research question. Credit goes to those who succeed in finding answers. But when Medawar advised us to focus on soluble problems, I don't think he meant that we should focus exclusively on those problems that are soluble with one privileged technique: his criterion was that they should be soluble *with some technique* – never mind which.

A second benefit from this change in attitude is that we stop trying to apply econometrics to problems for which it is not suited. When we do that, the results are usually disappointing. In fact, economic journals have been quite forgiving to the authors of such work, and do not apply the Medawar criterion very rigorously. As a result, quite a lot of the econometric results we find in journals – even the journals that are usually considered the top journals – are disappointing. I don't think this has helped our reputation outside our own discipline. If such results represent the cream of our work, then we can't be surprised that other disciplines may not give us the respect we would like.

A third benefit of the change in attitude is that we may rediscover the art of enhancing econometric work by using other techniques in combination. Chapter 6 showed that one serious problem in much applied econometrics (especially with complex multivariate models) was what we called the problem of the signal-to-noise ratio. But we also saw in Chapter 6 (and the appendix at the end of the book) that extraneous information from other applied research techniques can increase the signal-to-noise ratio, and thus improve the quality of econometric estimates.

A fourth benefit of the change in attitude has been discussed at length in Chapters 2 and 5. Our almost exclusive focus on one research technique has increased our isolation from other disciplines and from the vernacular economists who provide much of our data. When we take a different attitude to applied economic research, we can come out of this professional isolation.

A fifth benefit is that we start to think seriously about innovation in research techniques. This is essential if we are to respond to Frisch's advice (Chapter 21) that we should constantly be on the look out for new ways of addressing the research questions of tomorrow.

A sixth benefit of this change in attitude is that it reminds us just how multifaceted are the research problems we look at, and that we should not be surprised that different research techniques may give very different answers. And, indeed, we start to respond positively to contradictory evidence from other disciplines using other research techniques. Instead of ignoring it, on the grounds that it 'isn't really economics', we can start to learn from such contradictions. This is the paradox-seeking approach to research, which I turn to shortly.

Now I will not deny that it is a substantial challenge to harness different research techniques together to achieve a deeper understanding. More often than not, our first sensation when we try to mix different research strategies is one of confusion. Different techniques have different origins, and researchers in the different communities have relatively little contact with each other, and speak different 'languages'. It may not be immediately obvious how to connect different techniques together so that they help each other.

It is rather like the problem faced by a computer engineer charged with connecting together several different systems. Each system may work well on its own, but the engineer encounters severe difficulties in passing data from one system to another. Either the connection doesn't work, or else only a very little of the structure or richness in one system is passed through to the other. There are three approaches that the engineer may take. One is to give up and conclude that it is simply impossible to pass data adequately from one system to another. Each distinct system will have to progress in splendid isolation. This solution seems wasteful, but at least it shifts the effort away from trying to solve an apparently insoluble interface problem. The second is to try to persuade colleagues to take a long view and harmonise their systems. But this seems doomed to failure, because such an approach will incur very large switching costs. And even more serious, no one system will be satisfactory for all users. The third and most realistic solution recognises that there will always be a plurality of systems, but we need to develop partial (and ad hoc) gateways between these different systems.[1]

Which of these three generic approaches is right for applied economics? The first is not right: it reinforces the isolation between economics and neighbouring disciplines, and I have argued throughout the book that this is not good for us – or for them. The second is the 'universal solvent' approach, and we have said that it will not work. So, once again, the third approach is probably the right one in applied economics. We recognise that a plurality of techniques is desirable, and we seek to develop gateways between the different communities. These gateways will be imperfect: the qualitative researcher will see things in a case study that are lost to the econometrician, and equally, the econometrician will see things in test results that are beyond the ken of the qualitative researcher. Nevertheless, any gateway is better than none.

A PARADOX-SEEKING RESEARCH STRATEGY

We have argued above that a common reaction when we encounter contradictory evidence produced by other research techniques is to sweep it under the carpet. We do this, because we are accustomed to feeling embarrassed by evidence that contradicts our theories or our econometric results, and we don't really know what to do with it.

This is all wrong. We saw in Chapter 19 that paradoxes can be a powerful learning experience. To learn from a paradox, we must engage with it confidently but not stubbornly. If we stubbornly stick to our starting hypothesis regardless of paradoxical evidence, then we learn little or nothing. At the other extreme, if exposure to contradictory evidence makes us lose all confidence in our starting hypothesis, then we learn little either. The most constructive response to the paradox is to maintain some confidence in the original hypothesis, but accept that it is incomplete. We saw in Chapter 19 how to use the paradox to extend our mental models.

I will not pretend that this is an easy process. Of course, it is uncomfortable when evidence from another source contradicts our theories or cherished empirical findings. It takes some self-confidence to face up to a contradiction of one's theory. Moreover, the solution to the paradox may not be immediately apparent. For two reasons, it was rather easy for the learning computer of Chapter 19 to learn from the paradox. First, the computer did not suffer any loss of face from the shortcomings of its understanding. Second, the computer could consult the human expert, who would provide the necessary explanation. The resolution of research paradoxes is not so easy, and there is rarely an oracle who knows all the answers. But despite this, the principle is the same: paradoxes are useful because they show us shortcomings in our existing models, and if we can resolve the paradox then we can produce a more powerful model.

If the confident handling of the paradox is such a powerful learning experience, then the most confident researchers may decide that they wish to pursue a paradox-seeking research strategy. How is that to be achieved? A paradox-seeking research strategy will involve a considerable diversity of research approaches. Why should that be?

Consider Figure 23.1. The outer circle represents the set of phenomena (**P**) to which a particular theory, generalisation or intuition applies. For the most part, these phenomena behave as expected, and we describe this as a correspondence (**Y**) between expectation and actuality. But for a small sub-set of phenomena (identified by the oval set), the theory, generalisation or intuition does not apply. We describe this paradox as a non-correspondence (**N**) between expectation and actuality. The smaller circles within the diagram labelled *A* to *H* represent some of the different research methods available. In this representation, all of the techniques have limited scope, meaning that they can only shed light on some of the phenomena to which the theory, generalisation or intuition applies. And in this simple illustration, the techniques are non-overlapping, meaning that different techniques illuminate different phenomena. That is not essential, but keeps the diagram simple.

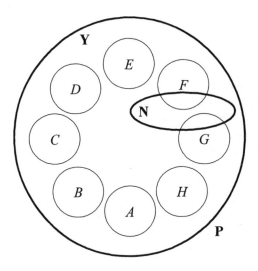

Figure 23.1   Paradox-seeking research strategy

We see immediately that only two of the technique sets (*F* and *G*) intersect with the negative set. Moreover, this intersection is incomplete in the sense that not all applications of techniques *F* and *G* will guarantee a paradox, and some parts of the negative set are outside the reach of any research method.

Suppose we do not know the location of the sub-set **N** within **P**. What is the best strategy to find it? Use of one technique only – even in an exhaustive way – is rather 'hit and miss'. We might be lucky and pick one of the techniques *F* or *G* that intersect with **N**. But if we pick one of the others, there is no chance of a paradox. A more reliable approach would be to iterate, to use each technique in turn (*A* to *H*) until a paradox is found. This will not necessarily happen automatically on the first use of technique *F* or *G*. Once a paradox is found using a particular technique, that technique can be repeated intensively, and some of these repetitions will generate other paradoxes.

CONCLUSION

To sum up, our attitude to research needs to change if we are to put applied economics back on the right track. We need to abandon the idea that econometrics, or any other technique, is a universal solvent for all applied research questions. We need to engage constructively with a plurality of techniques, and to take the vernacular seriously. We need to embrace the paradox as a route to enhancing our learning. We need to change all of these together, because the universal-solvent approach tends to encourage us to shun contradictions and paradoxes. If we take a more open attitude which recognises plurality of research techniques as a good thing, then we shall encounter many more paradoxes, and start to learn from these. We should try to reach a point where we can say: 'This evidence contradicts my earlier evidence: how interesting, I wonder why?' When we have reached this point of enlightenment, then we are well on the way to a proper understanding of applied economics.

To return to the wise words of Somers (1951), cited at the start of this chapter, econometrics cannot be better than the econometrician. The best way to develop what we get from econometrics is to broaden the education of the applied economist, to encompass the vernacular knowledge of ordinary people and the unfamiliar techniques and approaches of adjacent fields.

NOTES

1. This was Berners-Lee's approach to designing the World Wide Web. The beauty of this is that it works as a network despite the subtle differences between the different computers that it joins together. In the language of standardisation, it is a relatively unambitious standard which can be implemented on all (or almost all) computers.

24. How do we make the future happen?

In this book, I have sketched a very different approach to applied economic research than the one that is usually taught in graduate school. I believe that applied economists will do better applied research if they re-orientate their approach to research along the lines described above. But as I said in the last chapter, to adopt this research approach involves a substantial change in attitude, and at times it seems that no wise person could really expect to bring about such a change. As G.B. Shaw (1903, p. 238) said: 'The reasonable man adapts himself to the world: the unreasonable one persists in trying to adapt the world to himself. Therefore all progress depends on the unreasonable man'.

Is this book an unrealistic and utopian vision? In a way, the book is less of a utopian vision than the vision of the founding fathers of the Econometric Society.[1] Their vision was that an elegant combination of theory, maths, statistics and data could help to achieve Jevons's dream of a real empirical science of economics. My vision is a more eclectic and informal approach to research, pragmatic rather than elegant. But the basic question still remains: is my vision ever going to become reality?

THE STATUS QUO AS AN OPTIMUM?

The mainstream reader might respond by saying that my vision should not become reality because it is mistaken. The curriculum for training applied economists has been shaped by many great minds with huge experience in applied economic research, and what we have now is some kind of optimum – taking into account the needs of a wide range of research areas. The mainstream reader might concede that classroom training is a bit narrow, but in practice, good applied economists pick up what they need of these alternative research techniques as they go along.

From my point of view, this sort of argument just doesn't work. The present mainstream curriculum for the training of applied economists is nowhere near an optimum. It is far too 'hit and miss' to expect young researchers to pick up all the additional techniques they need without giving these a proper place in the curriculum.

IS THERE LOCK-IN?

If the research approach described here is indeed better, and is a long distance from the orthodox approach, then we must ask: why has the mainstream settled on a sub-optimal solution?

A natural response is the idea of lock-in. As we saw in Chapter 14, the literature on standards (following David, 1985) argues that we may get locked into sub-optimal solutions when product competition exhibits three special characteristics: network effects, coordination costs and switching costs.

Suppose that we are currently using a particular computer system A, but it would be better that we switch to a new system B which will perform better. If network effects are important, however, then we want to use the same system as everyone else, and if they continue to use A, then so will we. But what if it would be better for everyone else to switch from A to B? Surely then it is worthwhile for all to switch? Maybe, but if coordination costs are high, then it may be very difficult to manage an orderly transition. Any one person will only switch if confident that all others will switch, but nobody believes that this coordination will work seamlessly. Accordingly, no one switches. Finally, the longer we use a particular system A, the higher the switching costs in moving to B.

Most models of standards races tend to find that, with these characteristics, a single standard will emerge. Much of the literature suggests that we can experience lock-in to a sub-optimal standard. By contrast, the work of Liebowitz and Margolis (1990) argues that lock-in is rarely if ever found. They argue that the status quo is an optimum.

So is the dominance of econometrics as the primary – and too often, exclusive – tool of applied economics an example of lock-in? The mainstream response might be that econometrics is the best technique, and this is not a lock-in but an optimum. The unorthodox response would be that this surely is a lock-in. It is interesting to follow the changing attitude of Ragnar Frisch on this question. In the 1930s he was an enthusiastic pioneer of econometrics, believing it to be superior to any existing tools. But by the 1950s, Frisch was starting to talk of something very like a lock-in to econometrics (Frisch, 1956, p. 300): 'for good or evil it has come to stay'. In my view there is a lock-in and we need to understand why it has arisen.

WHY IS THERE LOCK-IN?

In my view, network effects play a very important part in this lock-in to econometrics as the dominant technique of applied economics. Our success as academic economists depends in the main on peer review. We are encouraged to clock up citations. We succeed if our work is published in what are generally reckoned to be the best journals and if other successful people cite our work. The best journals are edited and refereed by people who have achieved success by orthodox standards. The probability that unconventional work will find its way into the best journals is small, and equally, such unorthodox work is unlikely to be cited by the mainstream. In short, our work is more likely to be regarded and cited if it relates to a field where influential people are currently active. By contrast, if our work is idiosyncratic, then it is unlikely to be widely cited. All of this produces considerable pressure to conform. Whether we like it or not, we are constrained to devote considerable energy to publication in leading journals, because these brand names are the currency of professional recognition.

These network effects contribute to the lock-in. Many unorthodox economists feel obliged to use a conventional research technique more often than they wish, not because it is the best, but because it is essential for professional survival to be seen using that technique.

To what extent do switching costs contribute to the lock-in? By way of answer, I would refer the reader once again to the remarks of Morishima (1984) cited in Chapter 5. The leaders of the mainstream have invested heavily in conventional intellectual capital, and are quite understandably reluctant to switch to a different ball game where they have little accumulated capital. They have much to gain from the persistence of the lock-in, and much to lose from a wholesale switch to another paradigm.

Finally, to what extent do coordination costs contribute to the lock-in? In general, it seems that the mainstream of any discipline faces much lower coordination costs than the unorthodox parts of that discipline. Partly, this is because the mainstream tends to control the most influential journals, professional societies and associations, while unorthodox researchers do not. Second, unorthodox researchers tend to have higher communication costs because they tend to be fragmented into different factions. However, we should not underestimate the power of the Internet in bringing together such fragmented unorthodox factions.[2]

CAN WE BREAK AWAY FROM THE LOCK-IN?

The literature on standards races suggests various features that may lead the market to break away from lock-in to one standard, and to switch over to another standard. It is instructive to see which, if any, of these is relevant here.

New cohort?

One such possibility arises when we have different cohorts in the network. The existing network effects apply to existing network users, but a new cohort may pay little attention to the form of the network amongst existing members, but consider instead only the form of the network in their own new cohort. A standard may be the particular choice of existing cohorts, but a new cohort can break away from that and adopt a different standard.

This, however, is unlikely to help us break away from lock-in in this particular case. As the training programmes of graduate schools become ever more orthodox, so the new cohort of young researchers is even more orthodox than their predecessors. Like Blaug (2001), I regret the passing of history of economic thought from most graduate programmes in economics. If that is true of the history of thought, then what chance is there for an unorthodox approach to applied economics? Indeed, the careful management of orthodoxy in the graduate school reminds me of Ruskin's assertion about the role of the academy in constraining the work of the great artist, J.M.W. Turner (Ruskin, 1904a, p. 389): 'The Academy . . . carefully repressed his perceptions of truth, his capacities of invention, and his tendencies of choice'.

Moreover, there is a life-cycle effect at work here. Hutchinson (1977, p. 164, n. 20) described how young researchers show 'optimistic youthful enthusiasm' for the latest technical work, but the older researchers show a certain scepticism, 'which may even swing too far the other way'. For this reason, the change to the econometric programme was easier than the change back to a pluralistic research programme will be. In the econometric revolution, enthusiastic young economists were displacing the tired older generation. To change back, it will have to be the older generation who displace the younger generation, and that seems more problematic.

I should add, however, that in business schools – as opposed to economics departments – it may be easier to change back to the pluralistic programme. Not only are the economists in business schools more heterodox – see below – but we find students who have actively moved away from conventional economics to business studies, because they do not like the approach taken in mainstream economics. However, most students of industrial economics in business schools are destined for careers outside academic economics. And those who proceed to graduate studies within a business school are unlikely to follow careers in departments of economics, because the latter rarely recruit staff from business schools. As a result, there is little chance of any cross-fertilisation this way.

Confident subcultures

The model of the standards race also suggests that minority standards may sometimes survive in self-contained communities or subcultures. Loosely speaking, this is one reason why the PC standard has never driven out the Apple Mac: there is a hard core of Apple users, fiercely loyal to their network, who would never switch to the PC format.

This argument works up to a point in the present context. There are various groups of economists in exile in other sorts of academic department. The group I know best is the community of economists in the business schools. But there are other groups in schools of public policy, multidisciplinary research centres (in innovation, for example) and engineering schools. Can these communities, at least, break the lock-in to econometrics described above? My sense is, 'yes', there is some scope for business school economists to break the rules of the mainstream, and indeed some necessity.

Broader definitions of network effects

The previous paragraph was about the possibility that subcultures (where network effects are defined over a smaller social network) might support diverse standards. But equally, we may find that a broader definition of the network can help us break away from lock-in. If the network is defined as 'applied economics' then the strongest network effects accrue to those who conform to mainstream conventions. But if the network is broadened to 'social sciences', then the network effects may be greatest for the interdisciplinary travellers whose work is recognised across disciplinary boundaries. We could observe a similar phenomenon if we broaden the concept of research network to include business and policy users of research, and other vernacular economists.

Sponsorship

A fourth way that we can break away from lock-in within the model of the standards race is if external agencies 'sponsor' a new and superior standard. This does happen to some extent within the social sciences. As noted above (in Chapter 19), government and business are generally more concerned about the credibility of research results than their methodological orthodoxy. Moreover, in deciding what sort of research they want, these sponsors are not unduly concerned about network effects amongst academics – except to the extent that academic orthodoxy is a useful counter-weight to political pressures to stay 'on message'. Government and industry will sometimes fund research that breaks some of the mainstream academic conventions. From time to time, the research councils have also sought to sponsor promising but as yet unconventional research approaches.

There is an idea in the creativity literature that sponsored research is less likely to be creative than traditional peer-oriented research. But, in this context, I believe the balance is the other way. Research sponsored from outside the academic world can sometimes achieve greater creativity because academics have greater liberty to ignore the academic network effects.

Customers more concerned with intrinsics than network effects

A related idea in some models of the standards race is that lock-in is less likely when users are more concerned about intrinsic characteristics of products than network effects. Taken to its logical limit, if there are no network effects then lock-in is much less likely. Here again, we note a distinction between the preferences of the academic sponsor of research and the non-academic sponsor of research. The former gives more attention to academic network effects than the latter.

Risk in the unconventional?

Finally, an important factor in lock-in is the idea that switching is risky when we are unclear about the switching intentions of others in our network. The words of G.B. Shaw at the start of this chapter capture this very well. So also did Machiavelli (1513/1908, Chapter 15) in his advice to the Prince: 'He who neglects what is done for what ought to be done, sooner effects his ruin than his preservation'. There is no doubt that switching to an unorthodox approach to applied economics involves career risk. Should we really advise young researchers to take such risks?

AN INCOMPLETE STORY

This is an incomplete story. I don't know when we can free applied economics from this lock-in. If economists of the stature of Frisch and Leontief could not end this lock-in, then who can hope to? However, I believe that at some point we will escape the lock-in.

I conclude with two observations by Keynes (1936), which come respectively from the beginning and the end of his *General Theory*. At first he describes the difficulty of getting a discipline to change direction: 'The difficulty lies, not in the new ideas, but in escaping from the old ones' (Keynes, 1936, p. viii). But at the end of the book he strikes a more optimistic tone: 'Soon or late, it is ideas, not vested interests, which are dangerous for good or evil' (Keynes, 1936, pp. 383–4). This latter observation leaves me optimistic that in the future we shall develop a healthier approach to applied economics, in which vernacular and formal work hand in hand.

NOTES

1. Indeed, Frisch (1981) himself talks of the Econometric Society vision as a 'Utopian theory'.
2. The website http://www.paecon.net/ is a striking example.

25. Conclusion

In the Preface, I said that my main objectives were these. I wanted to persuade economists to take vernacular economics seriously, and to explain what we gain from doing that. I wanted to show that it was perfectly natural to expect economic agents to have their own models of how the world works, and that we could learn much from these. And I said that a different attitude to economic research was essential if we were to achieve a proper re-combination of divided intellectual labour.

In the Introduction, I said that my aim was to move away from the current orthodoxy where applied economics means (essentially) applied econometrics. Instead, I described an attitude to applied research where plurality is centre stage and the vernacular plays a prominent role. Four major arguments for this were that: (1) economics has no monopoly of wisdom about the economy; (2) econometrics is not a universal technique; (3) the reliance on one technique limits essential dialogue, and leads to intellectual isolation; (4) the applied economist's desk should contain many more activities than applied econometrics.

The approach to research described here is one in which we embrace a plurality of techniques, not simply to show that other techniques endorse the findings of one preferred technique, but so that we can appreciate the multi-faceted character of most applied economic research questions, and so that we start to learn from paradoxes.

We saw that the vernacular is much more than crude anecdote, but can be quite a rich source of empirical information. We have seen that we can learn very different things from using a variety of techniques. We have argued that the right attitude is to enjoy this diversity rather than try to 'bend' different techniques towards our preferred technique.

We argued that the present trajectory of applied economics is in danger of putting cleverness in conflict with wisdom. The new approach to applied economics described in this book is about getting cleverness and wisdom to pull in the same direction. I have suggested that this approach requires a new attitude to applied economics, but that to some degree we are locked into our present research trajectory, and it is not easy to break this lock-in.

I said in the Preface and Introduction that my overriding objective was to describe a new direction in applied economics: a pluralistic and vernacular approach to economics. I argued that the mainstream economist's preoccupation with econometrics has become a major obstacle in the path of this new direction, and that is why *putting econometrics in its place* is so essential. Some readers may think I have been unduly critical of econometrics, but I don't think I have.

Econometrics has become a dominant technique, and in the name of econometrics many older research methods have been driven into disuse. Some econometricians have been very dismissive about these 'obsolete' methods, so econometrics has to be prepared to receive some criticism in return. The complaint against econometrics is about what it has driven out rather than what it does. As we said before, these are sins of omission rather than sins of commission. If the status of econometrics were just one tool amongst many, which we used in those cases where it is suitable, then there would be little need to criticise it. But the situation is different. Economics has treated econometrics as a universal technique which makes other techniques redundant. It is this attitude that provokes my criticism and my insistence on a new direction. As Frederick the Great observed, 'You can't make an omelette without breaking eggs'.[1]

Shortly after completing the first full draft of this book, I re-read some of Babbage's (1835) painstaking work gathering data on the economy of machinery and manufactures. Until its rediscovery by Rosenberg, this work was ignored by almost all economists, apart from Mill and Marx. In his research, Babbage spent a lot of time talking to manufacturers and other business people – the vernacular economists of my book. The research approach taken by Babbage died many years ago, and forms no part of the education of the modern economist. And yet, there are very few works that tell us so much about the empirical microeconomics of production and innovation. It is a great pity that the formal revolution in economics has driven out that sort of study. I hope that the present book may encourage a new generation of economists to rediscover such approaches to research, and just how much we have to learn from them.

NOTES

1.   Here quoted from Lynn and Jay (1983, p. 99).

Appendix

This appendix describes the mathematics of the signal-to-noise ratio, and collects the results cited in Chapter 6.

RESULT 1: MEASUREMENT ERROR BIAS

Assume an underlying bivariate regression model with two normalised variables (y and x), with zero means, and a disturbance term u:

$$y = bx + u \qquad \text{(A.1)}$$

But x cannot be measured exactly, only with error:

$$\tilde{x} = x + v \qquad \text{(A.2)}$$

where v is random error (or noise). The usual ordinary least squares (OLS) estimator using the measured (rather than the true) values of x can be written:

$$\hat{b} = \frac{\hat{\sigma}_{\tilde{x}y}}{\hat{\sigma}_{\tilde{x}\tilde{x}}} \qquad \text{(A.3)}$$

where $\sigma_{\tilde{x}y}$ is a sample covariance, and $\sigma_{\tilde{x}\tilde{x}}$ is the sample variance of the *measured* signal. If the noise v is independent of u, x and y, then:

$$\sigma_{\tilde{x}y} = \sigma_{xy} \qquad \text{(A.4)}$$

$$\sigma_{\tilde{x}\tilde{x}} = \sigma_{xx} + \sigma_{vv} \qquad \text{(A.5)}$$

and the probability limit of $\hat{b}$ can be written:

$$\text{plim } \hat{b} = \frac{\sigma_{xy}}{\sigma_{xx} + \sigma_{vv}} = \frac{\sigma_{xy}}{\sigma_{vv}} \cdot \frac{1}{1 + \sigma_{vv}/\sigma_{xx}} = \frac{b}{1 + \sigma_{vv}/\sigma_{xx}} \quad \text{(A.6)}$$

where σ_{xy} is the population covariance of x and y, σ_{xx} is the population variance of x, and σ_{vv} is the population variance of the noise (or measurement error). The extent of the bias can therefore be described as follows:

$$\frac{\text{plim } \hat{b}}{b} = \frac{1}{1 + \sigma_{vv}/\sigma_{xx}} = \frac{1}{1 + \dfrac{1}{\sigma_{xx}/\sigma_{vv}}} \quad \text{(A.7)}$$

where σ_{xx}/σ_{vv} is the true population signal-to-noise ratio.

RESULT 2:   TWO EXPLANATORY VARIABLES

For simplicity, we present the case of two explanatory variables. Assume an underlying regression model with three normalised variables (y, x and z), with zero means:

$$y = xb + zc + u \quad \text{(A.8)}$$

where x is measured with error as in equation (A.2) while the other explanatory variable (z) is measured accurately.

Using the Frisch–Waugh theorem (1933), the usual OLS estimator for b, using the measured values (rather than the true values) of x, can be written:

$$\hat{b} = \frac{\hat{\sigma}_{\tilde{x}y.z}}{\hat{\sigma}_{\tilde{x}\tilde{x}.z}} \quad \text{(A.9)}$$

where $\hat{\sigma}_{\tilde{x}y.z}$ is the (sample) partial covariance of $\tilde{x}$ and y, independent of z; and $\hat{\sigma}_{\tilde{x}\tilde{x}.z}$ is the (sample) partial variance of $\tilde{x}$, independent of z.

What is the interpretation of these partial variances and covariances? The partial variance in x is a measure of the signal in x which is unrelated to variations in z. More precisely:

$$\sigma_{\tilde{x}\tilde{x}.z} = \sigma_{\tilde{x}\tilde{x}}\left(1 - R^2_{\tilde{x}.z}\right) \quad \text{(A.10)}$$

where $R^2_{\tilde{x}.z}$ is the *R*-squared from a regression of $\tilde{x}$ on *z*. Clearly, if $\tilde{x}$ and *z* are unrelated, then this *R*-squared is approximately 0, and in that case the partial variance is roughly equal to the full variance. But if $\tilde{x}$ and *z* are very closely related, so that this *R*-squared is nearly 1, then the partial variance of $\tilde{x}$ is much less than the full variance. (The partial covariance is defined in an analogous way.)

Assuming that the noise *v* is independent of *u*, *x* and *y*, then:

$$\sigma_{\tilde{x}y.z} = \sigma_{xy.z} \tag{A.11}$$

$$\sigma_{\tilde{x}\tilde{x}.z} = \sigma_{xx.z} + \sigma_{vv} \tag{A.12}$$

and the probability limit of $\hat{b}$ can be written:

$$\text{plim}\,\hat{b} = \frac{\sigma_{xy.z}}{\sigma_{xx.z} + \sigma_{vv}} = \frac{b}{1 + \sigma_{vv}/\sigma_{xx.z}} \tag{A.13}$$

where σ_{xy} is the (population) partial covariance of *x* and *y*, independent of *z*; $\sigma_{xx.z}$ is the (population) partial variance of *x*, independent of *z*; and σ_{vv} is the (population) variance of the noise. The extent of the bias can therefore described as follows:

$$\frac{\text{plim}\,\hat{b}}{b} = \frac{1}{1 + \sigma_{vv}/\sigma_{xx.z}} = \frac{1}{1 + \dfrac{1}{\sigma_{xx.z}/\sigma_{vv}}} \tag{A.14}$$

where $\sigma_{xx.z}/\sigma_{vv}$ is the true (population) partial signal-to-noise ratio. The interpretation of this result is similar to the interpretation of equation (A.7), except that here the relevant signal-to-noise ratio is the *partial* signal-to-noise ratio.

RESULT 3: MANY EXPLANATORY VARIABLES

Result 2 easily generalises to the case of an arbitrary number of explanatory variables (*k*) – so long as only one of these variables (*x*) is measured with error, and all the $k - 1$ others (**Z**) are measured accurately. The steps of the proof are just the same as in Result 2, except that the single variable *z* is replaced by a vector **Z** of dimension $k - 1$.

The basic character of the result is the same as equation (A.14), but the partial signal in x is liable to be smaller in this case. That is because the R-squared in equation (A.10) refers to a regression of x on *all* the $(k - 1)$ explanatory variables in **Z**. This R-squared is liable to be higher than the R-squared from a regression of x on one variable (z).

RESULT 4: CRITICAL LEVELS

It is common to say that a variable x is accurate to $\pm p$ per cent. This band is often interpreted as a 95 per cent confidence interval for the real value of x. If σ_{vv} is the variance of the noise in the measured value of x, then this 95 per cent confidence interval for the true value of x is given by (Swann, 1985a):

$$p = \begin{cases} \dfrac{2\sqrt{\sigma_{vv}}}{\bar{x}} & \text{when x is in levels} \\ \\ 2\sqrt{\sigma_{vv}} & \text{when x is in logs} \end{cases} \qquad (A.15)$$

where $\bar{x}$ is the mean value of $\tilde{x}$. Here we are using the rule of thumb convention that a 95 per cent confidence interval is plus or minus two standard deviations.

The 'Critical Level of Measurement Error' (CLME) is the level of noise that would drive the true (partial) signal-to-noise ratio towards 0. In this case, the measured partial signal is all noise. Using equation (A.12), it is clear that this is:

$$\sigma_{vv} = \sigma_{\tilde{x}\tilde{x}.z} \qquad (A.16)$$

This would mean that the measured value $\tilde{x}$ is accurate to $\pm p$ per cent, where:

$$p = \begin{cases} \dfrac{2\sqrt{\sigma_{\tilde{x}\tilde{x}.z}}}{\bar{x}} & \text{when } \tilde{x} \text{ and x are in levels} \\ \\ 2\sqrt{\sigma_{\tilde{x}\tilde{x}.z}} & \text{when } \tilde{x} \text{ and x are in logs} \end{cases} \qquad (A.17)$$

The 'Half-critical Level of Measurement Error' (HCLME) is the level of noise that would drive the true (partial) signal-to-noise ratio towards 1. In this case, the measured signal is half true and half noise. Using equation (A.12), it is clear that this is:

$$\sigma_{vv} = \frac{\sigma_{\tilde{x}\tilde{x}}}{2} \tag{A.18}$$

This would mean that the measured value $\tilde{x}$ is accurate to $\pm p$ per cent, where:

$$p = \begin{cases} \dfrac{\sqrt{2\sigma_{\tilde{x}\tilde{x}.z}}}{\overline{x}} & \text{when } x \text{ is in levels} \\[3mm] \sqrt{2\sigma_{\tilde{x}\tilde{x}.z}} & \text{when } x \text{ is in logs} \end{cases} \tag{A.19}$$

RESULT 5:   GINI RANGE AND CONFIDENCE INTERVAL

Consider the model defined in Result 1. (We can also generalise the result to the models defined in Results 2 and 3.) As described in Chapter 6, the Gini range is:

$$\left\{ \hat{b}, \frac{1}{\hat{c}} \right\} \tag{A.20}$$

where:

$$\hat{b} = \frac{\hat{\sigma}_{\tilde{x}y}}{\hat{\sigma}_{\tilde{x}\tilde{x}}} \tag{A.21}$$

$$\hat{c} = \frac{\hat{\sigma}_{\tilde{x}y}}{\hat{\sigma}_{yy}} \tag{A.22}$$

are, respectively, the parameter estimates from a regression of y on $\tilde{x}$ and a regression of $\tilde{x}$ on y. As described in Chapter 6, this Gini range is a measure of our uncertainty about the value of b due to our uncertainty about the character of errors in our equation.

Appendix

This Gini range is conceptually quite distinct from the standard confidence interval due to sampling uncertainty. However, Swann (1985b) showed that the width of this Gini range could easily be compared to the width of the standard 95 per cent confidence interval describing the sampling uncertainty in a regression estimate.

For the simple regression model in Result 1, the confidence interval is defined by (again using the same rule of thumb convention as in Result 4):

$$\left\{ \hat{b} - 2se(\hat{b}), b + 2se(\hat{b}) \right\} \tag{A.23}$$

The width of this confidence interval is simply:

$$CI = 4se(\hat{b}) \tag{A.24}$$

The width of the Gini range is given by:

$$GR = \frac{\hat{\sigma}_{yy}}{\hat{\sigma}_{\tilde{x}y}} - \frac{\hat{\sigma}_{\tilde{x}y}}{\hat{\sigma}_{\tilde{x}\tilde{x}}} = \frac{\hat{\sigma}_{yy} - \hat{\sigma}_{\tilde{x}y}\hat{\sigma}_{\tilde{x}\tilde{x}}^{-1}\hat{\sigma}_{\tilde{x}y}}{\hat{\sigma}_{\tilde{x}y}} \tag{A.25}$$

Note also that:

$$var(\hat{b}) = \frac{\hat{\sigma}_{yy} - \hat{\sigma}_{\tilde{x}y}\hat{\sigma}_{\tilde{x}\tilde{x}}^{-1}\hat{\sigma}_{\tilde{x}y}}{(T-k)\hat{\sigma}_{\tilde{x}\tilde{x}}} \tag{A.26}$$

where $T - k$ defines the number of degrees of freedom in the regression. (In the simple model of Result 1, $k = 1$.) Note that the numerator of the right-hand side in equations (A.25) and (A.26) are the same, so these two equations can be solved to obtain the following expression for the width of the Gini range:

$$GR = \frac{(T-k)\hat{\sigma}_{\tilde{x}\tilde{x}} var(\hat{b})}{\hat{\sigma}_{\tilde{x}y}} = \frac{(T-k) var(\hat{b})}{\hat{b}} \tag{A.27}$$

And we solve equations (A.24) and (A.27) to obtain the following:

$$\frac{GR}{CI} = \frac{(T-k) var(\hat{b})}{4se(\hat{b})\hat{b}} = \frac{(T-k)se(\hat{b})}{4\hat{b}} = \frac{(T-k)}{4t} \tag{A.28}$$

where t is the conventional t-statistic for the null hypothesis that $b = 0$. From equation (A.28), we can conclude:

$$
\begin{array}{ll}
\text{If } t < (T-k)/4 \text{ then } GR > CI \\
\text{If } t = (T-k)/4 \text{ then } GR = CI \\
\text{If } t > (T-k)/4 \text{ then } GR < CI
\end{array}
\qquad \text{(A.29)}
$$

RESULT 6: VALID RESTRICTIONS

Suppose we have a general multivariate model:

$$
y = \mathbf{X}\beta + u \qquad \text{(A.30)}
$$

where $\mathbf{X}$ is of dimension k. Suppose also that we have extraneous information (perhaps from another research technique) which suggests the following relationships between the parameters:

$$
r = \mathbf{R}\beta \qquad \text{(A.31)}
$$

where r and $\mathbf{R}$ are both known. Restricted least squares can use this extra information to provide a more efficient estimator. Let us denote this restricted least squares estimator by β^*, while the ordinary least squares estimator is denoted by $\hat{\beta}$.

An elegant theorem due to Goldberger (1964, pp. 256–7) proves that:

$$
\text{var}(\beta^*) = \text{var}(\hat{\beta}) - \mathbf{C} \qquad \text{(A.32)}
$$

where $\mathbf{C}$ is a positive semi-definite matrix. In short, the variance of the restricted least squares estimator of any parameter is less than or equal to the variance of the ordinary least squares estimator.

Now, by using the generalised Frisch–Waugh Theorem (Stone, 1970), we can show the following relationship for the variance of a specific element of $\hat{\beta}$, say $\hat{\beta}_1$:

$$
\text{var}(\hat{\beta}_1) = \frac{\sigma_{uu}}{(T-k)\sigma_{11.(2\ldots k)}} \qquad \text{(A.33)}
$$

where $\sigma_{11.(2\ldots k)}$ is the partial variance in variable 1, independent of variables $2\ldots k$. In short, the variance of a particular parameter ($\hat{\beta}_1$) is inversely proportional to the partial variance in the corresponding variable (1).

This means that the use of restrictions and restricted least squares can reduce the variance of a particular parameter estimate, by increasing the partial variance of the corresponding variable. A corollary follows from this. If restrictions increase the partial variance of a variable in a particular regression, then they will also increase the signal-to-noise ratio for that variable.

References

Abra, J. and G. Abra (1999), 'Collaboration and Competition', in M.A. Runco and S.R. Pritzker (eds), *Encyclopedia of Creativity: Volume 1*, San Diego, US: Academic Press, pp. 283–94

Adelman, I. (1988), 'Simulation Models', in J. Eatwell, M. Millgate and P. Newman (eds), *The New Palgrave: A Dictionary of Economics*, London: Macmillan, pp. 340–42

Adelman, I. and F.L. Adelman (1959), 'The Dynamic Properties of the Klein–Goldberger Model', *Econometrica*, **27**, 596–625

Alchian, A.A. (1950), 'Uncertainty, Evolution, and Economic Theory', *Journal of Political Economy*, **58**, 211–21

Alchian, A.A. (1953), 'Biological Analogies in the Theory of the Firm: Comment', *American Economic Review*, **43**, 600–603

Aldridge, A. and K. Levine (2001), *Surveying the Social World*, Buckingham: Open University Press

Amman, H.M., D.A. Kendrick and J. Rust (eds) (1996), *Handbook of Computational Economics: Volume 1*, Amsterdam: Elsevier

Arthur, W.B. (1989), 'Competing Technologies, Increasing Returns, and Lock-In by Historical Events', *Economic Journal*, **99**, 116–31

Ashcraft, M.H. (1989), *Human Memory and Cognition*, Glenview, US: Scott, Foresman and Company

Babbage, C. (1835), *On the Economy of Machinery and Manufactures*, 4th edition, London: Charles Knight

Barber, W.J. (1997), 'Reconfigurations in America's Academic Economics: A General Practitioner's Perspective', *Daedalus*, **126** (1), 87–103

Barnard, C. (1942), *The Functions of the Executive*, Cambridge, US: Harvard University Press

Barten, A.P. (1964), 'Consumer Demand Functions under Conditions of almost Additive Preferences', *Econometrica*, **32**, 1–38

Barten, A.P. (1969), 'Maximum Likelihood Estimation of a Complete System of Demand Equations', *European Economic Review*, **1**, 7–73

Becker, G.S. (1996), *Accounting for Tastes*, Cambridge, US: Harvard University Press

Berg, J. and H. Schumny (eds) (1990), *An Analysis of the IT Standardisation Process*, Amsterdam: North-Holland

Binmore, K. and P. Klemperer (2002), 'The Biggest Auction Ever: The Sale of the British 3G Telecom Licences', *Economic Journal*, **112**, C74–C96

Birke, D. and G.M.P. Swann (2005), 'Social Networks and Choice of Mobile Phone Operator', *Industrial Economics Division Occasional Paper*, No. 2005–14, Nottingham, UK: Nottingham University Business School

Blaug, M. (1992), *The Methodology of Economics: Or How Economists Explain*, 2nd Edition, Cambridge, UK: Cambridge University Press

Blaug, M. (2001), 'No History of Ideas, Please, We're Economists', *Journal of Economic Perspectives*, **15** (1), 145–64

Bonini, C.P. (1963), *Simulation of Information and Decision Systems in the Firm*, Englewood Cliffs, US: Prentice-Hall

Boulding, K. (1970), *Economics as a Science*, New York: McGraw-Hill

Boulding, K. (1971), 'After Samuelson, Who Needs Adam Smith?', *History of Political Economy*, **3** (2), 225–37

Bronowski, J. (1973), *The Ascent of Man*, London: BBC Publications

Brunak, S. and B. Lautrup (1990), *Neural Networks: Computers with Intuition*, Singapore and London: World Scientific

Burns, P. (1985), 'Experience and Decision Making: A Comparison of Students and Businessmen in a Simulated Progressive Auction', in V.L. Smith (ed.), *Research in Experimental Economics: Volume 3*, Greenwich, US: JAI Press, pp. 139–57

Cairncross, F. (1997), *The Death of Distance*, Boston, US: Harvard Business School Press

Carey, J. (ed.) (1999), *The Faber Book of Utopias*, London: Faber and Faber

Cargill, C.F. (1989), *Information Technology Standardisation: Theory, Process and Organisations*, Bedford, US: Digital Press

Catchpole, C.K. (1980), 'Sexual Selection and the Evolution of Complex Songs among European Warblers of the Genus *Acrocephalus*', *Behaviour*, **74**, 149–66

Chenery, H. (1953), 'Process and Production Functions from Engineering Data', in W. Leontief (ed.), *Studies in the Structure of the American Economy: Theoretical and Empirical Explorations in Input–Output Analysis*, New York: Oxford University Press, pp. 297–325

Christensen, L.R., D.W. Jorgenson and L.J. Lau (1975), 'Transcendental Logarithmic Utility Functions', *American Economic Review*, **65**, 367–83

Cipolla, C. (1967), *Clocks and Culture: 1300–1700*, London: William Collins and Sons

Cook, E.T. and A. Wedderburn (1907), 'The Economist of Xenophon', in E.T. Cook and A. Wedderburn (eds), *The Works of John Ruskin: Volume 31*, London: George Allen, pp. 33–93

Cyert, R.M. and J.G. March (1963), *A Behavioural Theory of the Firm*, Englewood Cliffs, US: Prentice-Hall

Dalby, A. (1998), *Dictionary of Languages*, London: Bloomsbury

Darnell, A. and J.L. Evans (1990), *The Limits of Econometrics*, Cheltenham, UK and Brookfield, US: Edward Elgar

Dasgupta, P. (2002), 'Modern Economics and its Critics', in U. Maki (ed.), *Fact and Fiction in Economics: Models, Realism and Social Construction*, Cambridge, UK: Cambridge University Press, pp. 57–89

Dasgupta, P. and P.A. David (1994), 'Toward a New Economics of Science', *Research Policy*, **23** (5), 487–521

David, P.A. (1985), 'Clio and the Economics of QWERTY', *American Economic Review*, **75** (2), 332–6

David, P.A. and S.M. Greenstein (1990), 'The Economics of Compatibility Standards: An Introduction to Recent Research', *Economics of Innovation and New Technology*, **1** (1/2), 3–41

Davis, D.D. and C.A. Holt (1993), *Experimental Economics*, Princeton, US: Princeton University Press

Deane, P. (1965), *The First Industrial Revolution*, Cambridge, UK: Cambridge University Press

Deaton, A.S. (1987), 'Consumers' Expenditure', in J. Eatwell, M. Millgate and P. Newman (eds), *The New Palgrave: A Dictionary of Economics*, London: Macmillan, pp. 592–607

Deaton, A.S. and J. Muellbauer (1980), 'An Almost Ideal Demand System', *American Economic Review*, **70**, 312–26

De Wilde, P. (1997), *Neural Network Models*, 2nd edition, Berlin: Springer-Verlag

Dogan, M. (1994), 'Fragmentation of the Social Sciences and Re-combination of Specialties', *International Social Science Journal*, **139**, 27–42

Dogan, M. (1999) 'Marginality' in M.A. Runco and S.R. Pritzker (eds), *Encyclopedia of Creativity: Volume 2*, San Diego, US: Academic Press, pp. 179–86

Dogan, M. and R. Pahre (1990), *Creative Marginality: Innovation at the Intersection of Social Sciences*, Boulder, US: Westview Press

Douglas, J.D. (1985), *Creative Interviewing*, Beverley Hills: Sage Publications

Dreyfus, H.L., S.E. Dreyfus and T. Anthaniou (1986), *Mind Over Machine: The Power of Human Intuition and Expertise in the Era of the Computer*, New York: Free Press

Duesenberry, J.S. (1960), 'Comment on An Economic Analysis of Fertility', in Universities–National Bureau Committee for Economic Research (eds), *Demographic and Economic Change in Developed Countries: A Conference*, Princeton, US: Princeton University Press, for the National Bureau of Economic Research, pp. 231–4

Duesenberry, J.S., O. Eckstein and G. Fromm (1960), 'A Simulation Model of the United States Economy in Recession', *Econometrica*, **28**, 749–809

Durkheim, E. (1893/1984), *The Division of Labour in Society*, translated by W.D. Halls, New York: Free Press

Encyclopaedia Britannica (2002), CD-Rom, London: Britannica.co.uk

Evans, C.D., B.L. Meek and R.S. Walker (eds) (1993), *User Needs in Information Technology Standards*, Oxford: Butterworth–Heinemann

Farrell, J. and G. Saloner (1985), 'Standardization, Compatibility and Innovation', *RAND Journal of Economics*, **16** (1), 70–83

Farrell, W. (1998), *How Hits Happen: Forecasting Predictability in a Chaotic Marketplace*, New York: Harper Collins Publishers

Feininger, A. (1973), *Principles of Composition in Photography*, London: Thames and Hudson

Feller, I. (1957), *An Introduction to Probability Theory and its Applications: Volume I*, 2nd edition, New York: John Wiley and Sons

Feyerabend, P. (1978), *Against Method*, London: Verso

Finlay, J. and A. Dix (1996), *An Introduction to Artificial Intelligence*, London: UCL Press

Foddy, W. (1993), *Constructing Questions for Interviews and Questionnaires: Theory and Practice in Social Research*, Cambridge, UK: Cambridge University Press

Forrester, J.W. (1971), *World Dynamics*, Cambridge, US: Wright–Allen Press

Frantz, R. (2003), 'Herbert Simon. Artificial Intelligence as a Framework for Understanding Intuition', *Journal of Economic Psychology*, **24** (2), 265–77

Friedman, D. and S. Sunder (1994), *Experimental Methods: a Primer for Economists*, Cambridge, UK: Cambridge University Press

Friedman, M. (1991), 'Old Wine in New Bottles', *Economic Journal*, **101** (404), 33–40

Frisch, R. (1934), *Statistical Confluence Analysis by Means of Complete Regression Systems*, Oslo: University of Oslo Economics Institute

Frisch, R. (1946), 'The Responsibility of the Econometrician', *Econometrica*, **14** (1), 1–4

Frisch, R. (1948), 'Repercussion Studies at Oslo', *American Economic Review*, **38** (3), 367–72

Frisch, R. (1956), 'Opening Address to the Kiel Meeting of the Econometric Society', *Econometrica*, **24** (3), 300–302

Frisch, R. (1963), 'Numerical Determination of a Quadratic Preference Function for Use in Macroeconomic Planning', in *Studi di Economia, Finanza e Statistica in Onore di Gustavo del Vecchio*, Padua: Edizione CEDAM, pp. 311–51

Frisch, R. (1970), 'Econometrics in the World of Today', in W.A. Eltis, M.F.G. Scott and J.N. Wolfe (eds), *Induction, Growth and Trade: Essays in Honour of Sir Roy Harrod*, Oxford: Clarendon Press: pp. 158–66

Frisch, R. (1981), 'From Utopian Theory to Practical Applications: The Case of Econometrics', *American Economic Review*, 71 (6), 1–16

Frisch, R. and F.V. Waugh (1933) 'Partial Time Regressions as Compared with Individual Trends', *Econometrica*, 1 (4), 387–401

Fuseli, H. (1831), *The Life and Writings of Henry Fuseli: Volume II*, London: Henry Colburn and Richard Bentley

Gabel, H.L. (ed.) (1987), *Product Standardization and Competitive Strategy*, Amsterdam: North-Holland

Gabel, H.L. (1991), *Competitive Strategies for Product Standards: The Strategic Use of Compatibility Standards for Competitive Advantage*, London: McGraw-Hill

Galbraith, J.K. (1971), *A Contemporary Guide to Economics, Peace and Laughter*, Boston, US: Houghton Mifflin

Gates, W.H. III (1999), *Business @ The Speed of Thought: Using a Digital Nervous System*, Harmondsworth, UK: Penguin Books Limited

Gilbert, N. and K.G. Troitzsch (1999), *Simulation for the Social Scientist*, Buckingham, UK: Open University Press

Gillham, B. (2000), *Case Study Research Methods*, London: Continuum

Gini, C. (1921), 'Sull'interpolazione di una Retta quandi i Valori della Variabile Independente sono Affeti da Errori Accidentali', *Metron*, 1, 63–82

Goldberger, A.S. (1964), *Econometric Theory*, New York: John Wiley and Sons

Gorman, W.M. (1976), 'Tricks with Utility Functions', in M. Artis and A.R. Nobay (eds), *Essays in Economic Analysis*, Cambridge, UK: Cambridge University Press, pp. 211–43

Griffiths, P. (1985), *Olivier Messiaen and the Music of Time*, Ithaca, US: Cornell University Press

Griliches, Z. (1974), 'Errors in Variables and Other Unobservables', *Econometrica*, 42 (6), 971–98

Grindley, P.C. (1995), *Standards Strategy and Policy: Cases and Stories*, Oxford: Oxford University Press

Hahn, F. (1991), 'The Next Hundred Years', *Economic Journal*, 101 (404), 47–50

Hamel, J., S. Dufour and D. Fortin (1993), *Case Study Methods*, Newbury Park, US: Sage Publications

Hansard (2004), 'Statement on GM Policy by the Secretary of State for Environment, Food and Rural Affairs', *Hansard (House of Commons*

Daily Debates), 9 March 2004, http://www.parliament.the-stationery-office.co.uk/pa/cm/cmhansrd.htm

Harré, R. (1986), *Varieties of Realism: A Rationale for the Natural Sciences*, Oxford: Basil Blackwell

Hayek, F. (1945), 'The Use of Knowledge in Society', *American Economic Review*, **35** (4), 519–30

Henderson, W. (1982), 'Metaphor in Economics', *Economics*, Winter, 147–53

Henderson, W. (1994), 'Metaphor and Economics', in R.E. Backhouse (ed.), *New Directions in Economic Methodology*, London and New York: Routledge, pp. 343–67

Henderson, W. (1995), *Economics as Literature*, London and New York: Routledge

Hendry, D.F. (1995), *Dynamic Econometrics*, Oxford: Oxford University Press

Hendry, D.F., E.E. Leamer and D.J. Poirier (1990), 'A Conversation on Econometric Methodology', *Econometric Theory*, 6, 171–261

Hicks, J.R. (1969), *A Theory of Economic History*, Oxford: Clarendon Press

Hicks, J.R. (1979), *Causality in Economics*, Oxford: Basil Blackwell

Holland, J.H. (1992), *Adaptation in Natural and Artificial Systems: An Introductory Analysis with Applications to Biology, Control and Artificial Intelligence*, Cambridge, US: MIT Press

Holmyard, E.J. (1956), 'Alchemical Equipment', in C. Singer, E.J. Holmyard, A.R. Hall and T.I. Williams (eds), *A History of Technology: Volume II*, New York and London: Oxford University Press, pp. 731–52

Holstein, J.A. and J.F. Gubrium (1995), *The Active Interview*, Thousand Oaks, US and London: Sage

Houthakker, H.S. and L.D. Taylor (1970), *Consumer Demand in the United States: Analysis and Projections,* 2nd edition, Cambridge, US: Harvard University Press

Howard, E. (1920), *Territory in Bird Life*, London: John Murray

Howard, R.D. (1974), 'The Influence of Sexual Selection and Interspecific Communication on Mockingbird Song (Mimus Polyglottos)', *Evolution*, **28**, 428–38

Hutchinson, T.W. (1977), *Knowledge and Ignorance in Economics*, Oxford: Basil Blackwell

Hutchison, T.W. (2000), *On the Methodology of Economics and the Formalist Revolution*, Cheltenham, UK and Northampton, US: Edward Elgar

Huxley, A. (1963), *Literature and Science*, London: Chatto and Windus

Ilich, I. (1982), 'Vernacular Values', in S. Kumar (ed.), *The Schumacher Lectures*, London: Abacus/Sphere Books Limited, pp. 70–79

Jackson, K. (ed.) (1996), *The Oxford Book of Money*, Oxford: Oxford University Press

Jevons, W.S. (1871/1970), *The Theory of Political Economy*, Harmondsworth: Penguin Books

Johnson, H.G. (1972), 'Individual and Collective Choice', in W.A. Robson (ed.), *Man and the Social Sciences*, London: George Allen and Unwin Limited, pp. 1–22

Jones, S. (ed.) (1999), *Doing Internet Research: Critical Issues and Methods for Examining the Net*, Thousand Oaks, US: Sage

Kagel, J.H. (1987), 'Economics According to the Rats (and Pigeons Too): What Have We Learned and What Can We Hope to Learn?', in A.E. Roth (ed.), *Laboratory Experimentation in Economics: Six Points of View*, Cambridge, UK: Cambridge University Press, pp. 153–92

Kalman, R.E. (1982a), 'System Identification from Noisy Data', in A.R. Bednarek and L. Cesari (eds), *Dynamical Systems II*, New York: Academic Press, pp. 135–64

Kalman, R.E. (1982b), 'Identification from Real Data', in M. Hazewinckel and A.H.G. Rinnooy Kan, *Current Developments in the Interface: Economics, Econometrics, Mathematics,* Dordrecht: D. Reidel Publishing Company, pp. 161–96

Katz, M.L. and C. Shapiro (1985), 'Network Externalities, Competition and Compatibility', *American Economic Review*, **75** (3), 424–40

Keynes, J.M. (1936), *The General Theory of Employment, Interest, and Money*, London and Basingstoke: Macmillan

Keynes, J.M. (1939), 'Professor Tinbergen's Method', *Economic Journal*, **49**, 558–68

Keynes, J.M. (1972), *The Collected Writings of John Maynard Keynes, Volume X: Essays in Biography*, London: Macmillan for the Royal Economic Society

Klamer, A. and T.C. Leonard (1994), 'So What's an Economic Metaphor?', in P. Mirowski (ed.), *Natural Images in Economic Thought: 'Markets Read in Tooth and Claw'*, Cambridge, UK and New York: Cambridge University Press, pp. 20–51

Klepper, S. and E.E. Leamer (1984), 'Consistent Sets of Estimates for Regression with All Variables Measured with Error', *Econometrica*, **52**, 163–83

Koestler, A. (1964), *The Act of Creation*, London: Hutchinson

Kohr, L. (1982), 'Tribute to Schumacher', in S. Kumar (ed.), *The Schumacher Lectures*, London: Abacus/Sphere Books Limited, pp. 182–192

Kotler, P., L. Fahey and S. Jatusripitak (1986), *The New Competition: Meeting the Marketing Challenge from the Far East*, Englewood Cliffs, US: Prentice-Hall International

Krebs, J.R. (1977), 'Song and Territory in the Great Tit, Parus Major', in B. Stonehouse and C.M. Perrins (eds), *Evolutionary Ecology*, London: Macmillan, pp. 47–62

Krebs, J.R., R. Ashcroft and M. Webber (1978), 'Song Repertoires and Territory Defence in the Great Tit', *Nature*, **271**, 539–42

Kripke, S. (1980), *Naming and Necessity*, Cambridge, US: Harvard University Press

Lakoff, G. and M. Johnson (1980), *Metaphors We Live By*, Chicago: University of Chicago Press

Landes, D. (1983), *Revolution in Time*, Cambridge, US: Belknap Press of Harvard University Press

Landes, D. (2003), *The Unbound Prometheus: Technological Change and Industrial Development in Western Europe from 1750 to the Present*, 2nd edition, Cambridge, UK: Cambridge University Press

Law, A.M. and W.D. Kelton (2000), *Simulation Modelling and Analysis*, 3rd edition, Boston, US: McGraw-Hill

Leamer, E.E. (1987), 'Econometric Metaphors', in T.F. Bewley (ed.), *Advances in Econometrics World Congress: Volume II*, Econometric Society Monographs No. 14, Cambridge, UK and New York: Cambridge University Press, pp. 1–28

Leontief, W.W. (ed.) (1953), *Studies in the Structure of the American Economy: Theoretical and Empirical Explorations in Input–Output Analysis*, New York: Oxford University Press

Leontief, W.W. (1971), 'Theoretical Assumptions and Non-observed Facts', *American Economic Review*, **61** (1), 1–7

Leontief, W.W. (1982), 'Academic Economics', *Science*, **217**, 104–7

Leontief, W.W. (1983), 'Academic Economics, Continued', *Science*, **219**, 904

Liebowitz, S.J. and S.E. Margolis (1990), 'The Fable of the Keys', *Journal of Law and Economics*, **33**, 1–25

Lovins, A. (1982), 'Soft Energy Paths', in S. Kumar (ed.), *The Schumacher Lectures*, London: Abacus/Sphere Books Limited, pp. 28–65

Lynn, J. and A. Jay (1983), *Yes Minister: The Diaries of a Cabinet Minister by the Right Hon. James Hacker: Volume 3*, London: BBC Publications

Lynn, J. and A. Jay (1986), *Yes Prime Minister: The Diaries of the Right Hon. James Hacker: Volume 1*, London: BBC Publications

McCloskey, D.N. (1985), *The Rhetoric of Economics*, 1st edition, Madison: University of Wisconsin Press

McCloskey, D.N. (1998), *The Rhetoric of Economics*, 2nd edition, Madison: University of Wisconsin Press

McGregor, P.K., J.R. Krebs and C.M. Perrins (1981), 'Song Repertoires and Lifetime Reproductive Success in the Great Tit (Parus Major)', *American Naturalist*, **118**, 149–59

Machiavelli, N. (1513/1908), *The Prince*, London: J.M. Dent and Sons

Maddala, G.S. (1983), *Limited-Dependent and Qualitative Variables in Econometrics*, Cambridge, UK: Cambridge University Press

Maddala, G.S. (1998), 'Econometric Issues Related to Errors in Variables in Financial Models', in S. Strøm (ed.), *Econometrics and Economic Theory in the 20th Century: The Ragnar Frisch Centennial Symposium*, Econometric Society Monograph, Cambridge, UK: Cambridge University Press, pp. 414–32

Malinvaud, E. (1980), *Statistical Methods of Econometrics*, 3rd edition, Amsterdam: North-Holland

Mandeville, B. (1723), *The Fable of the Bees; or, Private Vices, Publick Benefits*, 2nd edition, London: Edmund Parker

Marshall, A. (1898), 'Distribution and Exchange', *Economic Journal*, **8** (29), 37–59

Mathias, P. (1983), *The First Industrial Nation: An Economic History of Britain, 1700–1914*, 2nd edition, London: Routledge

Maurice, R. (1968), *National Statistics: Sources and Methods,* London: HMSO

May, T. (2001), *Social Research: Issues, Methods and Process*, 3rd edition, Buckingham: Open University Press

Mayer, T. (1980), 'Economics as a Hard Science: Realistic Goal or Wishful Thinking?', *Economic Inquiry*, **18**, 165–78

Mayer, T. (1993), *Truth vs. Precision in Economics*, Cheltenham, UK and Brookfield, US: Edward Elgar

Meadows, D.H., D.L. Meadows, J. Randers and W.W. Behrens III (1972), *The Limits to Growth*, New York: Universe Books

Medawar, P.B. (1982), *Pluto's Republic*, Oxford: Oxford University Press

Mill, J.S. (1859/1929), *On Liberty*, London: Watts and Co.

Mirowski, P. (1988), *Against Mechanism: Protecting Economics from Science*, Totowa, US: Rowman & Littlefield

Mirowski, P. (1989), *More Heat than Light Economics as Social Physics: Physics as Nature's Economics*, Cambridge, UK and New York: Cambridge University Press

Mirowski, P. (1994), 'Doing What Comes Naturally: Four Meta-narratives on What Metaphors are For', in P. Mirowski (ed.), *Natural Images in Economic Thought: 'Markets Read in Tooth and Claw'*, Cambridge, UK and New York: Cambridge University Press, pp. 3–19

Moggridge, D. (ed.) (1973), *The Collected Writings of John Maynard Keynes, Volume XIV: The General Theory and After, II*, London: Macmillan for the Royal Economic Society

Morgenstern, O. (1963), *On the Accuracy of Economic Observations*, 2nd Edition, Princeton, US: Princeton University Press

Morishima, M. (1984), 'The Good and Bad Uses of Mathematics', in P.J.F. Wiles and G. Routh (eds), *Economics in Disarray*, Oxford: Basil Blackwell, pp. 51–73

Mumford, L. (1934), *Technics and Civilization*, New York: Harcourt, Brace and Company

Mumford, L. (1952), *Art and Technics*, London: Oxford University Press

Mumford, L. (1961), *The City in History*, New York: Harcourt Brace and Company

Mumford, L. (1967), *The Myth of the Machine: Technics and Human Development*, London: Secker and Warburg

Mumford, M.D. and P.P. Porter (1999), 'Analogies', in M.A. Runco and S.R. Pritzker (eds), *Encyclopedia of Creativity: Volume 1*, San Diego: Academic Press, pp. 71–8

Orcutt, G.H. (1988), 'Simulation of Microanalytic Systems', in J. Eatwell, M. Millgate and P. Newman (eds), *The New Palgrave: A Dictionary of Economics*, London: Macmillan, pp. 342–44

Orcutt, G.H., M. Greenberger, J. Korbel and A.M. Rivlin (1961), *Microanalysis of Socioeconomic Systems: A Simulation Study*, New York: Harper and Row

Oxford Dictionary of Quotations (1953), 2nd edition, London: Oxford University Press

Parsons, D.W. (1997), *Keynes and the Quest for a Moral Science: A Study of Economics and Alchemy*, Cheltenham, UK and Lyme, US: Edward Elgar

Penrose, E.T. (1952), 'Biological Analogies in the Theory of the Firm', *American Economic Review*, **42**, pp. 804–19

Pevsner, N. (1960), *Pioneers of Modern Design*, Harmondsworth: Penguin Books

Phelps Brown, E.H. (1972), 'The Underdevelopment of Economics', *Economic Journal*, **82** (325), 1–10

Phillips, A.W. (1957), 'Mechanical Models in Economic Dynamics', *Economica*, 17, 283–305

Pidd, M. (1984), *Computer Simulation in Management Science*, Chichester, UK: Wiley

Plott, C.R. (1987), 'Dimensions of Parallelism: Some Policy Applications of Experimental Methods', in A.E. Roth (ed.), *Laboratory Experimentation in Economics: Six Points of View*, Cambridge: Cambridge University Press, pp. 193–219

Popper, K.R. (1957), *The Poverty of Historicism*, London: Routledge Kegan Paul

Porter, M. (1983), *Cases in Competitive Strategy*, New York: Free Press

Power, E. (1941), *The Wool Trade in English Medieval History*, London: Oxford University Press

Price, D.J. (1957), 'The Manufacture of Scientific Instruments: From c 1500 to c 1700', in C. Singer, E.J. Holmyard, A.R. Hall and T.I. Williams (eds), *A History of Technology: Volume III*, New York and London: Oxford University Press, pp. 620–47

Pust, J. (2000), *Intuitions as Evidence*, New York: Garland Publishing

Rabinovich, S. (1993), *Measurement Errors: Theory and Practice*, New York: American Institute of Physics

Roethlisberger, F.J. (1941), *Management and Morale*, Cambridge, US: Harvard University Press

Ruskin, J. (1904a), 'Modern Painters: Volume III', in E.T. Cook and A. Wedderburn (eds), *The Works of John Ruskin: Volume 5*, London: George Allen, pp. 3–439

Ruskin, J. (1904b), 'The Stones of Venice: Volume II', in E.T. Cook and A. Wedderburn (eds), *The Works of John Ruskin: Volume 10*, London: George Allen, pp. 3–349

Samuelson, P.A. and W.D. Nordhaus (1985), *Economics*, 12th edition, New York: McGraw-Hill

Samuelson, P. A. and W. D. Nordhaus (1989), *Economics*, 13th edition, New York: McGraw-Hill

Scherer, F.M. (1979), 'The Welfare Economics of Product Variety: An Application to the Ready to Eat Breakfast Cereals Industry', *Journal of Industrial Economics*, **28**, 113–34

Schmalensee, R. (1978), 'Entry Deterrence in the Ready to Eat Breakfast Cereal Industry', *Bell Journal of Economics*, **9**, 305–27

Schumacher, E. (1974), *Small is Beautiful*, London: Abacus/Sphere Books Limited

Seligman, B.B. (1962), *Main Currents in Modern Economics, Volume III: The Thrust Towards Technique*, New York: Free Press

Shaw, G.B. (1903), *Man and Superman: Maxims for Revolutionists*, London: Constable and Company

Shepherd, W.G. (1990), *The Economics of Industrial Organisation*, 3rd edition, Englewood Cliffs, US: Prentice-Hall International

Shurmer, M. and G.M.P. Swann (1995), 'An Analysis of the Process Generating De Facto Standards in the PC Spreadsheet Software Market', *Journal of Evolutionary Economics*, **5**, 119–32

Silverman, D. (2001), *Interpreting Qualitative Data: Methods for Analysing Talk, Text and Interaction*, London: Sage Publications

Simon, H.A. (1982), *The Sciences of the Artificial*, 2nd edition, Cambridge, US: MIT Press

Simon, H.A. (1983), *Reason in Human Affairs*, Stanford, US: Stanford University Press

Simon, H.A. (1987), 'Making Management Decisions: The Role of Intuition and Emotion', in W. Agor (ed.), *Intuition in Organizations*, Newbury Park, US and London: Sage Publishers, pp. 23–39

Simon, H.A. (1996), *Models of My Life*, Cambridge, US: MIT Press

Simon, H.A. (1997), *Administrative Behavior*, 4th edition, New York: Free Press

Simon, H.A. and K. Gilmartin (1973), 'A Simulation of Memory for Chess Positions', *Cognitive Psychology*, **5**, 29–46

Skelton, R.A. (1958), 'Cartography', in C. Singer, E.J. Holmyard, A.R. Hall and T.I. Williams (eds), *A History of Technology: Volume IV*, Oxford: Clarendon Press, pp. 596–628

Skinner, F.G. (1954), 'Measures and Weights', in C. Singer, E.J. Holmyard and A.R. Hall (eds), *A History of Technology Vol. I: From Early Times to Fall of Ancient Empires*, London: Oxford University Press, pp. 774–84

Smith, A. (1776/1904), *An Inquiry into the Nature and Causes of the Wealth of Nations: Volumes I and II*, London: Methuen

Smith, V.L. (1982), 'Microeconomic Systems as an Experimental Science', *American Economic Review*, **72** (5), 923–55

Solow, R.M. (1974), 'Is the End of the World at Hand?', in A. Weintraub, E. Schwartz and J.R. Aronson (eds), *The Economic Growth Controversy*, London: Macmillan, pp. 39–61

Somers, H.M. (1951), 'Foreword', in J. Tinbergen, *Econometrics*, London: George Allen and Unwin Ltd, pp. vii–viii

Stone, J.R.N. (1954a), *The Measurement of Consumers' Expenditure and Behaviour in the United Kingdom, 1920–1938: Volume 1*, Cambridge, UK: Cambridge University Press

Stone, J.R.N. (1954b), 'Linear Expenditure Systems: An Application to the Pattern of British Demand', *Economic Journal*, **64**, 511–27

Stone, J.R.N. (1970), 'A Generalisation of the Theorem of Frisch and Waugh', in J.R.N. Stone, *Mathematical Models of the Economy and Other Essays*, London: Chapman and Hall, pp. 73–4

Stone, J.R.N. (1978), 'Introduction', in J.R.N. Stone and W. Peterson (eds), *Econometric Contributions to Public Policy*, London: Macmillan, pp. 1–10

Stone, J.R.N. and G. Stone (1961), *National Income and Expenditure*, London: Bowes and Bowes

Strøm, S. (ed.) (1998), *Econometrics and Economic Theory in the 20th Century: The Ragnar Frisch Centennial Symposium*, Econometric Society Monograph, Cambridge, UK: Cambridge University Press

Summers, L.H. (1991), 'The Scientific Illusion in Empirical Macroeconomics', *Scandinavian Journal of Economics*, **93** (2), 129–48

Swann, G.M.P. (1985a), *Quality Innovation and Demand: A Study of Microelectronics*, PhD Thesis, University of London

Swann, G.M.P. (1985b), 'Uncertainty in Regression Estimates: The Relative Importance of Sampling and Non-Sampling Uncertainty', *Oxford Bulletin of Economics and Statistics*, **47** (3), 303–10

Swann, G.M.P. (1986), *Quality Innovation: An Economic Analysis of Rapid Improvements in Microelectronic Components*, London: Frances Pinter Publishers

Swann, G.M.P. (2002a). 'There's More to the Economics of Consumption than (Almost) Unrestricted Utility Maximisation', in A. McMeekin, K. Green, M. Tomlinson and V. Walsh (eds), *Innovation By Demand: An Interdisciplinary Approach to the Study of Demand and its Role in Innovation*, Manchester: Manchester University Press, pp. 23–40

Swann, G.M.P. (2002b), *Engineering Economics: A Feasibility Study*, Report to Department of Trade and Industry: Innovation, Economics, Statistics and Evaluation Division (November)

Swann, G.M.P. and M. Taghavi (1992), *Measuring Price and Quality Competitiveness: A Study of 18 British Product Markets*, Aldershot, UK: Avebury Press

Symonds, R.W. (1947), *A History of English Clocks*, Harmondsworth: Penguin Books Limited

Szostak, R. (1999), *Econ-Art: Divorcing Art from Science in Modern Economics*, London: Pluto Press

Taylor, E.G.R. (1957), 'Cartography, Survey and Navigation 1400–1700', in C. Singer, E.J. Holmyard, A.R. Hall and T.I. Williams (eds), *A History of Technology: Volume III*, New York and London: Oxford University Press, pp. 530–57

Theil, H. (1965), 'The Information Approach to Demand Analysis', *Econometrica*, **33**, 67–87

Theil, H. (1975), *Theory and Measurement of Consumer Demand: Volume 1*, Amsterdam: North Holland

Thomas, A.B. (2004), *Research Skills for Management Studies*, London: Routledge

Tinbergen, J. (1938), *Statistical Testing of Business-Cycle Theories, I: A Method and its Application to Investment Activity*, Geneva: League of Nations

Tinbergen, J. (1951), *Econometrics*, London: George Allen and Unwin Ltd

Travers, M. (2001), *Qualitative Research through Case Studies*, London: Sage

von Hippel, E. (2005), *Democratizing Innovation*, Cambridge, US: MIT Press

von Neumann, J. and O. Morgenstern (1953), *Theory of Games and Economic Behaviour*, 3rd edition, Princeton, US: Princeton University Press

Waldrop, M.M. (1994), *Complexity: The Emerging Science at the Edge of Order and Chaos*, Harmondsworth, UK: Penguin Books Ltd

Ward, B. (1972), *What's Wrong with Economics*, London: Macmillan/Basic Books

Warde, A. (2002), 'Social Mechanisms Generating Demand: A Review and Manifesto', in A. McMeekin, K. Green, M. Tomlinson and V. Walsh (eds), *Innovation By Demand: An Interdisciplinary Approach to the Study of Demand and its Role in Innovation*, Manchester: Manchester University Press, pp. 10–22

Whitehead, A.N. (1929), *The Aims of Education and Other Essays*, London: Williams and Nordgate

Wiener, N. (1964), *God and Golem, Inc.: A Comment on Certain Points Where Cybernetics Impinges on Religion*, Cambridge, US: MIT Press

Wilde, O. (1899/1954), 'The Importance of Being Earnest', in *Oscar Wilde Plays*, Harmondsworth: Penguin Books Limited

Wiles, P.J.F. (1984), 'Epilogue: The Role of Theory', in P.J.F. Wiles and G. Routh (eds), *Economics in Disarray*, Oxford: Basil Blackwell, pp. 293–325

Williams, R. (2000), *Lost Icons: Reflections on Cultural Bereavement*, Edinburgh: T&T Clark Limited

Witt, U. (2001), 'Learning to Consume: A Theory of Wants and the Growth of Demand', *Journal of Evolutionary Economics*, **11** (1), 23–36

Worswick, G.D.N. (1972), 'Is Progress in Economic Science Possible?', *Economic Journal*, **82** (325), 73–86

Yin, R.K. (1994), *Case Study Research: Design and Methods*, 2nd edition, Thousand Oaks, US: Sage

Index of names

Index of topics